THE CROSS
AND THE SPIRIT

THE CROSS
AND THE SPIRIT

A Study in the Argument
and Theology of Galatians

Charles H. Cosgrove

PEETERS

MERCER

ISBN 0-86554-317-8 [CASEBOUND EDITION]
ISBN 0-86554-347-X [PAPERBACK EDITION]

The Cross and the Spirit
Copyright © 1988
Mercer University Press
Macon, Georgia 31207
All rights reserved
Printed in the United States of America

Library of Congress Cataloging-in-Publication Data

Cosgrove, Charles H.
    The cross and the Spirit : a study in the argument
and theology of Galatians / Charles H. Cosgrove.
        xv + 216 pp. 15 × 23 cm. (6 × 9 in.)
        Bibliography : p. 195.
        Includes indexes.
        ISBN 0-86554-317-8 (alk. paper)
        ISBN 0-86554-347-X (alk. paper)
        1. Bible. N.T. Galatians—Criticism, interpretation, etc.
        2. Bible. N.T. Galatians—Theology.   I. Title.
        BS2685.2.C67   1988   88-32273
        227'.406—dc19   CIP

Contents

Preface

This study of Galatians grows out of my Princeton dissertation, "The Law and the Spirit: An Investigation into the Theology of Galatians" (Princeton Theological Seminary, 1985). Significant portions of that work are included here in revised form, together with considerable amounts of new material that give the present investigation a different focus. I set out to write a dissertation on the law in Paul. I ended up writing a book on Galatians.

No study of this sort takes shape in a theological vacuum. It is therefore appropriate that I say something here, however summary, about what I regard to be the theological significance of my work on Galatians. It was an interest in ethics that initially led me into the research out of which this book now finally emerges. Over the intervening years I have become increasingly preoccupied with issues relating to the gospel and social justice. Thus, as I write this preface, it happens that I am about to depart for a sabbatical in Buenos Aires in order to be in conversation with representatives of Latin American theology as I think through the challenges of liberation theology for constructive theological reflection on Paul. A number of the remarks that follow reflect concerns growing out of this current direction of my work, which is a way of indicating that not everything I am about to say is treated *directly* in the present study.

Today perhaps the two most dominant ways of understanding Galatians—aside from the classical interpretation of it as a discussion of "faith" and "works"—are (1) the view that the letter treats the question of whether "the law" stipulates the appropriate ethic for those "in Christ," and (2) the one that considers the status of the Gentiles among the people of God to be the burning issue in Galatians. Both reconstructions of the problem have much to commend them. It can scarcely be disputed that Galatians reveals significant dimensions of Paul's view of Jews and Gentiles in the light of the gospel. Certainly the letter also clarifies important facets of the way Paul relates the Torah and ethical conduct in Christ. Moreover, these two reconstructions are quite compatible, inasmuch as "works of the law" represent both a badge of Jewish identity and an ethic for God's people in the world. And the early church engaged in intense debates regarding the extent to which that identity and that ethic ought to be constitutive for God's people in Christ. Nevertheless, I do not think that prevailing identifications of the issue in Galatians, including the classical understanding of the problem, get at the central focus of the letter. As I see it, the question Paul addresses is stated explicitly in 3:5: "Does the one who supplies (sustains) you with the Spirit and works wonders among you do so because of works of the law or because you heard (the gospel) and believed?" The letter is concerned with the grounds of life in the Spirit, including the specific question of whether the powerful work of the Spirit can be promoted by lawkeeping. Paul's answer is that the Galatians enjoy the work of the Spirit solely because they are "in Christ," an idea that he can express with a number of metaphors: justification, sonship, putting on Christ in baptism, and co-crucifixion with Christ. Yet the emphasis of the letter falls on the last of these: "participation in Christ's cross" as the sole condition for life in the Spirit.

In the closing chapter of this study I pursue this relation of the cross and the Spirit by considering their interconnection in the light of Paul's other letters, especially the Corinthian correspondence. I am keenly aware of the fact that in my own American context "prosperity gospels" of every stripe serve to reinforce the notion that "blessings," especially material ones, are a sign of God's favor and approval. The assumption that right living has its more or less immediate temporal rewards is deeply rooted in the American ethos. I am reminded here of a passage from *Habits of the Heart* by Robert Bellah and others, in which a certain Margaret speaks about what "the universe" expects from her and expresses the following confidence: "If I'm the best person I know how to be according to my lights, then something good will happen."[1] Christian versions of this philosophy betray Paul's gospel of the cross,

---

[1]Robert N. Bellah, William M. Sullivan, Ann Swidler, and Steven M. Tipton, *Habits of the Heart: Individualism and Commitment in American Life* (New York: Harper & Row, 1985) 14-15.

in which the old connection between the law and blessing is replaced by the new relation of the cross and the Spirit.

Yet in a certain sense my own interpretation of Galatians could be labeled "enthusiastic," since I understand the idea of "living by the Spirit" in Galatians to mean above all the "miraculous" activity of the Spirit (exactly the sort of things Paul's opponents in 2 Corinthians appear to celebrate) and go so far as to distinguish this "life in the Spirit" from ethical conduct in Christ ("walking by the Spirit"). The Spirit, which embodies the power of the new creation, works not only in the noetic but also in the bodily sphere, hence Paul's pneumatology cannot be limited to deontology anymore than his apocalyptic gospel can be reduced to "justification by faith" or even Christology.[2] Yet precisely because Paul's understanding of the Spirit is apocalyptic in character, his enthusiasm is essentially related to his ethics at a deeper level, which is just what the complementary expressions, "living" and "walking" by the Spirit, are designed to indicate. Paul believes that God is already powerfully at work in the world bringing about realities that anticipate the final transformation of the earth, and on the basis of this faith he summons believers to live out the righteousness of the kingdom among themselves, "doing good to all" as they have "opportunity" (Gal 6:10). It is therefore fair to say that both aspects of the Spirit's work—its war against the "flesh" and its conflict with the power of "death"—constitute dynamic manifestations of the "righteousness of God," which is the "power of God unto salvation" (Rom 1:16-17).

Paul qualifies his conviction that the new creation is present in power not by trimming back to a realized eschatology of the Word alone, a favored way of a good deal of twentieth-century theology, but by anchoring the miraculous life of the Spirit in the cross. This does not mean that the Spirit's power gets redefined paradoxically *as* weakness. It means that Paul "locates" the powerful work of the Spirit where the crucifixion of Christ extends itself into the world. According to this understanding, the Spirit helps those who share Christ's sufferings. At the same time the new creation, to the extent that it is materialized in the world through the power of the Spirit, remains subject, like its earthly Lord, to the power of death. The same Spirit that sustains the church in suffering and delivers it from extremity is the Spirit of the crucified

---

[2]On the *essentially* apocalyptic character of Paul's gospel, see J. Christiaan Beker, *Paul the Apostle: The Triumph of God in Life and Thought* (Philadelphia: Fortress Press, 1980).

Christ, who leads the church in costly and risky forms of service in the world.

It is my impression that certain Anabaptist interpretations of Paul show special affinity for the apostle's view of the cross and the Spirit. It also seems to me that an Anabaptist reading of Paul may have more in common with Latin American liberation theology than do more mainstream Protestant understandings of the apostle. To be sure, there are significant differences among Paul, the Anabaptists, and the liberation theologians, not to mention the fact that the latter two groups also have important differences among themselves. Yet, generally speaking, all have at least this much in common: an "enthusiasm" grounded in the conviction that the gospel touches the whole of creation through Christ's death and life, which are already powerfully at work in the world. This "spiritualism," rooted in conceptions of the cross and resurrection as "ongoing events," led the Anabaptists to expect more from the present in the way of visible or external forms of "new creation" than either Luther's theology of the cross or Calvin's anthropology would allow. Today both political theology in Europe and liberation theology in Latin America are receiving the same sort of criticism that exponents of the so-called magisterial Reformation levelled at the Anabaptists, although it should be noted that on the question at hand, Calvin and the Reformed branch of the classical Reformation stand closer to the Anabaptists than they do to many of their modern theological heirs. From a latter twentieth-century vantage point, not only exponents of the Radical Reformation but also Reformers like Calvin appear to have been all too optimistic about the transformative power of the gospel in both church and society. Of course, one ought to have learned something from 450 years of Protestant history, and indeed I myself am well schooled by my education in the dangers of an "overly realized" eschatology. But I tend to agree with Karl Barth that "even (and especially) in theology the fear of impending dangers is always a bad teacher."[3]

With the preceding still in view, I wish to make a set of closing comments about the epigraph for chapter 6, the chapter from which this study gets its title. For a long time I did not have a suitable epigraph for this chapter, because I couldn't find one that linked suffering with Christ and the power of the Spirit in what I judge to be their Pauline logic. Again

---

[3]*Church Dogmatics* IV.2, trans. G. W. Bromiley (Edinburgh: T. & T. Clark, 1958) 10.

and again I came across potential candidates that did justice to the Pauline "theology of the cross" without reckoning sufficiently with the apostle's "theology of glory." At length I began searching in what some might regard as rather unconventional and perhaps even unsuitable places from which to cull an epigraph for a chapter in a scholarly monograph. The quotation I have selected comes from a book on divine healing by A. B. Simpson, a Presbyterian pastor who founded the Christian and Missionary Alliance. Simpson did most of his work toward the end of the nineteenth century and belongs squarely in the tradition of nineteenth-century "evangelicalism." It was thanks to the education I have received on the latter subject from my colleague and friend Donald Dayton that it ever entered my head to read the writings of a Simpson and expect to profit by it. The quotation from Simpson's book associates the power of Christ to heal the body with the sustaining presence of Christ among those who share his sufferings. I regard this citation as providing an ecumenical balance to the quotation from Albrecht Ritschl, which precedes it in chapter 5. Simpson's faith in God's power to touch the concrete world of bodily existence seemed to provide an appropriate complement to Ritschl's spiritual idealism. It is especially worth noting here that in the nineteenth century it was in large measure a confidence in the present power of the Spirit that inspired, within the same traditions, both radical abolitionism and "the gospel of healing" among churches in North America influenced by holiness theology. Faith in the power of God to mend the body formed the natural corollary of faith in the power of God to transform society and cure social ills.[4]

Today the cry for justice is heard on every side, and the ensuing debates about justice and the kingdom of God often involve competing interpretations of the cross and its relation to power, as well as conflicting understandings of what one ought to expect from God in the world. I cannot but think in this connection of Rudolf Bultmann's description of radical faith as a trust in God that refuses to objectify hope and remains always ready to walk into the darkness. There is a profound element of truth in this understanding of faith, especially in the implication that faith

---

[4]See Donald W. Dayton, *Theological Roots of Pentecostalism,* with a foreword by Martin E. Marty (Metuchen NJ: The Scarecrow Press, 1987); also, idem, "Yet Another Layer of the Onion: Or Opening the Ecumenical Door to Let the Riffraff in," *The Ecumenical Review* 40/1 (1988): 87-110.

is only genuine when we put ourselves at risk in obedience to God.[5] But perhaps it is just this sort of obedient "faith working through love" (Gal. 5:6) that requires also a certain worldly "objectification" of what the gospel makes historically possible. Perhaps one ought dare to "say something about that quality of life—personal and communitarian—that corresponds to the kingdom and therefore has eschatological significance" and to affirm "the quest for historical realizations (however partial and ambiguous) of this quality of life" that "carry the direction or dynamic of the kingdom."[6] These words of José Míquez Bonino point to some of the most significant questions confronting Christians today. Certainly among these questions are how the power and possibility of the gospel impinge on the sociopolitical sphere of human life in the world and what place "objectification" through discerning the "signs of the times" and imagining a "new future" ought to have in conceiving the presence and activity of God in history.

The theological concerns raised in these prefatory remarks can hardly be settled simply by exegesis. There are complicated hermeneutical issues that impinge upon the discussion at every point. But it remains my conviction that good exegesis offers an indispensable source of inspiration as well as correction to good theology. The present study is offered with both forms of service in mind.

Northern Baptist Theological Seminary
Lombard, Illinois
4 July 1988

---

[5]See, for instance, Bultmann's 1928 essay "Faith as Venture" ("Der Glaube als Wagnis") in *Existence and Faith: Shorter Writings of Rudolf Bultmann*, trans. Schubert Ogden (New York: Meridian Books, 1960). A useful presentation of Bultmann's eschatology is given by Walter Schmithals, *An Introduction to the Theology of Rudolf Bultmann*, trans. John Bowden (London: SCM Press, 1968) 301-24.

[6]José Míquez Bonino, "El Reino de Dios y la historia: reflexiones para una discusión del tema," in *El Reino de Dios y America Latina*, ed. C. René Padilla (Buenos Aires: Casa Bautista de Publicaciones, 1975) 87-88.

Acknowledgments

While my scholarly indebtedness to many others is documented in the notes, here a general word about sources is in order. Except as otherwise indicated, all translations of ancient texts are my own. Citations of the Greek text of the New Testament are from *Novum Testamentum Graece,* 26th ed., ed. Erwin Nestle and Kurt Aland (Stuttgart: Deutsche Bibelgesellschaft, 1979). Citations from the Septuagint are from *Septuaginta,* editio minor, 2 vols., ed. Alfred Rahlfs (Stuttgart: Deutsche Bibelgesellschaft, 1979; reprint of 1935 edition). Citations from Greek and Latin authors in the original language are from the Loeb Classical Library.

I wish to thank my teachers at Princeton, notably Paul Meyer, J. Christiaan Beker, and David Adams, for the contributions they have made to my intellectual development as a student of the New Testament and theologian of the church. At an early stage in the research for this study I spent two unforgettable years in Tübingen and wish to acknowledge the kindness and encouragement shown to me during this time by Peter Stuhlmacher. I am also indebted to Brian Roots, Scott Smith, and Sherri Smith for their invaluable assistance in checking citations and proofreading. I have been very fortunate to have the editorial assistance of Susan M. Carini, managing editor at Mercer University Press. I would also like to express my gratitude to Northern Baptist Theological Seminary and its board of trustees for financial assistance in support of this project. Finally, I wish to dedicate this book to my wife, Debbie, in deep appreciation for her love and support all along the way.

To

Debbie

Abbreviations

The majority of abbreviations occurring herein are standard. Most are cited in Siegfried Schwertner, *Internationales Abkürzungsverzeichnis für Theologie und Grenzgebiete* (Berlin; New York: Walter de Gruyter, 1974) and in "Instructions for Contributors," *Journal of Biblical Literature* 107/3 (September 1988): 579-96 (also in the Society of Biblical Literature's *Member's Handbook,* 1980). In addition, note the following.

AGAJU Arbeiten zur Geschichte des antiken Judentums und Urchristentums.

BAGD Arndt, William F., and F. Wilbur Gingrich. *A Greek-English Lexicon of the New Testament and Other Early Christian Literature.* A translation and adaptation of Walter Bauer's *Griechisch-Deutsches Wörterbuch zu den Schriften des Neuen Testaments und der übrigen urchristlichen Literatur.* Second edition. Revised and augmented by F. Wilbur Gingrich and Frederick W. Danker from Walter Bauer's fifth edition, 1958. Chicago/London: University of Chicago Press, 1979.

FB Forschung zur Bibel.

HNTC Herder's New Testament Commentaries.

NA Neutestamentliche Abhandlungen.

NF Neue Folge.

NS New Series.

NTG Jacob Wettstein, *Novum Testamentum Graecum* (Amsterdam: Dommerian, 1752).

OBO Orbis Biblicus et Orientalis.

OTP *The Old Testament Pseudepigrapha.* Edited by James H. Charlesworth. Two volumes. Garden City NY: Doubleday & Company, Inc., 1983 and 1985. Vol. 1. *Apocalyptic Literature and Testaments.* Vol. 2. *Expansions of the "Old Testament" and Legends, Wisdom and Philosophical Literature, Prayers, Psalms, and Odes, Fragments of Lost Judeo-Hellenistic Works.*

Introduction

> The White Rabbit put on his spectacles.
> "Where shall I begin, please your Majesty?" he asked.
> "Begin at the beginning," the King said, very gravely,
> "and go on till you come to the end: then stop."
>
> —Lewis Carroll, *Alice's Adventures in Wonderland*[1]

WHAT IS FOR THE READER a place of beginning is typically a place of ending for the author of a book. Having faced the question of *where to begin* at numerous points along the way, the author usually confronts this question for the last time in the introduction, since most of us are wise enough to put off the preparation of any opening remarks until we have become fully acquainted with the work ourselves. In the case of the present study, however, the question of where to begin is also an explicit methodological theme of the investigation, and the central thesis of this book hinges on the answer to the question of *entry point* in gaining access to the logic of Paul's argumentation in Galatians.

Stated succinctly the method and central thesis of this study[2] are as follows. Since we stand outside the circle of Paul's conversation with the Galatians and are privy to only one-half of what is said, we must begin by getting our bearings on the discussion (What is Galatians

---

[1]Lewis Carroll, *Alice's Adventures in Wonderland* and *Through the Looking-Glass*, ed. Roger Lancelyn Green (Oxford: Oxford University Press, 1971) 106.

[2]The present study (especially chs. 1 and 2) revises material from my Princeton dissertation, which focuses on Paul's view of the law in Galatians: "The Law and the Spirit: An Investigation into the Theology of Galatians" (Ph.D. diss., Princeton Theological Seminary, 1985). But much of the material presented here is new, and where there is overlap with the dissertation the perspective is generally different.

about?). These "bearings" must then guide our interpretation of the letter as a whole. This methodological consideration, which is the subject
of chapter 1 ("Joining the Conversation"), leads to the following decision: The place for us to "enter" Paul's conversation with the Galatians is 3:1. Chapter 2 ("The Law and the Spirit") then acts upon this
decision and develops the following thesis regarding the "occasion" of
Galatians: Galatians is not about whether justification is by works or by
faith, but about whether believers can promote their ongoing experience
of the Spirit by doing the law.

I take Galatians 3:1-5 as the decisive clue to Paul's view of the
"problem at Galatia." This passage is often quickly passed over by
readers of Galatians who are eager to get on to Paul's "Scripture arguments" in 3:6ff. But I am impressed with Paul's question in 3:2, "I
only want to know one thing: Did you receive the Spirit by works of the
law or by hearing and believing (the gospel)?" When Paul says, "I only
want to know one thing," he suggests that what he is about to ask goes
to the very heart of "the problem at Galatia." Moments later, in 3:5,
Paul draws a conclusion: "*Therefore,* does the One who gives you the
Spirit and works miracles (by the Spirit) among you do so because you
are lawkeepers or because you heard and believed in the gospel?" It
sounds as if Paul wants the Galatians to see that God keeps on supplying
them with the power of the Spirit because they are believers, not because they keep the law.

Chapter 2 ("The Law and the Spirit") establishes and defends the
foregoing interpretation by focusing on the flow of argumentation in
Galatians 3–4. In 3:1–4:7 Paul's conclusions[3] have to do again and again
with how believers come into possession of the *Spirit,* which is treated
in Galatians as the substance of the Abrahamic promise (blessing, inheritance). Furthermore, the apostle introduces themes expressive of
status (justification, being in Christ, sonship) not for their own sake but
in order to make his point about the grounds of life in the Spirit. This
means that the theme of justification, for instance, never becomes an
object of reflection in Galatians, and much of what Paul says about top-
ics such as justification, faith, and sonship rests upon assumptions that

---

[3]See Gal 3:5; 3:9; 3:14; 3:16-17 in the light of 3:22; 3:29; 4:7.

he shares with his audience regarding these themes and their application to the Galatians.

In each of the subsequent chapters of this study I am guided by the basic methodological insight of chapter 1, that the interpreter's understanding of "the problem at Galatia" not only tends to determine but must determine his or her reading of the letter, especially when it comes to those portions of the letter which *by their very nature* admit multiple, competing interpretations (the autobiography and the paraenesis).[4] Therefore, chapter 1, which establishes the method of this study, and chapter 2, which establishes its central thesis about the problem at Galatia, constitute the critical foundation of this book. Thus, the decision to "enter" Paul's conversation with the Galatians at 3:1, a decision toward which chapter 1 leads and upon which chapter 2 rests, represents the fundamental beginning that grounds this entire investigation. And this is a beginning that must first be *discovered* before it is possible to "begin at the beginning . . . go on till you come to the end: then stop."

---

[4]The autobiography, as story, is multivalent, and, to the extent that it covers a history in which the Galatians do not figure explicitly, its relevance for their situation cannot be established from 1:11–2:21 alone. Instead one must listen to the autobiography from the "Galatian" standpoint. The paraenesis, insofar as it consists of general, traditional materials, does not disclose its specific occasion, and what Paul says in Gal 5–6 could in principle serve a number of different occasions.

CHAPTER 1

Joining
the Conversation

But we return now to deliberative oratory. . . .
Private deliberation does not require a narration of facts,
at least when it comes to the question that calls for a decision,
since everyone is familiar with the issue under debate.
—Quintilian, *Institutio Oratoria* 3.8.10

THE AIM OF THIS FIRST CHAPTER can be put very precisely. I intend to show that as third parties to Paul's "conversation" with the Galatians we must join that conversation at Galatians 3:1 and nowhere else. This means that we must get our bearings on the "occasion" of Galatians (what Galatians is *about*) at this specific point of entry and allow those bearings to determine our reading of the letter as a whole.

In what follows, this case will be made in two ways, one negative and the other positive. The negative line of argument may resemble at points a "history of research" ("Forschungsgeschichte"), and it is intended to serve the same function as this traditional method of introducing a scholarly monograph, which is to justify the need for the present study by pointing up inadequacies in previous investigations. But the history of research presented here is not carried out in the traditional fashion. It is highly selective and, as it progresses, departs more and more from the traditional format of chronological report and critique. The purpose of this discussion is therefore not to provide a comprehensive treatment of previous investigation. Instead the aim is to identify moments in the history of the letter's interpretation that illustrate the relative *malleability* of the text in the hands of a given interpreter operating under a given conception of the "problem at Galatia." With the help of certain insights gleaned from linguistics and literary criticism, this notion of the text's malleability will be pressed in order to show that the methods by which interpreters get their basic orientation to the themes and problems taken up in the letter not only often do determine but *must* determine their respective interpretations of the letter in decisive ways. That being the case, one must subject this process of orientation to criticism and rigorous control, and in this respect previous investigations of the letter are found wanting.

This last comment announces the constructive task of this chapter, namely, to identify through rigorous and systematic analysis an "appropriate place to begin" in interpreting Galatians. Toward this end we shall subject the letter to formal analysis, examining Paul's discourse in the light of ancient rhetorical and epistolary conventions. This investigation will lead to the insight that 3:1 is the appropriate point to "join the conversation," a conclusion that will set the exegetical agenda for chapter 2.

What Is Galatians About?

The crisis that evokes Paul's letter to the Galatians has long been attributed to an infiltration of the Galatian churches by "Judaizers"[1] of a Jewish-Christian stripe, who seek to bring the community under the yoke of the Torah. The burden of their message is said to be that acceptance of the law, and especially circumcision, is a necessary requisite for full participation in the salvation wrought by God in Christ. The law is the means of righteousness before God, and the one who takes up the

---

[1] The Greek term Ἰουδαΐζειν (Gal 2:14b) means to "live as a Jew" or "adopt the lifestyle of a Jew." See A. E. Harvey, "The Opposition to Paul," in *Studia Evangelica*, vol. 4, ed. F. L. Cross, TU 102 (Berlin: Akademie Verlag, 1968) 322. The English word "Judaize" has this sense as well but is also used typically to mean "promote a Jewish lifestyle." The agitators at Galatia are generally understood to have been Judaizers in both senses. For a brief survey of theories on the occasion of Galatians, see George Howard, *Paul, Crisis in Galatia: A Study in Early Christian Theology*, SNTSMS 35 (Cambridge/New York: Cambridge University Press, 1979).

Torah through circumcision becomes a son of Abraham. Part of the Judaizers' strategy is to discredit Paul by accusing him of opportunism and failure to remain faithful to the gospel he received from the Jerusalem apostles, upon whom he is dependent. To this extent the Judaizers are opponents of Paul.[2]

If this sketch of the "agitators" (see Gal 5:10; 5:12) has a certain prima facie appeal in its straightforwardness, it is also misleading. We may be certain that the agitators urged the Galatians to accept circumcision (6:12-13; cf. 5:2-3), but it is not immediately clear whether they defined circumcision as an entrance requirement, a matter of obedience toward God expected of those regarded as already members of his people, a necessary step toward "full membership," or an initiation rite, as some have suggested, into a higher plane of Christian spirituality.[3]

Nor is it immediately apparent from the letter what relationship exists between receiving circumcision and doing the works of the law, for Paul or for the agitators. Representatives of more or less traditional views of the Galatian crisis tend to define circumcision as an entrance requirement by which one takes up the Torah and to understand Paul's rejection of the former under his attack on the latter. According to this view, righteousness through the Torah brings with it the status of "sonship" before God, and this status itself depends on justification under the law. Thus, as we shall see in chapter 2, the statements on status in Galatians 3 and 4 are conceived as part of Paul's attack on the opponents' theology of "justification on the basis of works of the law." Consequently, the heart of the apostle's criticism of the Torah is said to rest in his rejection of the opponents' "works-righteousness," their attempt, in his judgment, to constitute life in Christ according to the soteriological structure of the law. When Paul speaks of death to the law (Gal 2:19)

---

[2]I do not mean to attribute this view of the agitators to anyone in particular. Werner Georg Kümmel's picture of the opponents approximates this one: *Introduction to the New Testament*, rev. English ed., trans. Howard Clark Kee (Nashville: Abingdon Press, 1975) 298-301.

[3]Compare the conflicting views of the following interpreters on these questions: E. P. Sanders, *Paul, the Law, and the Jewish People* (Philadelphia: Fortress Press, 1983) 20; J. Christiaan Beker, *Paul the Apostle: The Triumph of God in Life and Thought* (Philadelphia: Fortress Press, 1980) 44. Robert Jewett, "The Agitators and the Galatian Congregation," *NTS* 17 (1971): 198-212.

he means not simply that the believer is no longer obligated to keep the requirements (or certain requirements) of the law, but that he has died to a particular kind of existence before God, an existence whose motive principle is "works." In a now-famous passage from his *Theology of the New Testament*, Rudolf Bultmann characterized this mode of existence ("the way of works of the law") as the human attempt to win salvation, an attempt that not only leads to sin but already is sin by virtue of its opposition to God's free grace.[4] Heinrich Schlier, whose commentary on Galatians is dedicated to Bultmann, offers a variation of this view when he proposes in the course of his comments on Galatians 3:10-14 that for Paul the problem with the law is that it must be *done* ("das ποιεῖν") and thereby becomes an occasion for human achievement.[5] Schlier has been justly criticized for reading Romans 7 into Galatians here. Even more important is an observation that E. P. Sanders makes in discussing Bultmann's position: "in Galatians, the reason for not keeping the law which Bultmann adduces (that keeping it is itself sinning, because it leads to sin: boasting before God) is notably not in evidence."[6] The point is telling, especially since the theme of boasting does eventually occur, in Galatians 6:4-5, where the hope of an authentic boast in one's own work is Paul's positive expectation for believers. The only association of boasting with the *law* occurs in 6:13, where the agitators are said not to keep the law but to promote circumcision solely "that they might boast in your flesh." But a polemical and ironic jab like this hardly warrants the conclusion that the law as the agitators taught it had a misdirection toward boasting for its false heart.

If the Galatian letter gives no hint that keeping the Mosaic law represents for Paul an attempt at autonomous existence or self-justification, do we have reason to believe that any such conception forms an

---

[4]*Theology of the New Testament*, vol. 1, trans. Kendrick Grobel (New York: Charles Scribner's Sons, 1951) 264.

[5]*Der Brief an die Galater*, 5th ed., MeyerK 7/14 (Göttingen: Vandenhoeck & Ruprecht, 1971) 134. Cf. Günter Klein, "Sündenverständnis und theologia crucis bei Paulus," in *Theologia Crucis—Signum Crucis: Festschrift für Erich Dinkler*, ed. Carl Andresen and Günter Klein (Tübingen: J. C. B. Mohr [Paul Siebeck], 1979) 270ff.

[6]*Paul and Palestinian Judaism: A Comparison of Patterns of Religion* (Philadelphia: Fortress Press, 1977) 482. See also Hans Hübner, *Law in Paul's Thought*, trans. James C. G. Grieg and ed. John Riches (Edinburgh: T. & T. Clark, 1984) 111.

assumption of the letter, taken for granted by the apostle? Had the Judaism of Paul's day come to regard the law as a legalistic system, poor in divine grace and rich in opportunity for establishing "one's own righteousness"? Since the appearance of E. P. Sanders's book, *Paul and Palestinian Judaism,*[7] New Testament interpreters have become increasingly less inclined to grant such an assumption.[8] If Sanders, in seeking to correct the traditional (Christian) portrait of ancient Jewish religion as a legalistic system, fails in some measure to do justice to the pluralism of Second Temple Judaism and refracts the interests of the literature he surveys through the lens of Pauline scholarship,[9] his work serves as an indispensable reminder of at least this much: Torah-obedience was understood in Palestinian Judaism to be grounded in and enabled by God's grace to no lesser degree than in early Christianity.

But the very question of whether the Torah was understood "legalistically" in first-century Judaism is already misconceived, if it aims to know the extent to which legalism, whether promoted in religious literature or incarnated in lived religion, forms a presupposition about the law's structure taken for granted by Paul. For this false direction ("verkehrte Richtung") of the law is supposed to be a Pauline insight, in which case it cannot comprise an assumption. Bultmann, it should be remembered, never argued from the nature of the law in its Jewish understanding, as he saw it, to the correctness of his interpretation of Paul's critique of that understanding. The character of the Mosaic law is not self-evident in Paul's situation. The apostle must first uncover it.[10]

---

[7]See n. 6 above. Sanders was by no means the first scholar to defend ancient Judaism against the charge of legalism or "works-righteousness," and he acknowledges his indebtedness to previous work throughout his study. See especially the opening chapter of *Paul and Palestinian Judaism.*

[8]For example, James D. G. Dunn can now speak of "the new perspective on Paul," by which he means the new way of looking at Paul inaugurated by Sanders. See Dunn's essay, "The New Perspective on Paul," *BJRL* 65 (1983): 95-122.

[9]See Jacob Neusner, "Comparing Judaisms," *HR* 18 (1978): 177-91; also Jerome Murphy-O'Connor, "Review of E. P. Sanders, *Paul and Palestinian Judaism,*" *RB* 85 (1978): 122-26.

[10]Bultmann, *Theology of the New Testament* 1:263-69. Bultmann never makes it clear whether this "perverted direction" of the law belongs to the Mosaic law in its givenness or consists in a misuse of it. He does appear to assume that Paul treats the Mosaic law

If an attack by Paul on the misdirection of the law cannot be inferred from Galatians and if the particular conception of the law's soteriological structure which is said to form the premise of this attack cannot be assumed to comprise an unexpressed presupposition in the debate, then it is extremely doubtful that the inner intent of the law or a "Jewish perversion" of that intent in "works" constitutes Paul's focus in the Galatian crisis. Appeal here to Romans will not do, even if such a focus is to be found there. It is scarcely plausible that matters that must be clarified in detail in Romans, the relation between boasting and the law (Rom 3–4) together with the law's role in the "revival of sin" (Rom 7), form unexpressed presuppositions of the Galatian controversy.

Bultmann always kept what he took to be Paul's qualitative critique of the law together with the impossibility of its quantitative demand ("no one can keep the whole law perfectly"), and he regarded the former as Paul's profoundest insight into the law. We should remember here that Luther himself, in his first lectures on Romans, identified the quantitative impossibility as the chief object of the apostle's criticism, but by the Galatians lectures of 1531 had deepened his conception of the problem, through a highly theocentric reflection, to precisely the same point at which Bultmann arrives. It was on the question of just this sort of "deepening" that Adolf Schlatter parted from Luther.[11] And on this same point Ulrich Wilckens dissents from Bultmann.

---

as 'verkehrt' in itself. The only Mosaic law that exists for Paul is this misdirected one, which Paul refuses to attribute to God: "Especially significant is the fact that in the polemic of Gal. 3:19f., Paul can take up the Gnostic myth of the giving of the Law by angels in order to prove that the Law of Moses is not attributable to God Himself. Paul can do that only because he views the Law as a matter of course in the role in which the Jew lets it encounter him." Ibid. 1:268.

[11]See Schlatter, *Der Glaube im Neuen Testament,* 6th ed. (Studienausgabe reprint of 1927 4th ed. Stuttgart: Calwer Verlag, 1982) 323-31. Schlatter rarely names the representatives of the positions he attacks. No doubt it is in the end Luther's understanding that comes in for criticism in the following passage from *Der Glaube im Neuen Testament:* "Aber auch dies war ein Missgriff, wenn man, um das negative Urteil über die Werke des Gesetzes verständlich zu machen, einen ethischen Mangel in sie hineinlegte, entweder so, dass man dem Werk dem Nebenbegriff des Äusserlichen gab. . . . oder so, dass man im Werken etwas Selbstisches suchte, ein Hervordrängen des menschlichen Ichs zur Überhebung über Gott" (328).

According to Wilckens, the Judaizers in Galatia seek to reestablish the law as the criterion of righteousness before God. This program is said to contradict the gospel not because the law comprises a false criterion of righteousness but because "all have sinned." The law does not deceive those who obey it about the will of God. "Paul says simply that *sinners* cannot be justified on the basis of works of the law."[12] The way of the law is not misdirected but misadapted to the situation of the sinner; hence Paul's position is not that no one in principle *should* obtain salvation by "works of the law," but that no one *can*.

Where Wilckens cannot find the Bultmannian idea of the law's misdirection in Paul's thought, E. P. Sanders questions whether the apostle's critique of the law touches essentially its *dysfunctionalism*. Sanders observes that the presupposition of such a view (that no one can keep the law) is nowhere explicitly stated in Galatians. Nor is such a presupposition self-evident. If the universality of human transgression is a commonplace in Judaism, it did not lead automatically to despair over righteousness in the law.[13] Since he finds no evidence in Galatians that Paul argued *from* the universality of human sin *to* the impossibility of justification by the law, Sanders concludes that Galatians 3:10-14 is a dogmatic scripture argument that does not disclose the real grounds for Paul's attack on the law.

According to Sanders, Galatians 3:10-14 is an *argument* against justification by works of the law in which the *reason* for Paul's view is neither stated nor clearly implied. The reason must be sought elsewhere.

In the midst of a sometimes bewildering series of arguments, quotations, and appeals, there seem to be two sentences in Galatians in which Paul states unambiguously not only what his position is (which is never in doubt), but *why* he holds it. These statements are the last two cited [2:21 and 3:21]. Put in propositional terms, they say this: God sent Christ; he did so in order to offer righteousness; this would have been pointless if righteousness were already available by the law (2:21); the

---

[12]"Was heisst bei Paulus: 'Aus Werken des Gesetzes wird kein Mensch gerecht?' " in *Evangelisch-Katholischer Kommentar zum Neuen Testament: Vorarbeiten*, Pamphlet 1, ed. E. Schweizer et al. (Neukirchen: Neukirchener Verlag, 1969; Zürich: Benziger Verlag, 1969) 64.

[13]See *Paul, the Law, and the Jewish People*, 20-25 and 27-29.

law was not given to bring righteousness (3:21). That the positive statement about righteousness through Christ grounds the negative one about
the law seems to me self-evident.[14]

Sanders never justifies his selection of these two sentences from Galatians as genuine *reasons,* to be distinguished from all the other secondary arguments. Nor does he ever document the assumption under which
he understands the meaning of Paul's "dogmatic" stance against the law,
that "the debate in Galatians is a debate about 'entry' in the sense of
what is required to be considered a member *at all.*"[15] In fact, Paul says
nothing explicit to this effect, and statements such as the one in Galatians 3:3 ("Having begun with the Spirit do you intend to finish up with
the flesh?") suggest that the debate has much to do with "maintenance" (to adopt Sanders's own terminology) in the Christian life. The
assumption becomes especially suspect when we are informed that although in Judaism the language of righteousness does concern "the
maintenance of status among the group of the elect," in Paul it serves
as "transfer" terminology.[16]

Whatever one makes of Sanders's own interpretation of Galatians,
the distinction between "reasons" and "arguments" is nonetheless
helpful.[17] It reminds us that an argument may not touch upon the point(s)
of dispute in such a way that the opposing viewpoint may be reconstructed simply through the argument's own reversal. It suggests rightly
that in uncovering the basic reasons for Paul's arguments we come closer
to comprehending the problem as he saw it. Most important, it points
up the fact that unless one knows the reason or motivation for an ar-

---

[14]*Paul, the Law, and the Jewish People,* 27.

[15]Ibid., 20.

[16]See *Paul and Palestinian Judaism,* 544; cf. *Paul, the Law, and the Jewish People,*
6.

[17]The distinction is broached on p. 4 of *Paul, the Law, and the Jewish People.* The
differentiation is not without its problems. Sanders never considers, for example, whether
initial "reasons" may lose their motive power and be replaced by subsequent reasons,
some of which may have started out as "arguments." It is, after all, characteristic of
human thought that it continually makes sure of its foundations, and secondary defense
("arguments") is constitutive not only for apologetics but also for the very definition
and articulation of a position. In short, tested arguments become reasons.

gument, the argument may be understood at a surface level without being really grasped. We will return to this.

It is a weakness of both the traditional approach, which finds the motive of Paul's thrust as a whole in Galatians 2:15-21 and 3:10-14, and the reconstruction of Sanders, which places so much weight on Galatians 2:21 and 3:21, that little attention is paid to justifying the choice of those passages which are treated as most revealing of the problem at Galatia as Paul sees it. Galatians 2:15-21 is notoriously difficult to interpret, and not simply because of the density of its argument. The more basic interpretive difficulty concerns its function in the letter as a whole. It is simply not evident from the passage itself how the argument, which takes its point of departure from the Antioch episode, touches specifically on the situation at Galatia. An adequate exegesis here requires a prior identification of the crisis at Galatia, hence Galatians 2:15-21 cannot serve as a starting point for reconstructing the occasion of the letter. Galatians 3:10-14, on the other hand, occurs in a section aimed directly at the Galatians (see 3:1). But why should we give this argument precedence over any other in Galatians 3–4 as providing the most direct insight into the heart of the debate? The same goes for Galatians 2:21 and 3:21.

In a letter like Galatians we are faced with a particularly tricky version of the problem of relating the part to the whole. For the whole includes the situation that occasions the letter, hence an understanding of the literary whole requires some reconstruction of the other side of the debate, to which it comprises a response. How we read any given part in the literary whole and how we relate it to that whole will be in large measure determined, *and must be so determined,* by our conception of the larger whole, which includes the situation itself. The interpreter who identifies a passage other than 2:15-21 or 3:10-14 as the clearest window into this global epistolary context may well read *loci classici* such as 2:15-21 and 3:10-14 in novel ways. And the history of Galatians research has not been without such nontraditional readings.

In a 1945 essay Frederic R. Crownfield[18] identified the opponents as Jewish-Christian syncretists who advocated circumcision as a vehicle of hidden power and therefore a means to transcendent spiritual life

---

[18]"The Singular Problem of the Dual Galatians," *JBL* 64 (1945): 491-500.

in Christ. A more detailed and systematic reconstruction of syncretistic Judaizing at Galatia was soon after attempted by Walter Schmithals,[19] whose ideas have been taken up and modified in varying degrees by Gustav Stählin, Dieter Georgi, Willi Marxsen, and Klaus Wegenast.[20]

Schmithals regards Paul's apostolic autobiography (1:11–2:21), with its appeal not to a chain of tradition but to direct pneumatic vocation, as a genuinely gnostic argument, necessitated by gnostic claims to authority on the part of his opponents. As Schmithals sees it, these gnostic agitators do not promote the law as such, much less keep it themselves (5:13); their interest touches only that aspect of the Torah which lends itself to gnostic reinterpretation: circumcision. Consequently, it falls to Paul to inform the Galatians that circumcision obligates one to keep the whole law (5:3). The agitators advocate a libertinistic spiritualism (6:1; 5:25), bound up in some way with certain astrological speculations, such as those familiar to us from the Colossian "heresy" (4:8-11).[21] Wilhelm Lütgert, and after him James Hardy Ropes, had already puzzled over the relationship between statements in the letter that suggest a pneumatic self-understanding on the part of the community (3:2-5; 5:25; 6:1) and those that suggest a nomistic one (4:21; 5:4).[22] On the assump-

---

[19]"Die Häretiker in Galatien," *ZNW* 47 (1956): 25-67; revised under the same title in *Paulus und die Gnostiker,* TF 35 (Hamburg and Bergstedt: Herbert Reich, 1965) 9-46; further revised by the author and translated by John E. Steely under the title "The Heretics in Galatia," in *Paul and the Gnostics* (Nashville and New York: Abingdon Press, 1972) 13-64. See now also his essay, "Judaisten in Galatien?" *ZNW* 74 (1983): 27-58.

[20]Stählin, "Galaterbrief," in *Religion in Geschichte und Gegenwart,* vol. 2, 3rd ed. (6 vols: Tübingen: J. C. B. Mohr [Paul Siebeck], 1958) cols. 1187-89; Georgi, *Die Geschichte der Kollekte des Paulus für Jerusalem,* TF 38 (Hamburg/Bergstedt: Herbert Reich, 1965) 35-37; idem, "Theologische Auseinandersetzung mit den Einwänden gegen die Thesen der Bruderschaften," in *Christusbekenntnis im Atomzeitalter,* ThEh 70 (Munich: Chr. Kaiser Verlag, 1959) 109-13 (111 n. 2); Marxsen, *Introduction to the New Testament,* trans. G. Buswell (Philadelphia: Fortress Press, 1968) 50-58; Wegenast, "Das Problem der Tradition im Galaterbrief und im 1. Thessalonicherbrief," in *Das Verständnis der Tradition bei Paulus und in den Deuteropaulinen,* WMANT 8 (Neukirchen: Neukirchener Verlag, 1962) 34-49.

[21]"The Heretics in Galatia," 29, 43-55.

[22]Lütgert, *Gesetz und Geist: Eine Untersuchung zur Vorgeschichte des Galaterbriefes* (Gütersloh: Bertelsmann, 1919); Ropes, *The Singular Problem of the Epistle to the Galatians,* HTS 14 (Cambridge MA: Harvard University Press, 1929).

tion that Judaistic nomism and the pneumatic state are mutually exclusive, the so-called Lütgert-Ropes theory posits two fronts in Galatia: a legalistic party and an enthusiastic-libertinistic party. Schmithals finds the evidence for ecstatic licentiousness convincing but sees no hint in the letter that Paul distinguishes between two groups when he addresses the Galatians. With these two considerations in mind, he turns the weakness of the Lütgert-Ropes hypothesis to his own advantage: "gnostic circumcision and the pneumatic state go well together."[23] His arguments have not been lost upon Schlier, who remains nevertheless guarded in his overall portrait of the opposition.[24]

It is not necessary here to criticize Schmithals's reconstruction. Its insufficiencies have already been adequately exposed by Jost Eckert and others.[25] But one aspect of Schmithals's interpretation deserves attention: what he makes of 3:6–4:7 and 4:21-31. According to Schmithals these sections contain current *topoi* belonging to previous debates with *Jews* over the question of the law. That is to say, Paul does not address the situation in Galatia directly in these passages. Schmithals has been accused of suggesting that Paul *misunderstood* the situation at Galatia and that he knows better than the apostle does the true state of affairs,[26] but this accusation misrepresents his position. Schmithals's view is that Paul introduces his "antisynagogal pieces" in Galatians 3:1–5:12 not because he mistakes the problem at Galatia for Judaizing but because he wishes to inform the community about the logical consequences which the adoption of circumcision entails:

> Paul's theological reflection in Galatians 3:1–5:12 on righteousness by works and righteousness by faith, for which Galatians 2:19-21 prepared the way, thus is not to be interpreted as though Paul is presupposing in

---

[23]"The Heretics in Galatia," 46.

[24]*Der Brief an die Galater*, 19-24.

[25]*Die urchristliche Verkündigung im Streit zwischen Paulus und seinen Gegnern nach dem Galaterbrief* (Regensburg: Friedrich Pustet, 1971) 64-71; also R. Mcl. Wilson, "Gnostics—in Galatia?" in *Studia Evangelica* 4/1, TU 102 (Berlin: Akademie-Verlag, 1968) 358-67.

[26]So Philip Vielhauer, "Gesetzesdienst und Stoicheiadienst im Galaterbrief," in *Oikodome: Aufsätze zum Neuen Testament*, vol. 2, ed. G. Klein, TBNT 65 (Munich: Chr. Kaiser Verlag, 1979) 184.

these theological statements that some *in Galatia* consciously intended to go the way of pure law-righteousness. . . . This central part of Galatians rather gives witness that *for Paul* the adoption of circumcision can mean nothing other than an attempt to achieve righteousness without faith through works. Therefore the circumcision being practiced in Galatia *must* have the same meaning for the Galatians *coram Deo,* regardless of whether they themselves know it or not (Gal. 5:3), whether they concern themselves with the fulfillment of the law or—incomprehensibly—neglect it, in spite of circumcision (Gal. 6:13).[27]

These remarks bring to light a methodological principle essential to a correct interpretation of Paul's argument in its epistolary context. Reconstruction of the opponents' position does not in itself tell us what is at stake in the letter. Not what the agitators or Galatians regard as the center of dispute but what Paul sees as the real issue must form the *presupposition* of exegesis. Not a reconstruction of the historical situation at Galatia but a reconstruction of the epistolary perspective on that situation comprises the prerequisite for interpreting the letter.

To say that the epistolary perspective on the Galatian situation comprises the prerequisite for interpreting the letter is a little like saying that we need to be briefed by Paul on the problem at Galatia before we can rightly *hear* the letter. And since Paul cannot favor us with such an "advance briefing" personally, we must manage it ourselves. The ancients conceived of the letter as only one half of a dialogue.[28] In order to hear what is being said in context, we must join the dialogue of which Galatians is a part. That will mean breaking into the conversation and getting our bearings. It will require subjecting the letter to *two distinct readings.* And the first reading must lead to a definitive *standpoint* from which the second reading can proceed.

The result of the first reading is to be distinguished from what interpreters call a "hunch" or "working hypothesis" to be tested exe-

---

[27]"The Heretics in Galatia," 41.

[28]Adolf Deissmann, *Light from the Ancient Near East,* trans. L. R. M. Strachan (Grand Rapids MI: Baker, 1978; based on the 4th German ed. of 1922) 228. See, e.g., Demetrius *de elocut.* 233ff. (εἶναι γὰρ τὴν ἐπιστολὴν οἷον τὸ ἕτερον μέρος τοῦ διαλόγου), as cited in Deissmann, *Bibelstudien* (Marburg: N. G. Elwert, 1895) 190 n. 1.

getically, even if such hunches often do exert the same sort of determinative influence that the first reading is *designed* to exercise. Furthermore, the result of the first reading must be conclusive rather than provisional and its application prescriptive rather than merely suggestive. A consideration of the nature of "meaning in context" reveals why this is so. Consider the following story told by literary theorist Stanley Fish.

> On the first day of the new semester a colleague at Johns Hopkins University was approached by a student who, as it turned out, had just taken a course from me. She put to him what I think you would agree is a perfectly straightforward question: "Is there a text in this class?" Responding with a confidence so perfect that he was unaware of it . . . , my colleague said, "Yes; it's the *Norton Anthology of Literature*," whereupon the trap (set not by the student but by the infinite capacity of language) was sprung: "No, no," she said, "I mean in this class do we believe in poems and things, or is it just us?"[29]

The question, as the student posed it, had for its context a class in which the objective meaning of the "text" was disputed by professor Fish who preaches "the instability of the text and the unavailability of determinate meanings."[30] The professor of the class she was about to take heard the question in its conventional (beginning-of-the-semester) academic context, where it means, "Is a textbook required for this class?"

The importance of situational context in the example just cited is obvious. And it should also be evident that if the student's question ("Is there a text in this class?") were encountered in a paragraph, it might still be misunderstood, especially by an uninformed reader. For paragraphs also depend on the unexpressed presuppositions of "situational contexts" (such as Stanley Fish's class). And no doubt a number of my own readers, if they are unacquainted with Fish's work, remain unclear about what the student was really asking, even though they understand the words and syntax of her question perfectly well. Now consider Ga-

---

[29]Stanley Fish, *Is There a Text in This Class? The Authority of Interpretive Communities* (Cambridge/London: Harvard University Press, 1980) 305.

[30]Ibid., 305. In citing Fish's anecdote I do not mean to suggest that I follow him in all of the implications for literary criticism that he develops out of this story.

latians 4:1-11, which appears to associate the law with the "cosmic elements."[31] An adequate interpretation of this paragraph depends on our ability to answer one very basic question. Is it the agitators (or the Galatians) or Paul who first makes this connection? If it is Paul, then we will conclude that "serving the elements" represents something unequivocally negative in context and functions in an argument aimed at discrediting the Galatians' law-observance by equating it with this given negative, perhaps the "world" as a sphere of bondage to sin and death.[32] If the agitators have made the connection, the point of the argument shifts fundamentally. In this case, serving the elements through the law designates for Paul's readers something desirable, at least in its effects, and is itself an express point of dispute between the apostle and the community.[33] The frustrating thing about this passage is that we seem to be in a poor position to determine with any degree of certainty who first brings "the law" and "the elements" together, Paul or the agitators (or the Galatians).[34]

The problem of ascertaining the situational context does not affect the interpretation of sentences and paragraphs alone. Larger complexes

---

[31]στοιχεῖα τοῦ κόσμου ("elements of the cosmos"). Since I choose this text only by way of illustration, I will not enter at this juncture into the debate whether or not it is observances of the law that are understood as stoicheia-service.

[32]So Vielhauer, "Gesetzesdienst und Stoicheiadienst im Galaterbrief," 193-95; cf. Bo Reicke, "The Law and the World according to Paul," JBL 70 (1951): 259-76; Josef Blinzler, "Lexikalisches zu dem Terminus στοιχεῖα τοῦ κόσμου bei Paulus," in Studiorum Paulinorum Congresus Internationalis Catholicus, vol. 2, AnBib 17-18 (Rome: Pontifical Biblical Institute, 1963) 429-43; G. Delling, στοιχέω, TDNT 7:666-87.

[33]See, for example, Robert Jewett, "The Agitators and the Galatian Congregation." "The widespread assumption that the στοιχεῖα (Gal. IV.9) ruled during certain periods through the stars and planets seems to have been connected by the agitators with the Jewish festivals. In celebrating the festivals at the proper times, the powers of the universe would be appeased and the success of human activity assured" (208).

[34]The idea of the στοιχεῖα τοῦ κόσμου as spiritual powers is present in Galatians, together with the equation of serving them with serving the law (see 4:3 in its larger context and 4:8-11). But it is not clear whether this particular understanding of the στοιχεῖα is a "given" of the debate or, as F. F. Bruce puts it, "Paul's own contribution to religious vocabulary" (The Epistle to the Galatians: A Commentary on the Greek Text, NIGTC [Grand Rapids MI: Wm. B. Eerdmans, 1982] 204; cf. G. Delling, στοιχέω, 685).

find their meaning in the context of certain situationally given assumptions. If these assumptions are in significant ways idiosyncratic and if the writing does not clue the outside reader into this idiosyncracy, an accurate interpretation will be impossible. Consider the concept of "sonship" in Galatians. Let us assume for the moment that its various expressions ("sons of Abraham," "sons of God in Christ Jesus," "seed of Abraham," "children of promise," "children of the free woman") all point to essentially the same idea, the status of "sonship" in the sphere of God's people. Now most interpreters agree that according to Galatians 3:6–4:7 a person receives "sonship" not by the law (or by "works of the law") but by faith. But what does this mean? We may sharpen this question with a semantic consideration.

Linguists designate as "unmarked" that meaning "which would be readily applied in a minimum context where there is little or nothing to help the receptor in determining the meaning."[35] In the story related by Fish, the professor took the terms of the student's question in their conventional "unmarked" signification. But for the student herself the terms of her question bore the meanings with which they had been "marked" by Fish's class. It would appear that the majority of interpreters have assumed that the language of "sonship" in Galatians is *unmarked*. That is, they do not think that the use of this terminology in Galatians is in any sense idiosyncratic. On this assumption, that minimum preunderstanding of "sonship" necessary to the most basic grasp of Galatians 3–4 is to be gotten from its use in early Christianity and Judaism. "Sonship" specifies *who* belongs to God's people. In Galatians, so the traditional interpretation goes, the concept assumes importance because the Galatians' status before God is at stake (hence the link with justification). That is straightforward enough, but the traditional viewpoint has not gone unchallenged.

Frederick Crownfield had this to say about the first reference to sonship in Galatians (3:7): "The contrast implied [sonship by faith and not by works of the law] is not with the Jews claiming to be sons of Abraham, but with a pretended higher stage of mystery."[36] And consider the more recent interpretation of the Galatian situation by Robert Jewett:

---

[35]J. P. Louw, *The Semantics of New Testament Greek,* SBLSS (Philadelphia: Fortress Press, 1982; Chico CA: Scholars Press, 1982) 33.

[36]"The Singular Problem of the Dual Galatians," 499.

> It was their [the Galatians'] desire to gain the final level of perfection which led to circumcision when they heard from the agitators that such an act would ensure entrance into the mythical seed of Abraham. And it was their instinctive respect for the cosmic powers which led them to a celebration of the calendar whose mystery was revealed by the wisdom of the Old Testament.[37]

In these reconstructions the meaning of "sonship" in Galatians is treated as "marked," in the first instance by the extra-epistolary context (at Galatia, in the antecedent communications to Paul) but also by the letter itself, where it provides clues to the situation. If the idea of sonship here has less to do with status and mostly to do with participation in what is spiritually ultimate, then the argument of Galatians 3:6–4:7 will be read much differently than we are accustomed to reading it. Statements on "the blessing" and "the promise" will no longer be construed as having "justification before God" as their essential content. And the meaning and function of the justification language itself may be cast in an entirely new light.[38]

Idiosyncratic or marked meanings are likely to resist ready identification in a document like Galatians. Since Paul writes to those who know the letter's occasion as participants, he need not define the terms used by the agitators or rehearse their arguments. Nor has the apostle any cause to summarize the Galatians' own thinking on the matter at hand. Whatever marked meanings belong to the debate will be disclosed only incidentally. Hence, it should come as no surprise that those who reconstruct a somewhat idiosyncratic theology of the agitators, a "syncretistic nomism," do so on the basis of clues scattered throughout

---

[37]"The Agitators and the Galatian Congregation," 212.

[38]See, e.g., Bernard Brinsmead, *Galatians—Dialogical Response to Opponents*, SBLDS 65 (Chico CA: Scholars Press, 1982). According to Brinsmead, the justification terminology in Galatians is mystery language (hence "marked"). It is said to function in the opponents' system as part of a "doctrine of cosmic deliverance on the basis of a program of 'works of the law,' " where justification by the law is subject to a "mystical understanding" (115). It is interesting to observe in this connection that Sanders in effect treats Paul's justification language as marked, when he alleges that the "righteous" word group concerns "maintenance of status" among the elect in Judaism but has to do with "getting in" or "transfer" to the body of the saved in Paul (*Paul and Palestinian Judaism*, 544).

the letter. Passages such as 3:19; 5:3; 6:13; 6:1 (with its reference to οἱ πνευματικοί) and especially 4:8-11 have figured decisively in such reconstructions.[39] It is unfair criticism to complain that this approach is illegitimate because it does not allow the contours of the debate to emerge from the letter as a whole. The method is in principle fully justified, *if* the letter assumes marked meanings for words that are of determinative significance in the debate.

This last qualification is important. One takes for granted that any discussion develops to some degree its own peculiarities in the usage of terms and concepts. At the same time communication always takes place in the context of meanings more broadly shared. A text never tells all it knows but, like every communication, depends heavily on what "goes without saying," that is, on assumed meanings that inform, one could say enable, its assertions. Consequently, even what the text tells remains meaningless apart from what it assumes. Therefore, the interpreter who seeks a "historical-critical" understanding of Galatians—and that means to some extent every interpreter who reads the text in Greek—must bring to the text a "prior" understanding of its language, based on the semantic world of the letter *beyond* its particular occasion. This preunderstanding is prerequisite to reading the text at all. But the interpreter must also gain access to the particular semantic world of the letter, which may include "marked" meanings of conventional language. It is at this point that we find ourselves as readers extremely disadvantaged. We may approximate, to be sure with severe limitations, the "world" of the Galatian letter beyond its immediate setting. If this were not the case we could not even *translate* the letter. But our approximation of the most immediate semantic context, the debate itself, is of a different order. For where the controls on establishing the more general semantic context (the Pauline mission, early Christianity, first-century Judaism, the Graeco-Roman world) consist of a multiplicity of sources, there is only one control on the immediate context of Galatians: the letter itself. This need not in principle pose an obstacle to an adequate interpretation of the letter. If there are no situationally marked meanings that we need to be aware of in order to follow Paul's argument, we may read the letter simply on the basis of our general under-

---

[39]See Kümmel, *Introduction to the New Testament*, 299-300.

standing of the language Paul employs. But if key terms and concepts have been marked idiosyncratically in the situation, we may not be able to understand the letter. Interpreters have always been reluctant to face up to this possibility.

Heinrich Schlier, for example, given pause by Schmithals's reconstruction, insists in the end that a precise identification of the agitators and their ideas is inconsequential for interpretation:

> For whoever his opponents may have been and whatever specific convictions they may have represented, Paul sees them, according to the reports he has received, as representatives of a Jewish-Christian nomism that is not consistent but ignores the decisive requirement of the law, namely Agape. Had another shading of a legalistic Jewish Christianity appeared in Galatia among the Christian communities, the apostle would scarcely have responded any differently. For his response is, as usual, based on "principle" [ist wie meist "prinzipiell" gehalten].[40]

When Schlier insists on the primacy of the apostle's viewpoint for interpreting Galatians, his method is sound. But the idea that Paul responds simply "on principle" is suspect. It is not altogether evident what is meant, but one gathers that behind the assertion is something like the assumption informing Schmithals's view of the arguments in 3:6–4:7 and 4:21-31 (those sections "in which the situation in Galatia is not directly addressed"[41]), namely, that we already know what these "antisynagogal" pieces mean, or better, that the use of language in these central passages of the letter does not presuppose anything which is not accessible to us from Paul's remaining letters, particularly Romans. If interpreters have become increasingly aware of the dangers entailed in reading Galatians in the light of the theology of Romans, less attention has been paid to those inherent in assuming that at least the semantic field is the same for both letters. Of course, in large measure it must be. But in certain respects, including some which may be critical to interpretation, it may not. The meaning of "sonship," discussed above, offers a potential case in point. This is another way of saying that the possibility of situationally marked meanings has not been fully reck-

---

[40]*Der Brief an die Galater*, 24.
[41]"The Heretics in Galatia," 41.

oned with, not even by interpreters who discern a measure of idiosyncracy (or "syncretism") in the theology of the agitators as Paul confronts it.[42]

Let us review and sharpen our understanding of the difficulties before us. We have learned how to restate Paul's arguments. "Justification," "sonship," "blessing," and "promise" are all to be had "by faith" and "not by (works of) the law." But we are not certain precisely what is meant here. We are not clear on where the point lies. We understand Paul's letter to be directed toward a concrete situation and assume that the point rests at that juncture where his arguments impinge upon the problem as he sees it. But the problem as he sees it appears to form an assumption of the letter. That is, the letter does not aim at its disclosure except in argument against it, where the nature of the problem at one level is presupposed at the same time that it is cast in a new light. We hope that we can reconstruct the occasion of the letter at least minimally from certain suggestive passages but know that this will be possible only if these sections of the letter do not include situationally marked meanings that we are unable to discern as such from the letter alone, which is all we have.

How Does an Outsider Join the Conversation?

The *impasse* we have reached in the interpretation of Galatians lies in the fact that we do not have a means of ascertaining *whether* significant terms of the debate carry situationally marked meaning, much less of fixing such meanings if they are there. But we have reason to believe that some of the language of Galatians may be just so marked. In short, we find ourselves excluded from the dialogical circle, where, to borrow Quintilian's words from the epigraph for this chapter "everyone is familiar with the issue under debate." But to put the problem this way is to suggest that it is in part a function of the "rhetoric" of Galatians, and not simply a matter of historical distance. In that case, a formal analysis of Galatians may shed light on the problem.

---

[42]E.g., Schmithals and Schlier (see above). Most theories of a syncretistic nomism at Galatia have been presented in such brevity that the precise consequences for understanding Paul's arguments in Gal 3 and 4 are not specified.

To this point we have not considered the genre or structure of Galatians, except to observe that a letter addressed to a specific situation and representing only one voice in a dialogue may not disclose to the outside reader information essential to its interpretation, or, if it does disclose this information, may not identify it in a way that will lead the outside reader to recognize it as such. But a recent analysis of the literary composition of Galatians suggests that we do not face this problem after all. According to Hans Dieter Betz,[43] Galatians belongs to the genre of epistolary self-defense. As an "apologetic letter" it yields to analysis according to the canons of judicial oratory as set forth by the ancient Greek and Roman rhetors, especially Quintilian (*Institutio Oratoria*).[44] If this is correct, the problem of securing a standpoint from which to read Galatians has an immediate solution. For the third part of the judicial speech is the *propositio* (also termed *divisio* or *partitio*), "where we ought first to make clear what we and our opponents agree upon, if there is agreement on the points useful to us, and what remains contested" (Cicero, *Rhet. ad Her.* 1.10.17).[45] Since the whole speech is directed toward the judge (an outside party), the *propositio* is preceded by a *narratio*, a narration of the facts leading up to the case. In this way the *propositio* is given an interpretive context. If Galatians belongs to the genre of judicial oratory, then it will contain a formal disclosure of the case designed specifically for an outside audience.

---

[43]*Galatians: A Commentary on Paul's Letter to the Churches of Galatia*, Hermeneia (Philadelphia: Fortress Press, 1979); idem, "In Defense of the Spirit: Paul's Letter to the Galatians as a Document of Early Christian Apologetics," in *Aspects of Religious Propaganda in Judaism and Early Christianity*, ed. Elisabeth Schüssler Fiorenza (Notre Dame IN: University of Notre Dame Press, 1976); idem, "The Literary Composition and Function of Paul's Letter to the Galatians," *NTS* 21 (1975): 353-79.

[44]Among the valuable modern studies of Graeco-Roman rhetoric are the following: Heinrich Lausberg, *Handbuch der literarischen Rhetorik: Eine Grundlegung der Wissenschaft*, 2 vols. (Munich: Max Hueber, 1960); Josef Martin, *Antike Rhetorik: Technik und Methode*, Handbuch der Altertumswissenschaft 2/3 (Munich: C. H. Beck, 1974); Edward P. J. Corbett, *Classical Rhetoric for the Modern Student* (New York: Oxford University Press, 1965); George A. Kennedy, *Classical Rhetoric and Its Christian and Secular Tradition from Ancient to Modern Times* (Chapel Hill: University of North Carolina Press, 1980); idem, *New Testament Interpretation through Rhetorical Criticism* (Chapel Hill and London: University of North Carolina Press, 1984).

[45]See Betz, *Galatians*, 114.

If we lay the conventional scheme of the judicial speech over the Galatian letter, it is evident that 1:11–2:14 recommends itself as the *narratio,* and if that is so, then 3:1ff. (where Paul begins to adduce "proofs") should be the *confirmatio* (or *probatio*), that part of the judicial defense in which the supporting arguments are presented. Paul's so-called "speech to Peter" (2:14b-21) would then represent the *propositio,* in which case the place to begin is with this paragraph, read in the light of 1:11–2:14. In other words, if Galatians follows the pattern of the judicial speech, then 2:14b-21 should provide us with the proper orientation to the whole letter, the *standpoint* from which it is to be read.

Curiously, Betz's own reconstruction of the "case" does not seem to derive from his interpretation of 2:14b-21.[46] But the more pertinent question is whether Galatians is in fact an "apologetic letter." We must return a negative answer to this question.[47] The apologetic speech aims at self-defense, but Paul's apostolic self-defense in Galatians is ancillary to his defense of the gospel.[48] His purpose is to persuade the Galatians not simply to change their minds about him but to change their present course of thinking and acting with reference to the gospel. Hence, Nils Dahl is right in stressing the affinities between Galatians and sym-

[46]Betz presents his rhetorical analysis of Galatians as a whole in outline form on pp. 16-23 of his commentary. According to Betz, the Galatians are turning to the law in order to combat problems with "the flesh," for which his foundation preaching has not (to their minds) prepared them. Paul is said to respond by defending the sufficiency of the Spirit for the ethical sphere (*Galatians,* 29). Betz reconstructs this dispute primarily from the paraenesis ("In Defense of the Spirit," 105-106). But the Spirit is not even *mentioned* in 2:15-21.

[47]Both Betz's reconstruction of the Galatian crisis and his rhetorical analysis of the letter have received sufficient and compelling criticism, hence there is no need to evaluate his arguments in their specifics here. See especially the reviews by Wayne A. Meeks (*JBL* 100 [1981]: 304-307), Paul W. Meyer (*RSR* 7 [1981]: 318-23), W. D. Davies (*RSR* 7 [1981]: 310-17), George A. Kennedy (*New Testament Interpretation through Rhetorical Criticism,* 144-52), and George Lyons, *Pauline Autobiography: Toward a New Understanding,* SBLDS 73 (Atlanta: Scholars Press, 1985) 113-19.

[48]See 1:8 ("Even if *we* or an angel from heaven should preach a gospel to you other than the one we preached to you, let him be accursed"); 1:11 ("The gospel preached by me is not κατὰ ἄνθρωπον); 2:5 ("To them we did not submit for one moment, in order that the truth of the gospel might remain for you"); 2:14 ("But when I saw that they were not walking straightforwardly before the truth of the gospel . . . ").

bouletic (deliberative) speech.[49] Further, if the narrative in Galatians 1:11–2:14 presents the facts leading up to a particular case, it is the history culminating in the case at *Antioch*. The particular relation of the "Galatian case" to this history is not immediately evident. Moreover, 2:14b-21 does not set forth points of contention, it *mounts an argument*.[50]

We take it for granted that form and content belong inextricably together and expect, accordingly, that formal analysis can tell us something about material content and vice versa. For example, the one who understands the form of Aquinas's *Summa Theologica* knows that the opening opinions given on any point represent opposing views to be refuted. Here the form of presentation is explicit and consistent, hence a sure guide to the nature of the content. But form is often one of the least obvious aspects of a piece of literature. In such cases formal matters will have to be settled for the most part in the end, rather than at the beginning. The question concerning the extent to which Galatians conforms to a given rhetorical genre belongs among these questions of form that depend upon prior material considerations for their answer. But there is one formal judgment that we can make with certainty at the outset: Galatians is a *letter*. As a letter it conforms to Hellenistic epistolary norms and is in many ways typical of Paul's own exploitation of epistolary convention.[51] But more important for purposes here are the altogether ordinary stylistic characteristics, and precisely because of their patentness. In a piece of literature unmarked by paragraph spacing or subheadings, a writing meant to be read aloud, stereotypical transitional

---

[49]Dahl's views are reported by George Lyons, *Pauline Autobiography*, 119. They are contained in an unpublished paper circulated among the members of the Society of Biblical Literature Paul Seminar in 1973. See further George Kennedy, who also describes the style of Galatians as "deliberative rhetoric" (*New Testament Interpretation through Rhetorical Criticism*, 145-47).

[50]It may be noted that we have hardly any examples of apologetic speeches and only Plato's *Ep*. 7 as an apologetic letter. Although Betz appeals to Arnaldo Momigliano's discussion of the apologetic letter (*Galatians*, 15), Momigliano himself is able to list only Plato's *Ep*. 7 as an extant example. See Momigliano, *The Development of Greek Biography* (Cambridge: Harvard University Press, 1971) 60-62.

[51]For a general discussion of Paul's distinctive epistolary style, see William G. Doty, *Letters in Primitive Christianity* (Philadelphia: Fortress Press, 1973).

phrases define sense units, and the listener is expected to pay attention
to them. Vocatives, for example, provide a ready means of signalling
transitions to auditors.[52] In the following epistolary analysis, it is the
obvious to which we will give greatest heed. And, as we shall see, this
modest reconstruction of the epistolary structure of Galatians will carry
us a long way toward identifying the place to begin in interpreting the
letter. Thus, epistolary analysis comprises the first step in what we have
called our *first reading*.

Galatians exhibits a conventional epistolary "frame": opening
(sender, addressee, and greeting) in 1:1-5, a postscript in the author's
own hand (6:11-18), which includes a closing benediction (v.18). There
is no "thanksgiving" (or προσκύνημα) a period that Paul likes to use
as an occasion to give thanks to God for the success of the gospel among
the letter's recipients, but 1:6-10 appears to serve as a kind of "thanksgiving parody." Instead of celebrating the success of the gospel among
the Galatians, Paul upbraids the community for deserting the gospel.[53]
The vocative in 1:11 signals a new start, hence we will treat 1:11–6:10
as the letter body.

The next major transition after 1:11 is 3:1, where Paul turns abruptly
from the narrative of 1:11–2:21 to the present situation of the Galatians.
A vocative (Paul's harsh "Oh foolish Galatians!") again marks the new

---

[52]John L. White has documented this for the nonliterary papyri letters of the Roman
period. See *The Body of the Greek Letter*, SBLDS 2 (Missoula MT: Scholars Press,
1972) 15-19. Examples are also forthcoming from Jewish literature. In the *Testaments
of the Twelve Patriarchs*, for instance, an analogous phrase, καὶ νῦν τέκνα (μου),
provides the most characteristic convention for introducing new beginnings. The same
holds true for Paul's own use of the vocative in his other letters, in particular his fre-
quent use of ἀδελφοί. This is not to suggest that vocatives cannot be employed for
emphasis or to draw attention to a conclusion (1 Cor 7:24; 7:29; 11:33; 14:39; 15:31;
15:50; 15:58; 1 Thess 1:4; 2:14; 3:7; 4:10; 5:4; 5:14; 5:25; Phlm 7, 20). See further,
Stanley K. Stowers, *The Diatribe and Paul's Letter to the Romans*, SBLDS 57 (Missoula MT: Scholars Press, 1981) 86.

[53]See 1 Thess 1:3, 6-9; 1 Cor 1:4-7; Rom 1:8; Phlm 4-5; Phil 1:3-5, 7. Considerable
attention has been devoted to the Pauline thanksgiving. For a recent comprehensive survey and discussion, see Peter Thomas O'Brien, *Introductory Thanksgivings in the Letters of Paul*, SNovT 49 (Leiden: E. J. Brill, 1977). The language of "thanksgiving
parody" was suggested to me by Edgar Krentz in a private conversation about Gal 1:6-
10.

start unmistakably. The listener is caught by surprise in 3:1. *Formally* there is no break in Paul's speech to Peter begun in 2:14 until this point, where the Galatians are addressed directly for the first time since 1:11. The turn in 3:1 defines 1:11–2:21 as a discrete larger whole within the letter body, inasmuch as the Galatian situation is kept explicitly in view from 3:1 onwards. We may call this section (1:11–2:21) the apostolic autobiography.[54]

Within the remainder of the letter body (3:1–6:10) two sections emerge clearly as relatively self-contained units: the appeal in 4:12-20 (note the vocative and change of subject in 4:12) and the so-called allegory in 4:21-30 (31). The only formal break within 3:1–4:11 occurs at 3:15 (Ἀδελφοί, κατὰ ἄνθρωπον λέγω). It is not immediately clear whether this marks a major or a minor transition within 3:1–4:11. From a thematic point of view one could argue that 3:15–4:7 comprises a self-contained reflection on "the inheritance." But it is also possible to take 3:19 ("Why then the law?") as a major turning point[55] and to construe 3:19–4:11 as a unified whole organized around the thematic opposition "slavery/sonship." An advantage of the latter division is that it does not leave 4:8-11 dangling. But both ways of organizing the material are legitimate, and we should not force Paul's discussion into contrived structures, especially since he weaves the themes of inheritance and slavery/sonship together in his argument.

F. C. Baur divided the letter into three parts: a personal-apologetic section, a dogmatic section, and a practical section.[56] Since the work of Martin Dibelius,[57] it has become customary to term the practical exhortation in Paul's letters *paraenesis*. Hence formal analysis requires that we determine where the paraenesis in Galatians begins: with 4:12; 4:21;

---

[54]This description of Paul's "autobiographical narrative" (Lyons, *Pauline Autobiography*, 136) is appropriate inasmuch as Paul writes self-consciously in the *apostolic* first person (1:1; cf. 1:15-16).

[55]So, e.g., Betz, *Galatians*, 162; John L. White, *The Body of the Greek Letter*, 56.

[56]*Paul, the Apostle of Jesus Christ*, ET of 2nd German ed. issued post. by E. Zeller, 2 vols. (London and Edinburgh: Williams and Norgate, 1873 and 1875) 1:263.

[57]*Der Brief des Jakobus*, MeyerK 15/7 (Göttingen: Vandenhoeck & Ruprecht, 1921); idem, *Geschichte der urchristlichen Literatur*, ed. F. Hahn, TB 58 (Munich: Chr. Kaiser Verlag, 1975) 140-52.

5:1; 5:2; 5:7; or 5:13?[58] Now paraenesis as a genre, whether literary or oral, includes diverse elements: moral topoi, catalogues of vices and virtues, household codes, and community regulations. According to this definition, the paraenesis in Galatians begins in 5:13 and extends to 6:10. This block of material contains a list of vices and virtues (5:19-23), maxims (6:1-10),[59] and a traditional summary of the law (5:14).[60] Such paraenetic elements are absent from preceding sections.

But if we ask not where the paraenesis begins but where the apostolic *exhortation* commences, then the answer is 5:1. This is not to say that there are no imperatives or implied imperatives up to this point. In 4:12, for example, we meet an imperative, and the question in 4:9 has implied imperative force. Nevertheless, "exhortation" as an epistolary section begins with 5:1.[61] And since 4:31 introduces the basis for the opening exhortation and contains a vocative διό ἀδελφοί (cf. Rom 12:1), we may tentatively treat 4:31 as the opening of the apostolic exhortation.

After the imperative in 5:1 we have what can be described only as an implementation of apostolic authority: "Look, I Paul say to you . . . " (5:2). F. F. Bruce rightly observes that here, as in Romans 15:14ff., Paul "is projecting his presence as effectively as he can among those to whom the letter is sent."[62] It is the mood of apostolic authority that one hears in the warnings of this section. The paraenetic section has

---

[58]See Otto Merk, "Der Beginn der Paränese im Galaterbrief," *ZNW* 60 (1969): 83-104.

[59]For a careful treatment of these from the perspective of their parallels in the Hellenistic literature, see Betz, *Galatians,* 292-311.

[60]We do not have here simply a quotation of Lev 19:18. There is no introductory formula and the use of the wording of Lev 19:18 in "summaries" of the law is widely attested in primitive Christianity and Judaism. See Franz Mussner, *Der Galaterbrief,* 4th ed. HTKNT 9 (Freiburg/Basel/Vienna: Herder, 1981) 369-73 and notes.

[61]As Jürgen Becker observes: "5,1ff. bringt nicht eigentlich Paränese, d.h. (allgemeine) Mahnungen zum christlichen Verhalten, sondern reflektiert den Grundsatzentscheid zwischen Gesetz und Freiheit." See *Der Brief an die Galater,* NTD 8 (Göttingen: Vandenhoeck & Ruprecht, 1981) 67.

[62]*The Epistle to the Galatians,* 229. So also Schlier: "Mit ἴδε ἐγὼ Παῦλος gibt er dieser Behauptung [5:1] das Gewicht seiner Autorität ähnlich wie mit dem αὐτὸς δὲ ἐγὼ Παῦλος 2 Kor 10,1 seiner Mahnung" (*Der Brief an die Galater,* 231).

the same tone ("But I say . . . " 5:16; "I warn you as I told you before
. . . " 5:21). Hence, the whole section, 5:1–6:10, may be termed apostolic exhortation. And we have here another indication that the rhetorical style of Galatians is deliberative, for it is the authority of the
speaker that carries the deliberative speech (Quintilian *Inst. Or.* 3.8.12).

Following the paraenesis we meet the statement: "Look, I am writing to you in my own hand with large letters!" (6:11). Gordon J. Bahr[63]
has shown that such a subscription in the author's own hand was common to letters in which an amanuensis was employed. Subscriptions in
the papyri letters frequently consist of no more than date, name, and address. But sometimes the author takes up personal matters or touches
upon matters not mentioned in the body of the letter. This last practice
evidently owes something of its character to legal "reports" (con-
tracts), in which each party to an agreement would add to the bottom of
the document his signature and a summary of the contents of the agreement, which was itself prepared by a professional scribe. Such docu-
ments were sometimes formulated in the style of the official Hellenistic
letter.

Galatians 6:11-18 appears to represent an example of a *subscription*
in which the author himself appends a personal note concerning matters
touched upon but not developed in the letter body. Subscriptions were
rarely summaries of the body of the letter,[64] hence Betz's suggestion that
6:11-18 constitutes a *peroratio* (the section of the Hellenistic "apology" in which the main points of the argument were summarized) should
be received with caution. In particular the following assertion is doubtful:

> It [6:11-18 as the *peroratio*] contains the interpretive clues to the un-
> derstanding of Paul's major concerns in the letter as a whole and should
> be employed as the hermeneutical key to the intentions of the apostle.[65]

To the extent that a postscript afforded the author an opportunity to
amplify ideas mentioned already, it provided the reader with further in-

---

[63]"The Subscriptions in the Pauline Letters," *JBL* 87 (1968): 27-41.

[64]Ibid., 33.

[65]*Galatians*, 313.

sight into the letter body. But a subscript could also raise an entirely new matter. Hence we must first establish whether the autograph in Galatians returns to an earlier theme or takes a new direction (or both). Then an assessment of its usefulness for interpreting parts of the letter body can be made more soundly.

The foregoing epistolary analysis indicates a division of the letter into parts as follows:

Opening (1:1-5)
Thanksgiving Parody (1:6-10)
Body (1:11–6:10)
    Part One. Apostolic Autobiography (1:11–2:21)
    Part Two. Central Argument (3:1–4:30)
    Part Three. Apostolic Exhortation (4:31–6:10)
        Opening (4:31–5:12)
        Paraenesis (5:13–6:10)
Postscript (6:11-17)
Closing Benediction (6:18)

Formal analysis directs us to certain portions of the letter as potential places to begin in seeking to ascertain the apostle's position regarding the nature of the problem, while excluding others. We may begin by identifying the parts that are excluded.

The apostolic autobiography affords no entree into the epistolary occasion, inasmuch as it is far from self-evident how this personal history applies to the Galatians. Even the ''speech,'' which crowns the narrative and broaches themes to be treated more extensively in what follows (the law,[66] justification, eschatological life, the death of Christ), offers the outside reader no firm clues as to where the Antioch horizon ends and the Galatian begins. That determination requires a prior delineation of the Galatian horizon itself. Indeed, even if we succeed in reconstructing the argument(s) of 1:11–2:21 with some measure of confidence, we are not necessarily any closer to ascertaining the purpose of the autobiography. For the same story can serve a variety of purposes.

---

[66]The term νόμος appears for the first time in the letter in 2:16, although Paul has spoken of ''the traditions of my fathers'' (1:14) and ''circumcision'' (2:3, 7, 8, 12).

This negative result on the viability of using the apostolic autobiography as a way to join the epistolary conversation is extremely important. It means that the "traditional" interpretation, which identifies "justification by faith" as the main theme of the epistle, loses its prima facie appeal. For the language of justification by faith (ἐκ πίστεως δικαιοῦσθαι) is used emphatically only here. To be sure, Paul employs this terminology again in 3:8, 11, and 24. But beyond these instances he speaks of justification only once more (in 5:4-5). And it is far from self-evident that in 3:1-14 "justification" comprises the central nerve of the argument. In 3:8 it appears in a dependent clause as a kind of presupposition of the main assertion. In 3:11 it occurs in the midst of a larger argument involving a variety of themes. In fact, a thematic analysis of Galatians reveals that other themes are equally or even more pervasive than "justification." We have already observed that the whole of 3:15–4:7 can be viewed as an argument centering around the idea of "the (Abrahamic) inheritance." Moreover, if we take seriously the identification of the inheritance with the Spirit, via the medial terms "blessing of Abraham" and "promise" (3:14), then we may view all of 3:1–4:7 as thematically unified: the Spirit (3:2; 3:3; 3:5; 3:14) = the blessing (3:8; 3:9; 3:14) = the content of the promise (3:14; 3:16; 3:17; 3:18; 3:19; 3:21; 3:29) = the inheritance/"realized heirship" (3:18; 3:29; 4:7). Only by treating the note repeated in 2:16 as the central theme ("no one is justified by works of the law") can one construe chapters 3 and 4 as comprising "a *locus classicus* for the doctrine of the *justificatio impiorum*" and treat this judgment as "a proposition too familiar to require demonstration."[67] But if we consider 3:1ff. apart from what precedes it, then it is by no means obvious that the defense of "justification by faith" is the *point* of the argument.

Having excluded the apostolic autobiography as a starting point, we must disqualify the apostolic exhortation as well. We need not decide at this juncture whether the paraenesis is calculated or diffuse in its application, since paraenesis, even when it serves specific aims, consists

---

[67]C. K. Barrett, "The Allegory of Abraham, Sarah, and Hagar in the Argument of Galatians," in *Rechtfertigung: Festschrift für Ernst Käsemann*, ed. J. Friedrich et al. (Tübingen: J. C. B. Mohr [Paul Siebeck], 1976; Göttingen: Vandenhoeck & Ruprecht, 1976) 1.

of general ("usuelle"[68]) traditional materials. Just as we cannot determine the relevance of the autobiography for the Galatian situation without a prior understanding of that situation, so we cannot identify the apostle's specific purposes in the paraenesis without at least a prior understanding of the problem at Galatia as he sees it.

The reconstruction of the Galatian crisis by H. D. Betz is especially vulnerable at this point. According to Betz, the community, having enjoyed "a period of initial enthusiasm," now faces "a concrete problem with the 'flesh' (σάρξ)." The appearance of "transgressions" in their midst has prompted them to ask how the "pneumatic" can "live with 'trespasses' in his daily life?" The agitators are said to offer the Galatians the Torah as an antidote to "the flesh." Paul responds by disputing the law's power to check the flesh and defends the sufficiency of the Spirit for ethical life in Christ.[69] As one can see, this reconstruction depends heavily on the paraenesis for its inspiration, and for that reason it falls short of conviction. Consider, for example, Galatians 5:16.

> But I say, walk by the Spirit
> and you will not gratify the desires of the flesh.

Assuming that οὐ μὴ τελέσητε is assertive rather than imperative in force, this sentence certainly states an argument for the Spirit and its ethical efficacy. But this sort of argument is applicable to a variety of conceivable situations. In fact, a community dominated by "enthusiasm" and *unconcerned* with ethics (the mirror opposite of Betz's reconstruction) might well benefit from such a word, especially if that word followed upon the heels of a warning like the one we meet in verse 13: "You have (indeed) been called to freedom, but do not let your freedom become an opportunity for the flesh." Moreover, if there were only these two alternatives to choose from—Betz's ethically concerned ex-enthu-

---

[68]Martin Dibelius, *Die Formgeschichte des Evangeliums*, 6th ed., photomechanical reprint of the 3rd ed. with an expanded epilogue by G. Iber, ed. G. Bornkamm (Tübingen: J. C. B. Mohr [Paul Siebeck], 1971) 239.

[69]The preceding quotations are taken from pages 8-9 and 29 of Betz's commentary. He presents his summary of Paul's response on pages 32-33 (cf. "In Defense of the Spirit," 105-108).

siasts or, say, Lütgert-Ropes's libertinistic spiritualists[70]—5:21 would certainly tip the scales in favor of the second option: ''I warn you as I told you before that those who do such things (the works of the flesh) shall not inherit the kingdom of God.'' Surely believers engaged in taking concrete steps against ''problems with the flesh'' would not need to hear the solemn warning that disobedience courts disinheritance. The truth is that the paraenesis, taken as it stands, admits a variety of interpretations as to its purpose. And although some are more successful than others in accounting for the content and arrangement of the material, the paraenesis itself offers the interpreter what are at best ambiguous clues as to its function in Galatians. In short, the specific application of traditional material is by definition not given in that material itself.

We have excluded the apostolic autobiography and the paraenesis as starting points. We are left with the opening, the thanksgiving parody, the central argument in 3:1–4:30 (the appeal in 4:12-20 standing somewhat apart), the opening of the apostolic exhortation (4:31–5:12), and the personal autograph in 6:11-17. It is characteristic of Paul that he expands the customary epistolary opening and thanksgiving in ways that reveal at the very outset his concerns in writing.[71] The emphatic self-description in 1:1, ''an apostle *not from human beings nor through human beings*,'' announces the theme of ''Paul the Apostle'' and shows that Paul's apostolate and not simply his person is at stake in what we have therefore rightly termed the ''apostolic autobiography'' (1:11–2:21).[72] But it is not yet clear whether Paul's focus on his apostleship is

---

[70]As we have noted, according to Wilhelm Lütgert and after him James Hardy Ropes, Paul fights on two fronts in Galatia, on one hand against lawkeeping legalists and on the other hand against law-ignoring libertinistic spiritualists. See Lütgert, *Gesetz und Geist: Eine Untersuchung zur Vorgeschichte des Galaterbriefes* and Ropes, *The Singular Problem of the Dual Galatians*.

[71]See Paul Schubert, *Form and Function of the Pauline Thanksgivings*, BZNW 20 (Berlin: Alfred Töpelmann, 1939) 24; also Robert Funk, *Language, Hermeneutic, and Word of God* (New York/Evanston/London: Harper & Row, 1966) 256-57.

[72]George Lyons's otherwise very useful treatment of the autobiography seems a bit one-sided on this question in its almost exclusive stress on the mimetic aims of the narrative: ''Paul's autobiographical narrative serves as a paradigm of the behavior he persuades his readers to imitate'' (*Pauline Autobiography*, 136). It is perhaps telling that Lyons can make no sense of Paul's oath in 1:20 (*Pauline Autobiography*, 160), a rhetorical feature which most interpreters have rightly related in some way to Paul's articulation of his distinct apostleship.

defensive or offensive, if not some combination of the two.[73] It is, however, evident from the language in 1:1 that Paul takes up the theme of his apostleship *not simply* to make the point that his gospel is not "human" in origin or content. Paul makes a case for his apostolic *authority*, and he issues the letter under the aspect of that authority. One thinks again of the mood that dominates the deliberative speech. In the opening we also find that Paul draws attention to the saving death of Jesus. The traditional conceptions presented by the formula in 1:4 ("who gave himself for our sins to deliver us from the present evil age") have echoes in 2:20 ("who loved me and gave himself for me"), 3:13 ("having become a curse for us"), and 4:5 ("born of woman, born under the law, to redeem those under the law"). The death of Jesus is referred to or alluded to in 1:4; 2:19-20; 2:21; 3:1; 3:13; 4:5; 5:11; 5:24; 6:12; 6:14; and 6:17. This distribution is impressive in itself. But we do not learn from the prescript how Paul sees the death of Jesus to be at stake in the problem at Galatia.

From the thanksgiving parody we learn that Paul thinks the Galatians have fallen prey to a fundamental perversion of the gospel (1:6). They are turning to an "anti-gospel" (that is, a gospel that is not the gospel, 1:6-7), and the preachers of this gospel deserve an anathema (1:8-9). But the parody provides no clue as to the *content* of this false gospel. At most we may conclude from the opening and thanksgiving parody that the alien gospel compromises the word of the cross in some fundamental way. At this point, however, even this insight remains at the level of *formal* description. We turn, therefore, to the remaining sections (3:1–4:30; 4:31–5:12; 6:11-18) to consider whether the epistolary occasion is disclosed in straightforward and sufficiently specific language at any point(s) in these sections.

But now we face another difficulty. The letter presupposes the Galatian situation throughout, but as it progresses it begins to assume *itself*

---

[73]Whereas Walter Schmithals ("The Heretics in Galatia"), among others, has treated Paul's autobiographical remarks as a *defense* against what his detractors were saying about him, more recent investigations have stressed those features of the account that suggest Paul is on the offensive. See especially John Howard Schütz, *Paul and the Anatomy of Apostolic Authority,* SNTSMS 26 (Cambridge: Cambridge University Press, 1975) 128-29.

as well. This is another way of saying that the argument builds upon itself. Already in 3:19 we encounter a rhetorical question provoked ostensibly by what precedes. We suspect that the next question in 3:21 is in some way related to it and that much of what follows responds to one or both of these queries.[74] Consequently, we must first understand 3:1-18 before we will be in a position to judge whether 3:19ff. arises more immediately from Paul's arguments or from questions provoked by the Galatian situation.

On the other hand, it appears that the personal appeal in 4:12-20 does not develop out of its immediate context but comprises a relatively independent and self-contained discourse. Unfortunately, here the apostle addresses specific problems using general categories ("the gospel," "truth-speaking," "being shut out," "Christ-formation"). We learn nothing beyond what we have already concluded from the letter opening and thanksgiving parody: the community's very participation in Christ is in jeopardy (4:19), and Paul's authority has been implicitly or explicitly challenged (especially 4:16). The specific form of this challenge and the material content of the Galatian apostasy are not disclosed. The difficulty for interpretation becomes apparent as soon as one attempts to define concretely the opening imperative, where both themes (the gospel and the apostle) may be present: "Become as I am, for I also have become as you are, brothers" (v.12). What is the "imitation" encouraged here supposed to entail? Schlier singles out Paul's freedom from the law.[75] Oepke thinks of mutual approach ("Entgegenkommen").[76] From the immediate context the idea of becoming like Paul in his weakness suggests itself (vv.13-14). But a final determination depends on decisions made elsewhere.

---

[74]It has been suggested, e.g., that the answer to 3:19a motivates the question of 3:21. So Betz, *Galatians,* 173; Schlier, *Die Brief an die Galater,* 163, with qualification; Franz Mussner, *Der Galaterbrief,* 250; M.-J. Lagrange, *Paul, Épître aux Galates,* 2nd ed. (Études biblique; Paris: J. Gabalda, 1925) 87. What must not be overlooked is that 3:21bff. represents more than an answer to 21a in response to 3:19b-20. The whole argument of 3:1 on, together with 2:14b-21, motivates the question of 3:19a (sharpened in 3:21a).

[75]*Der Brief an die Galater,* 208; also Betz, *Galatians,* 222.

[76]*Der Brief des Paulus an die Galater,* 4th ed., posthumously edited and enlarged by J. Rohde, ThHK9 (Berlin: Evangelische Verlagsanstalt, 1979) 141.

The "allegory" in 4:21-31 engages themes already broached earlier, hence we cannot be certain whether we are to read it simply on its own or in light of the development of those themes up to this point. This is no idle question, inasmuch as many commentators treat 4:21-31 as an argument for "justification by faith," even though this terminology occurs nowhere in the pericope. In effect this is to assume that the argument proceeds here at a level of discourse once removed from the immediate terms of the debate at hand. In that case the problem at Galatia is not laid bare here; rather the interpreter must know the nature of the problem in advance in order to see how 4:21-31 addresses it.

One might well expect that the initial thrust of apostolic exhortation in 5:1-12 would zero in on the epistolary occasion at its most basic level. And certainly it becomes explicitly evident here for the first time that the Galatians are (contemplating?) getting circumcised (5:2-3, 6, 11). But the meaning of this circumcision is bound up somehow with what are by now well-developed themes in the epistle. Consider, for example, what appear to be critically important statements on the matter in 5:4-5.

> You are cut off from Christ, you who would be justified in the law; you have fallen from grace. For by the Spirit received by faith we wait for the hope of righteousness.

Even in the effort to *translate* these lines—one may well quarrel with my own rendering—it becomes apparent that the development of their thematic content in the preceding chapters is assumed. The same holds for the postscript (6:11-18). At just those points in the autograph where we find Paul issuing his final comments on themes familiar from the preceding discussions we are compelled to recognize that precisely *as final* comments these remarks *presuppose* the prior developments of those themes. For example, under which of its various aspects does Paul introduce the cross of Christ in 6:14? Does the cross signify here primarily the justification of sinners? The end of the Jew-Gentile distinction? A new order of ethical existence in Christ? The beginning of new creation as being in the Spirit?[77] The answer to these questions depends

---

[77]This last view is the one proposed in this study (see ch. 6). As for the interpretive

on decisions made about the meaning of Christ's death in 2:15-21 and 3:1-14, not to mention judgments about the nature of the "problem at Galatia." The postscript itself affords no immediate entree into the inner logic of the epistle.[78]

The Place to Begin

It is natural in attempting to understand a piece of literature to begin at the beginning, but the sort of departure point we seek for interpreting Galatians cannot be had in this way. Having read the epistle from beginning to end, we have learned that we must begin elsewhere than the beginning. But it has also become clear to us that it will not do to mount initial simultaneous forays into disparate regions of the letter in order to gather orientation material on its concrete occasion. The forward movement of the text must be respected. The place *for us* to begin in Galatians is with the *first unit that addresses the Galatian problem with directness and specificity.* The letter opening and thanksgiving parody exhibit directness without sufficient specificity. The apostolic autobiography is specific but not direct. The first unit that displays both specificity and direct focus on the Galatian situation is 3:1-14. It remains to be seen whether the specificity and directness of this passage signal the presence of discourse from which we can recover the epistolary occasion. But the passage looks initially promising for two reasons. First, Paul "marks" the blessing-promise terminology by specifying the content of the promise as *the Spirit* (v.14). Second, at the very outset Paul speaks in a way that suggests he is not approaching the central issue obliquely but head-on: "I only want to know one thing . . . " (v.2). We have almost joined the conversation.

---

options that precede it, each has defenders. E.g., see, respectively, the following authors: E. D. Burton, *A Critical and Exegetical Commentary on the Epistle to the Galatians,* ICC (Edinburgh: T.&T. Clark, 1921) 354; James D. G. Dunn, "The New Perspective on Paul," 117; Schlier, *Der Brief an die Galater,* 282-83.

[78]See, for example, the starting point taken by J. Louis Martyn in his essay, "Apocalyptic Antinomies in Paul's Letter to the Galatians" (*NTS* 31 [1985]: 410-24): "In a state of some ignorance,then, we turn to the text of the letter, taking our bearings initially from its closing paragraph" (412). One should note, however, in fairness to Martyn, that this essay develops out of a much larger work on Galatians, namely, a commentary now in progress for the Anchor Bible series.

CHAPTER 2

The Law and the Spirit

The beginning appears to be more than half of the whole,
and much of what is under investigation is illumined by it.
—Aristotle, *Nichomachean Ethics* 1.7.23

I only want to know one thing: Did you receive the Spirit
by doing the law or by hearing and believing?
—Galatians 3:2

IN THE PRECEDING CHAPTER the decision was made to enter Paul's conversation with the Galatians at 3:1-14. This means that we will allow our reading of this passage to determine our understanding of the "problem" at Galatia and Paul's response to it. To that extent we conclude our "first reading" with the interpretation of this text. But since this interpretation will guide us directly into the remainder of Paul's line of argument in Galatians 3 and 4, we commence here almost simultaneously with our "second reading." That is, the moment we have our bearings on the specific nature of Paul's dispute with the Galatians we will have begun our second reading.

The Mediation of the Spirit
as Crux of the Dispute (3:1-14)

Galatians 3:1-5 comprises Paul's first *specific* word addressed *directly* to the Galatian situation. If structural considerations have led us to expect here an open window into the problem at Galatia, the content of 3:1-5 bears out this expectation. It is a curious feature of the history of the letter's interpretation that this passage has been read so consistently from the perspective of what are regarded as the weightier and more pointed arguments of 2:15-21 and 3:6-14.[1] This approach has inclined interpreters to regard the argument of 3:1-5 as bearing only indirectly (by analogy) upon the controversy at hand. At issue is said to be how a person finds *justification:* on the basis of works or faith. On this assumption 3:1-5 is construed as an oblique introductory attack in service of the thesis that justification is based on faith alone. Paul's readers are supposed to draw the following conclusion: "If we received the Spirit from faith, are we not accepted by God and justified on the basis of faith?"

One difficulty with the traditional interpretation of 3:1-5 is that the passage never mentions "justification." But an even more serious problem is that the traditional approach gives primary consideration to 2:15-21 and 3:6-14 before listening to 3:1-5. The arguments of 3:6-14 *follow* 3:1-5. Should we not therefore give primary attention to the possibility that 3:1-5 sheds light on Paul's disagreement with the Galatians in such a way as to recommend itself as determinative for the perspective from which 3:6-14 is to be understood? The antecedent position of 2:15-21, which appears to share certain themes with 3:6-14, does not speak against this approach, inasmuch as the specific relevance of the speech to Peter for the argument at hand is obscured by the passage's ostensible focus on a situation other than that at Galatia. To what extent and in what manner 2:15-21 draws the Galatian problem into view cannot be ascertained until firm bearings on Paul's dispute with the Galatians have been secured. Perhaps it is the case of Antioch, with its stress on justification by faith, that offers the occasion for an argument by *analogy.*

The foregoing considerations do not in themselves disprove the traditional interpretation of 3:1-5, even if they call into question the way in which the passage has commonly been approached. What speaks de-

---

[1]See, for example, Heinrich Schlier, *Der Brief an die Galater,* 5th ed. MeyerK 7/14 (Göttingen: Vandenhoeck & Ruprecht, 1971) 126. Schlier's treatment of 3:1-5 shows that he regards the argument from Abraham not only as weightier but also as the clue to interpreting the appeal to the experience of the Spirit.

cisively against this interpretation is its failure to do justice to Paul's own characterization of his argument. After the transitional sentence in 3:1 ("O foolish Galatians, who has cast this spell over you—you, before whose very eyes Jesus Christ was placarded as crucified?"[2]), which links up with 2:21 and prepares for the argument from Christ's death in 3:10-14, the apostle poses a question that he introduces with the words, "I only want to know one thing from you" (τοῦτο μόνον θέλω μαθεῖν ἀφ' ὑμῶν). This sentence has verbal parallels in Greek literature, and one suspects that this sort of opening was typical both in formal diatribe and everyday speech.[3] The closest parallels uncovered to date are from Dionysius of Halicarnassus (d. 8 B.C..). Of these, only one instance provides an example of the expression used rhetorically. In *Ant. Rom.* 3.3.4-6 a certain Cluilius is portrayed as undone in debate over treaty violations by a question from the chief of a Roman assembly sent to get satisfaction from him. The question goes to the heart of the argument and brings the discussion to a close. It is introduced by the following words (the account is in indirect discourse): "This alone he determined to hear from him" (τουτ' ἠξίωσεν ἀκοῦσαι παρ' αὐτοῦ μόνον).[4]

Judging from the words themselves, including the fact that Paul places the phrase "this alone" (τοῦτο μόνον) in emphatic first position, and the parallel from Dionysius, we have a rhetorical device in Galatians 3:2 that signals a question regarded by the speaker as sufficient

---

[2]On the meaning of προγράφειν in Gal 3:1, see F. F. Bruce, *The Epistle to the Galatians* (Exeter: Paternoster Press, 1982; Grand Rapids MI: Eerdmans, 1982) 148; H. D. Betz, *Galatians* (Hermeneia; Philadelphia: Fortress Press, 1979) 131 (esp. nn. 36 and 39). Paul must be thinking of his own preaching and teaching among the Galatians.

[3]Jacob Wettstein listed the following texts in his note on v. 2 in *NTG:* Euripides *Iph. Taur.* 493; *Tr.* 63; Dionysius of Halicarnassus 3.60.1; 3.3.4; 5.54.3; Libanius *Ep.* 450. Betz supplies in addition: Sophocles *Oed. Col.* 505 [504?]; Plato *Phdr.* 262D; *Georg.* 494D; *Phd.* 63E; Philo *Her.* 33; *Fug.* 8; 164; *Dec.* 59; *Spec.* 1.36; 1.42; *Flacc.* 363 [sic?]; *Corp. Herm.* 1.3 (*Galatians,* 132 n. 42). Few of these are real parallels. The closest derives from Epictetus (*Disc.* 1.7.6), although the sentence is not rhetorical: ἆρ' οὖν ἀρκεῖ τοῦτο μόνον μαθεῖν.

[4]*Dionysius of Halicarnassus,* vol. 2, tr. Earnest Cary, LCL (London: William Heinemann, 1961; Cambridge: Harvard University Press, 1961).

to decide the whole matter at hand.[5] Therefore, the decisive test of any interpretation of 3:2-5 is whether it succeeds in bringing to light the sufficiency of the apostle's question in 3:2b. On this point the interpretation of the passage as an argument for "justification by faith" must be found wanting, as a closer examination of its several variations reveals.

A number of commentators find in 3:2-5 a contrast between "faith" and "works" as two diametrically opposed principles of life before God, a polarity they regard as fundamental to Paul's idea of "justification by faith and not by works of the law."[6] But even if the second assumption is granted, it remains unclear how the Galatians' reception of the Spirit by faith must lead necessarily to the conclusion that "faith" and "works" comprise mutually exclusive ways of relating to God. The Galatians put their faith in Jesus and experienced the signs of the Spirit in their midst, an occurrence manifestly *extra nos* and *sola gratia*. But where in this experience is disclosed an antithesis between faith and works as principles of existence before God? What in this experience, whether it is viewed as an event of conversion or an ongoing aspect of the community's life (see v. 5), militates against, for example, a synthesis in which God is understood to supply the motive power for existence as an unconditional gift and to justify those empowered with the Spirit on the basis of their works? Conceived as an argument against "works" as a principle of life before God, the passage comes off as singularly *indecisive*. And it is apparently just this element of ambiguity that prompts Heinrich Schlier, the staunchest advocate of the interpretation, to conclude that the apostle "must speak more fundamentally."[7]

Andrea van Dülmen suggests that the appeal to the Spirit provides a proof of Paul's law-free gospel based on a manifestation of divine

---

[5]Albrecht Oepke comments: "*Eine* Frage schon, wenn sie verständig ehrlich beantwortet würde, müsste alles entscheiden." See *Der Brief des Paulus an die Galater*, 4th ed., ThHK 9 (Berlin: Evangelische Verlagsanstalt, 1979) 100.

[6]Oepke, *Der Brief des Paulus an die Galater*, 101; H. Schlier, *Der Brief an die Galater*, 122 and 126; Jürgen Becker, *Der Brief an die Galater*, NTD 8 (Göttingen: Vandenhoeck & Ruprecht, 1981) 32-33. Betz, *Galatians*, 130 (Betz hears only a hint in 3:1-5 of what he regards to be the more specific problem, p. 136).

[7]*Der Brief an die Galater*, 126.

confirmation.[8] But the apostle does not ask whether his preaching did not find immediate confirmation in the coming of the Spirit; he inquires after the conditions of the Galatians' reception of the Spirit.

David Lull accords 3:1-5 a kind of primary consideration, but he does so by in effect lifting one sentence (v. 3) out of its rhetorical context and relating it with other clues in the letter from which his view of the problem at Galatia is constructed. This sentence "fits" his theory that the agitators "had almost persuaded Paul's converts that the Spirit was good for 'beginners', but to be [perfect] they had to perform the rites required by the Mosaic law. . . . "[9] But the logic of 3:1-5 as a unified argument is not allowed to emerge as guide to either the sense of verse 3 or, more importantly, the values of the law and the Spirit in Galatians, which Lull, following H. D. Betz, interprets primarily on the basis of the paraenesis.[10]

Although he has never developed the idea exegetically, E. P. Sanders has suggested that 3:2-5 addresses the issue whether a person can be said to belong to the body of Christ without taking upon himself the yoke of the Torah.[11] Considered in this light, Paul's rhetorical query does evince a prima facie sufficiency. The Galatians' reception of the Spirit marks their acceptance in God's sight. Since they received the Spirit in consequence of faith alone without works of the law, entering the body of Christ must not hinge on taking up the law. But the appeal of this reconstruction is deceiving. Primitive Christianity understood itself as a people upon whom God had poured out the Spirit of the last days. The manifest presence of the Spirit among them, perhaps more than any-

---

[8]*Die Theologie des Gesetzes bei Paulus,* SBM 5 (Stuttgart: Verlag Katholisches Bibelwerk, 1968) 30 (for the expression "law-free gospel," see p. 15).

[9]*The Spirit in Galatia: Paul's Interpretation of PNEUMA as Divine Power,* SBLDS 49 (Chico CA: Scholars Press, 1980) 42.

[10]See Lull, *The Spirit in Galatia,* 7-10, 30-39, 42-43, 53. Lull substantially modifies Betz's theory but agrees with the basic thesis of Betz that Galatians is a defense of the Spirit's sufficiency for the ethical life of the community in Christ. Cf. Betz, *Galatians,* 5-9 and 28-33; idem, "In Defense of the Spirit: Paul's Letter to the Galatians as a Document of Early Christian Apologetics," in *Aspects of Religious Propaganda in Judaism and Early Christianity,* ed. E. Schüssler Fiorenza (Notre Dame: University of Notre Dame Press, 1976) 99-114.

[11]*Paul, the Law, and the Jewish People* (Philadelphia: Fortress Press, 1983) 17-21.

thing else, gave the church as a whole its sense of distinct "eschatological identity" over against the synagogue and the world at large.[12] This fact lends the theory under consideration its force, but it also betrays its fundamental weakness. If the agitators disputed the Galatians' very status in Christ, their being in Christ per se, then they must have disputed the authenticity of the Galatians' experience of the Spirit. How else could they have convinced a community that knew the ongoing presence of the Spirit in its midst that *entrance* into the people of God requires reception of the Torah? But in that case Paul's argument from the Spirit only begs the question. Even more telling against Sanders's interpretation is the fact that Paul never once defends the authenticity of the Spirit's presence at Galatia. He takes for granted that all parties are agreed that the Galatians live by God's Spirit.

There is only one sort of dispute that the apostle's question in 3:2b could be said to sufficiently settle: a disagreement over the relationship of life in the Spirit to keeping the law. Where the Galatians connect their present experience of the Spirit with their newly adopted[13] practice of law, Paul seeks to reveal the illogic of this by reminding them of the circumstances under which they first received the Spirit. They received the Spirit not while they were practicing the law but when they heard and believed in Jesus (v. 2). Therefore (οὖν), God's present activity among them (supplying the Spirit and working miracles) can hardly be understood as dependent upon works of law but remains a consequence of their initial "hearing and believing" (v. 5). That is, God sends the Galatians the Spirit and works wonders among them because they are believers, not because they are lawkeepers.[14]

---

[12]See Jacob Jervell, "Das Volk des Geistes," in *God's Christ and His People: Studies in Honour of Nils Alstrup Dahl,* ed. J. Jervell and W. Meeks (Oslo/Bergen/Tromsö: Universatetsforlaget, 1977).

[13]Paul's exclamation in 4:10 is suggestive of this, even if it represents rhetorical exaggeration: "You are observing days and months and seasons and years!" The community has already taken concrete steps with the law, even if they have not yet (all?) received circumcision (5:2,3; 6:12).

[14]To my knowledge, no one has sought to interpret Galatians on the basis of this reconstruction of the "problem." At most, certain interpreters have suggested in passing or as a minor component of a larger hypothesis that the Galatians and/or agitators

In chapter 3, we will consider the *historical* plausibility of the idea that the Galatians, under pressure from the agitators, came to understand life in the Spirit as dependent somehow on lawkeeping, despite the fact that they were not under the Torah when they first received the Spirit. The important thing to see at this point is that *Paul argues as if* this were the problem, which is another way of saying that this *is* the problem as far as the letter is concerned. Therefore, we will leave open for now the question whether (and to what extent) the apostle responds to what are *in fact* the explicit views of the Galatians. For it may be that Paul is simply projecting this "problem" on the Galatians or addressing what he sees as the *implicit* theological assumptions behind what they are doing and saying about the law.

Paul himself treats the idea of getting the Spirit "from" the works of the law as rather incredible:

> Oh foolish Galatians! Who has bewitched you? . . . Look how foolish you are: Having begun with the Spirit, you are now (in fact) ending up with the flesh. Have you undergone so much in vain, if it is in vain? (3:1,3-4).

This translation assumes, on the basis of verse 5, that the community has not somehow forgotten the Spirit. Paul's closing question loses its intelligibility if the community no longer knows the ongoing manifestations of the Spirit in its midst.[15] In view of this, the apostle's statement

---

may have connected the law and the Spirit. See Klaus Wegenast, *Das Verständnis der Tradition bei Paulus und in den Deuteropaulinen*, WMANT 8 (Neukirchen: Neukirchener Verlag, 1962) 38; Donald Stoicke, " 'The Law of Christ': A Study of Paul's Use of the Expression in Galatians 6:2" (Th.D. diss., Graduate School of Theology at Claremont, 1971) 148 and 248. More suggestive is the recent essay by J. Louis Martyn, "A Law-Observant Mission to Gentiles: The Background of Galatians," *Michigan Quarterly Review* 22 (1983): 228-29. Martyn proposes that powerful manifestations of the Spirit accompanied the agitators' reading of the Torah in the worship service and that such demonstrations represented part of a larger program for recommending the law to the Galatians. Martyn does not mention this hypothesis in his more recent essay on Galatians, hence its present place in his overall conception remains unclear. See "Apocalyptic Antinomies in Paul's Letter to the Galatians," *NTS* 31 (1985): 410-24.

[15]So also Schlier (*Der Brief an die Galater*, 125) and most commentators. The δυνάμεις are to be understood as workings of the Spirit as well (cf. 1 Cor 12:10). Note Schmithals's criticisms of Betz on this point ("Judaisten in Galatien?" *ZNW* 74 [1983]: 43-44 n. 58).

in verse 3 is best taken as an ironic warning to the effect that the Galatians' present fascination with the Torah, far from fostering pneumatic
existence, courts its loss: ending up with the flesh or, as verse 4 has it,
ending up with *nothing* (εἰκῇ). The language in verses 3-4 does not
permit the interpreter to speak already of "justification by faith" versus
"justification by works of the law." The Spirit/flesh antithesis is put to
a wide variety of uses by the apostle; it is not simply another way of
expressing the polarity between faith and works of the law (see 1 Cor
3:1-3; Gal 5:16ff.; Gal 6:8). This fact in itself should caution us, moreover, against assuming that if Paul polarizes "beginning with the Spirit"
and "ending with the flesh," then the Galatians must be turning to the
law without thought for the Spirit, or perhaps even to make up for certain shortcomings of life in the Spirit. That would be to treat the verse
in isolation from its rhetorical context and to miss the *irony* in what Paul
says.

We find strong confirmation for our interpretation in verse 5, where
Paul draws his conclusion and does so by speaking in the present tense
about life in the Spirit. Interpreters have invariably understood the
"therefore" (οὖν) in verse 5 to be resumptive,[16] and that is not altogether unjustified. The closing question does take up the theme of verse
2. But the use of οὖν in rhetorical questions is characteristically illative. A survey of the New Testament itself, for example, reveals no instances of questions introduced by οὖν where the particle is purely
resumptive or continuative. The οὖν in a question always signals a logical connection with what precedes, suggesting that what has gone before in some way evokes the question. Similarly, in over one hundred
instances (every one inferential) Epictetus employs οὖν in rhetorical
questions lacking, as Paul's does in verse 5, any interrogative particle.[17]

---

[16]So, for example, Schlier, *Der Brief an die Galater,* 125 (see his n. 2); Oepke, *Der
Brief des Paulus an die Galater,* 101-102; Ernest De Witt Burton, *The Epistle to the
Galatians,* ICC (Edinburgh: T. & T. Clark, 1921) 151; J. B. Lightfoot, *The Epistle of
St. Paul to the Galatians* (Grand Rapids MI: Zondervan, 1957 reprint of 1865 ed.) 136.

[17]In his concordance to Epictetus, H. Schenkl lists over one hundred examples of
οὖν with questions unintroduced by question words. See the "Index Verborum" in
Epicteti: Dissertationes ab Arriano Digestae (Stuttgart: Teubner, 1916). An analysis of
these reveals three general uses: (1) to introduce questions which follow as false infer-
ences to be refuted, (2) to introduce inferential questions with obvious answers, and (3)
to open a further line of inquiry arising out of the previous debate.

We may note also that in their discussion of οὖν with questions, Kühner and Gerth appear to assume that such uses are illative and not resumptive.[18] Likewise, Liddell and Scott classify οὖν with questions under the larger category of its inferential and not its resumptive use.[19] One might conclude from this that a resumptive οὖν with a question is unnatural. But the evidence suggests that when used with questions οὖν is characteristically illative (it carried that ring in the Greek ear) and may in some cases be at the same time resumptive, depending upon the structure of the context.

Another example from Paul of a resumptive-illative οὖν in a question is found in Romans 4: "Does, then (οὖν), this blessing fall upon the circumcised alone, or also upon the uncircumcised?" (v.9a). As verse 9b shows ("For we say, 'Faith was reckoned to Abraham unto righteousness' "), Paul's question is to be answered on the basis of the Scripture citation (Gen 15:6) adduced all the way back in verse 3. The intervening example of David offers no support for the possibility that the blessing could be shared by the uncircumcised. For that Paul must reach back to Abraham.

In Galatians 3:5 the "therefore" takes up the question of verse 2 and builds upon its implied answer as a premise. If the community received the Spirit by hearing and believing the message of Christ, not by works of the law, then the grounds of their present experience of the Spirit must be the same. This explains Paul's shift in verse 5 to the present tense (ὁ ἐπιχορηγῶν . . . καὶ ἐνεργῶν). The present participle with the article may be "general," hence Burton suggests "the worker" and "the supplier" as possible translations of 3:5 and fills in the ellipsis with a *past tense* finite verb.[20] But an iterative sense is just as natural. Since Paul and early Christians in general thought of God's giving of the Spirit

---

[18]See Raphael Kühner, *Ausführliche Grammatik der griechischen Sprache*, vol. 2, 3rd ed., ed. B. Gerth (Hannover: Hannsche Buchhandlung, 1904) 154-63. The use of οὖν with questions is taken up for discussion under the inferential use of the particle and not in connection with its resumptive use.

[19]Henry G. Liddell and Robert Scott, *A Greek-English Lexicon*, 9th ed., rev. H. S. Jones and R. McKenzie (Oxford: Clarendon Press, 1940). *BAGD* lists only 1 Cor 8:4 and 11:30 as examples of the resumptive οὖν in Paul.

[20]*The Epistle to the Galatians*, 152.

not only as a once-for-all occurrence (in the life of the group or the individual) but also as a repeated act of benefaction (1 Cor 14:12; Phil 1:19; 1 Thess 4:8; Luke 11:13), we should take the present tense in 3:5 at face value. The reference to the working of "wonders" (δυνάμεις) confirms that the giving of the Spirit (literally "supplying" or "sustaining") is to be understood as an ongoing action. God is the one who keeps on supplying his people with the power of the Spirit, an idea that we shall have occasion to consider more fully in chapters 3 and 6 below. Furthermore, if Paul is making the point in verse 5 that the grounds of the Galatians' present life in the Spirit are the same as those of their initial reception of the Spirit, this also illumines his use once again of the expression "the hearing of faith" (ἀκοὴ πίστεως), which refers to an event of the Galatians' past (Paul's founding of the community), in a construction that speaks of God *continually* supplying them with the Spirit (cf. 1 Thess 4:8).

The preceding interpretation of 3:1-5 is confirmed by the logic of the argument in 3:6-14. Paul's discussion in these verses is structured more or less chiastically and weaves together the most prominent themes of Galatians 3–4:

> (*Spirit* by *faith* 3:5)
> people of *faith* are *sons* (of Abraham) (3:6-7)
> people of *faith* (incl. *Gentiles*) are *blessed* (3:8-9)
> people of works of the law *cursed* (3:10)
> no one in the law justified (3:11)
> law not of faith (3:12)
> Christ has redeemed *us* from *curse* of the law (3:13)
> *blessing* comes upon *Gentiles*,
> we receive promise of *Spirit* through *faith* (3:14)

This reconstruction is based on Paul's own statements, as interpretations of the Scripture passages cited, and does not take its cue from the quotations themselves. As far as the argument is concerned, Paul's own use of the citations is decisive; his conclusions ("You know, therefore," v. 7; "So then," v. 9) mark the train of thought. One notices immediately that the chiasm does not possess perfect symmetry, an aspect of the argument's structure that helps determine where the emphases lie. The thought of verses 6-7 is not picked up again, and the sentences in verses 11-12 are not parallel. Although the assumption is sometimes made that the center of a chiasm is its focal point, the focus of a chiastic *argument* is given by its internal logic. As we shall see, verses 11-12 are part of a proof supporting the negative thesis of verse 10. Not the blessing of the Spirit but a *curse* falls on those in the law. Verse 14 recapitulates verse 9 and at the same time returns to the thesis of verse 5: reception of the Spirit through faith. Thus we discover that the final aim of the argument is to confirm the point made in 3:1-5.

The preceding analysis shows that the central focus of the passage is not how a person becomes justified.[21] The conclusion of the argument in verse 14, together with its parallel in verse 9, makes this clear. Instead, the motif of justification serves as a helping theme, and in verses 6-9 the justification theme provides simply a link in an argument whose interest is not justification per se but how one shares in "the blessing." Let us examine this link more closely.

E. P. Sanders wisely advises that in order to interpret Paul's argument from Scripture we must take our cue from what Paul says, the use he makes of the texts that he cites, and not from the texts themselves alone. Unfortunately, Sanders does not follow his own advice. He states—and here the vast majority of commentators would concur with him—that Paul's thesis in Galatians 3:6ff. can be summarized with the words, "*Gentiles* are *righteoused* by *faith.*"[22] According to Sanders, it was Paul's interest in linking these three terms together (Gentiles, justification, and faith) that led the apostle to select his proof texts from

---

[21]Contra Franz Mussner, *Der Galaterbrief,* 4th ed., HTKNT 9 (Freiburg/Basel/Vienna: Herder, 1981) 212; Oepke, *Der Brief des Paulus an die Galater,* 106; Becker, *Der Brief an die Galater,* 31 (entitles all of 3:1-5:12 "Glaubensgerechtigkeit und Freiheit als Gegensatz zu Gesetz und Knechtschaft"); Hans Hübner, *Law in Paul's Thought,* trans. James C. G. Greig and ed. John Riches (Edinburgh: T. & T. Clark, 1984) 17-18; E P. Sanders, *Paul, the Law, and the Jewish People,* 21; Burton, *The Epistle to the Galatians,* 142, 153, 163, 175 (esp. p. 175, where he interprets the blessing of Abraham to mean specifically "the blessing of justification by faith"). According to Schlier, however, the focus of the passage is not so much the theme of justification as the contrast between "faith" and "works" as opposing principles of life (*Der Brief an die Galater,* 127 and passim). But Schlier does interpret v. 8 to mean that δικαιοῦν is not the presupposition but the act of εὐλογεῖν (131).

[22]*Paul, the Law, and the Jewish People,* 21.

the Abraham story. But close examination of the flow of Paul's argument reveals that the terms "justify" and "righteousness" are not treated as key words. Paul does not draw the conclusion from Genesis 15:6 (Gal 3:6) that the Gentiles are justified by faith. He writes in his own words: "Know (or "you know"), therefore, that people of faith are sons of Abraham" (3:7). Furthermore, the proof from Abraham does not come to rest once Paul has joined faith and sonship. The sonship motif forms a median idea in the argument, a stepping-stone to the conclusion, "So, then, those of faith are *blessed* with Abraham in his faith" (3:9). This inference (v. 9) depends not only on the Old Testament text referred to in verse 8 (Gen 12:3; cf. 18:18) but also on the preceding proof. The two texts (Gen 15:6 and 12:3) together facilitate the connection of faith with the blessing.[23] Although the language of justification appears in 3:8a, it does not show up in Paul's conclusion (v. 9). Its presence in the participial clause of verse 8 serves to forge explicitly the link between Genesis 15:6 (Abraham justified by faith) and Genesis 12:3/18:18 (all the nations blessed in Abraham). As verse 14 indicates, the blessing of Abraham is above all the gift of the Spirit. The idea that God justifies the Gentiles by faith serves here as a piece of common ground in an argument whose interest lies elsewhere.

The tendency among interpreters to equate the themes of sonship, blessing, and promise with "justification by faith"[24] belies Paul's careful use of this terminology. Paul identifies the promise (explicitly) and the blessing (by implication) with the gift of the Spirit (3:14). He never

---

[23]The two are associated already in Genesis, since 18:18 recalls 15:5 (to which 15:6 forms Abraham's response). The connection of Abraham's faith with the blessing was frequently made in Judaism, but typically from the perspective of Gen 22:16-18. See, for example, Sir 44:20-21 (καὶ ἐν πειρασμῷ εὑρέθη πιστός· διὰ τοῦτο ἐν ὅρκῳ ἔστησεν αὐτῷ ἐνευλογηθῆναι ἔθνη ἐν σπέρματι αὐτοῦ).

[24]See Burton, *The Epistle to the Galatians*, 175; Betz, *Galatians*, 142-43 (here Betz identifies the blessing with "justification," but on pages 152-53 the blessing, as the content of the promise, is said to be the Spirit); Hübner, *Law in Paul's Thought*, 16-17; Bruce, *The Epistle to the Galatians*, 157; J. S. Vos, *Traditionsgeschichtliche Untersuchungen zur paulinischen Pneumatologie* (Assen: Van Gorcum, 1973) 90. Compare also the view of Nils Dahl, who is right to stress that "[j]ustification and the gift of the Spirit are inseparable from one another" but goes too far when he alleges that "Paul makes no distinction between the forensic and the pneumatic." See *Studies in Paul: Theology for the Early Christian Mission* (Minneapolis: Augsburg, 1977) 133.

equates the blessing (promise or inheritance) with justification. Even in 3:8-9, the joining of Genesis 15:6 (justification by faith) with Genesis 18:18 (the blessing upon the Gentiles) serves not to identify *justification* as the blessing in which the Gentiles share but to establish a connection between *faith* and the blessing of Abraham prophesied for the nations. Thus the coherence of 3:1-14 as a whole emerges with clarity. At each point of conclusion in the argument Paul emphasizes the same thing: *the Spirit* (as the eschatological blessing/promise) comes by faith (3:5; 3:9; 3:14). Those under the law have no share in this blessing. On the contrary, they find themselves under its opposite: a curse.

This same interest in joining the gift of the Spirit with faith and divorcing it from the law is evident throughout 3:19–4:7 and 4:21-30. In these passages the relation of sonship to the Spirit and realized heirship must be carefully marked. Interpreters have become accustomed to understanding the emphasis on "sonship" in Galatians to concern a dispute over membership or status in the people of God. "Sonship," they point out, defines a particular *standing,* which one may conceive as including the status of being righteous in God's sight. And it is this question of righteousness or justification that is at stake in the apostle's statements about sonship.[25] Or, as Sanders has it, "justification" and "sonship" have to do with the question of *membership.*[26] It speaks against Sanders's thesis that there is no reference in Galatians 3–4 to *circumcision,* an indisputably key term in questions about joining God's people. But more important, the structure of Paul's arguments in 3:23–4:7 and 4:21-30, where the theme of sonship figures significantly, tells against any theory that treats the Gentile Galatians' "status" as the *issue* of Galatians. It is again important to pay attention to Paul's *conclusions.*

The argument of 3:23-29 reaches its climax in verse 29, and it is followed by a variation in analogy (4:1-7) that arrives at the same conclu-

---

[25]See, e.g., Burton, *The Epistle to the Galatians,* 210. Most commentators also stress that the question of the Galatians' status forms the focal point of the discussion (Betz, *Galatians,* 181; Bruce, *The Epistle to the Galatians,* 191), particularly as it turns on the dispute about whether one must become a Jew in order to count as a (full) member of God's people in Christ (Becker, *Der Brief an die Galater,* 46; Oepke, *Der Brief des Paulus an die Galater,* 126).

[26]*Paul, the Law, and the Jewish People,* 19-20.

sion in 4:7. In 3:29 Paul argues from "belonging to Christ" (= sonship) that the Galatians are on that basis *heirs according to promise*. The argument from sonship has as its main interest not so much the *status* of Gentile believers (that they are sons) as the benefits which accrue automatically to that status. To be a son is to be an *heir,* in possession of the inheritance given to Abraham by *promise* (3:18; that is, the promise of the Spirit, 3:14). That is precisely what 4:7 says, and once more the flow of the argument reveals that the idea of sonship is introduced not for its own sake but in order to link the Spirit with sonship as effected by redemption in Christ: "And *because* you are sons, God has sent his *Spirit* into our hearts, . . . " (4:6).[27] The Spirit comes with sonship in Christ; it is in no way dependent on lawkeeping. Indeed it is given to those redeemed from the law's curse (see v. 5). As verse 7 puts it, the Galatians are no longer slaves but sons, *and if sons also heirs.* Inheritance in Galatians means "realized heirship" as life in the Spirit. In a similar way the discussion of Abraham's two wives in 4:21-30 takes the Galatians' sonship as its *presupposition* (4:28 is no conclusion, as the use of δέ shows), aligning it with Sarah-Isaac, freedom, promise, and so forth. The point lies in the disassociation of the law from freedom and the Spirit, in the law's being aligned with Hagar-Ishmael and depicted as a slave bearing children for slavery.

We have previewed the arguments in 3:23–4:7 and 4:21-30, and we shall proceed shortly to a more detailed examination of the argumentation in 3:15–4:30 as a whole. But first we must consider a *crux interpretum* in 3:1-14 to which we have paid very little attention thus far, namely, the argument about the "curse of the law" in verses 10-12.

The Curse of the Law (3:10-12)

Although most interpreters have identified 3:11-12 as the nerve of Paul's argument, since they speak of justification, faith, and the law, the analysis presented above reveals that these statements make a subordinate point in Paul's argument. They support the thesis of verse 10a:

---

[27]Oepke construes the syntax of the sentence correctly (ὅτι = "weil") but then turns the sense around: "Aus dem erfahrenen Geistesempfang (s.z. 3,2) kann man daher auf die Annahme an Kindes Statt schliessen" (*Der Brief des Paulus an die Galater,* 133). But Gal 4:6 is not Rom 8:16.

"All who are from works of the law are under a curse." In verses 10-12 the apostle argues *e contrario* against the idea that the eschatological *blessing* attaches to lawkeepers by maintaining that dependence on the law[28] brings not a blessing but a *curse,* namely, the curse of the law itself.

Paul defends his thesis by citing Deuteronomy 27:26 (LXX), a highly provocative rhetorical move on his part. For the proof from Deuteronomy appears at first sight not to support but to contradict what he asserts in verse 10a. Paul maintains that lawkeepers as such stand under a curse, but Deuteronomy 27:26 pronounces a curse not upon those who *do* the law but upon those who *do not* do it. A common solution to this puzzle is to assume that the argument depends upon the unexpressed premise that even those who make it their business to keep the law fail to meet its uncompromising demand for blamelessness.[29] This solution is only as persuasive as the demonstrable self-evidence of such an assumed premise, which many interpreters judge to be anything but self-evident.[30] Another solution is to make a qualitative distinction between "works of the law" and what the law itself (speaking in Deut 27:26) really requires (faith or love).[31] But if one understands the expression

---

[28]The expression ὅσοι ἐξ ἔργων νόμου εἰσίν speaks of those who do what the law requires. But the ἐκ-construction with εἰσίν suggests that Paul views them in their dependence on the law (cf. ἐπαναπαύῃ νόμῳ, Rom 2:17).

[29]See, for example, Hübner, *Law in Paul's Thought,* 18-19.

[30]See, for instance, Schlier, *Der Brief an die Galater,* 132. Schier's own solution is to argue from vv. 11-12 that the curse attaches to ποιεῖν itself as it is determined by the law (134). But this is simply to ignore the fact that Deut 27:26 applies the curse not to those who *do* the law but to those who *do not.*

[31]See Ragnar Bring, "Die Erfüllung des Gesetzes durch Christus," *KD* 5 (1959): 1-22; idem, "Die Erfüllung des Gesetzes und der geknechtete Wille," *Vierhundertfünfzig Jahre Luthersche Reformation: Festschrift für Franz Lau* (Göttingen: Vandenhoeck & Ruprecht, 1967) 80-89; idem, *Der Brief des Paulus an die Galater* (Berlin/Hamburg: Luthersches Verlagshaus, 1968) 109-15; Daniel Fuller, "Paul and the 'Works of the Law,' " *WTJ* 38 (1975–1976): 28-42. I held the same opinion as Fuller once myself: "The Mosaic Law Preaches Faith: A Study in Gal. 3," *WTJ* 41 (1978–1979): 146-71. Cf. also James D. G. Dunn, "The New Perspective on Paul," *BJRL* 65 (1983): 95-122; "Works of the Law and the Curse of the Law (Galatians 3:10-14)," *NTS* 312 (1985): 523-42. Dunn takes "works of the law" to refer to a nationally exclusivistic Jewish understanding of the law as a boundary marking them off from other peoples, a "narrow" understanding of the law that does not allow full weight to be given to its central demand of love.

"(the) works of the law" (ἔργα νόμου) as Paul's own "technical phrase" for a wrong understanding of the law, then it becomes impossible to explain why he does not employ this phrase in 3:12, where this misunderstanding of the law is supposed to be in view. In fact, far from shielding the term "law" (νόμος) from any association with what is said to be a perversion of the law, Paul erects in 3:12 a polarity that overthrows any attempt to draw a distinction here between the two when he declares, "*The law* is not of faith."

Neither the appeal to an unexpressed premise nor the arbitrary distinction between "the law" and the "works of the law" is necessary, however, since Paul himself provides the required major premise of his argument in the explanation (δέ) that follows verse 10. In verse 11a Paul rephrases [32] the thesis of verse 10 with the statement, ἐν νόμῳ οὐδεὶς δικαιοῦται παρὰ τῷ θεῷ (v. 11a). For one schooled in the Septuagint the wording of this sentence represents a most natural way of expressing the thought, "in the law no one is just before God." [33] This statement contains more than an allegation that all lawkeepers transgress the law, a problem with which the law itself, with the cult and confession, is able to deal. The transgressor, like the tax collector of Luke 18:9-14, may go down to his house justified. But Paul understands the situation of those "who are from works of the law" to be more desperate. Righteousness in the law is simply excluded on any terms for those in the law. "No one is righteous in the law."

Paul defends the categorical statement of 3:11a by appealing to Habakkuk 2:4 (3:11b). As we shall see, Habakkuk 2:4 represents a fundamental article of the gospel, hence Paul can appeal to it without even

---

[32]The construction, ἔστιν δῆλον ὅτι, and especially its variation, δῆλον . . . ὅτι (as here), almost invariably takes up or completes a preceding idea. Very rarely does a speaker use this expression to introduce a new thought or additional argument. See Hermann Hanse, "ΔΗΛΟΝ: Zu Gal 3, 11," *ZNW* 34 (1935): 299-303.

[33]In the Septuagint, the middle and passive forms of the verb δικαιοῦν ("to justify") regularly express the idea "to be just" (translating the Qal form צָדֵק). See Ps 142:2; Gen 38:26; Ps 18:10; Isa 42:21; Tob 6:12; 6:13; 12:4. Compare *Pss. Sol.* 8:23 and 10:5. Marie-Joseph Lagrange observes that the other Greek versions sometimes translate the Qal צָדֵק in Job with δικαιοῦσθαι where the LXX has an adjective (δίκαιος or ἄμεμπτος with εἶναι). The passages are Job 10:15 (Aquila); 22:3 (Sym); 15:14 (Aquila; Th). See Lagrange, *Épître aux Romains* (Paris: Gabalda, 1950) 126.

marking it as a quotation from Scripture (for example, through the use of an introductory formula). The point of the argument is as follows. If the just shall live by faith, then (at least since the advent of eschatological faith) the just are not to be found among "those who are from works of the law." Who are these persons? Although the implication is that the agitators fall into this group and that the Galatians are in danger of doing so, those "from works of the law" are in the first instance the mass of Jews who continue to live "in the law" rather than "in Christ." That is, Paul's argument does not stand on its own but depends on his readers' affirmation of Habakkuk 2:4 as a fundamental article of the gospel applicable to Jews and Gentiles alike (cf. 2:16). The apostle builds his case on general "Christian" assumptions.

We have good reason to think that "Habakkuk 2:4" represents common ground between Paul and his readers. "Faith" was the characteristic term used by early Christians in speaking about the reception of the gospel[34] and it also served as a metonymy for the gospel itself. In Galatians alone we meet the following instances of the latter:

"faith" as content of preaching (1:23)
"the faith of (Jesus) Christ" (2:16; 3:22; cf. 2:20)
"faith" hypostatized (3:23, 25)
"the household of faith" (6:10)

Although "faith" (πίστις) is associated closely with its cognate verb "to believe" (πιστεύειν), it is clear that the substantive does not always mean simply "believing." This point has been made with special emphasis by those who take the phrase πίστις Χριστοῦ to refer to Christ's own faith-obedience.[35] But a number of considerations

---

[34]See Rudolf Bultmann, *Theology of the New Testament*, vol. 1, trans. Kendrick Grobel (New York: Charles Scribner's Sons, 1951) 89-92.

[35]Johannes Haussleiter, *Der Glaube Jesu Christi u. der christliche Glaube: Ein Beitrag zur Erklärung des Römerbriefes* (Leipzig, 1891). For a recent defense and substantial modification of Haussleiter's theory, see Richard B. Hays, *The Faith of Jesus Christ: An Investigation of the Narrative Substructure of Galatians 3:1-4:11*, SBLDS 56 (Chico CA: Scholars Press, 1983) 157-76; also Sam K. Williams, "The 'Righteousness of God' in Romans," *JBL* 99 (1980): 241-90 (271-76) and "Again *Pistis Christou*," *CBQ* 49 (1987): 431-47.

militate against construing the expression primarily of Christ's πίσ-τις. In those contexts where it is clear that Paul has Christ's faithful obedience in view, the apostle speaks of Christ's "obedience" (ὑπ-ακοή) but not of his "faith" (Rom 5:18-21; Phil 2:5-11). Paul's use of Habakkuk 2:4 as a prophecy of eschatological Faith also counts against the theory. Both the Septuagint and the Hebrew text qualify the word "faith" in Habakkuk 2:4 with a possessive adjective. The Septuagint has "my faith" and the Hebrew text (MT) reads "his faith," both referring evidently to God's own faithfulness. At Qumran "his faith" was taken to refer to the faith of the Torah-faithful person who aligns himself with the Teacher of Righteousness. But in his own citations of Habakkuk 2:4 (Gal 3:11 and Rom 1:17), Paul follows neither the Septuagint nor the Hebrew text. In fact, he does not modify the word "faith" in any way, even though he would certainly have been free to explicate this faith as Christ's own faithfulness by adding a possessive pronoun if there were none in the text tradition familiar to him.[36] This suggests that we are not to understand "the faith of Jesus Christ" (Gal 2:16; 3:22) primarily as a particular way of believing or being faithful, even if such is included in the notion by virtue of the fact that Paul can use this expression to refer to the whole of the eschatological reality of salvation inaugurated by God in Jesus Christ.

Of particular interest for our understanding of Habakkuk 2:4 in the argument of Galatians 3:11-12 is the use of the term "faith" in 3:23-26, where Paul speaks of faith as "coming" and "being revealed." The alternation between statements about faith and statements about Christ suggests that the former term functions almost as a synonym for the latter. Faith is conceived here as an eschatological reality, which enters the world with God's action in Christ. And this should not surprise us when we consider what a short step it is from the traditional expression in Galatians 2:16, where "faith" and "Christ" are joined in what is clearly a description of a single eschatological reality (πίστις 'Ιησοῦ Χριστοῦ), to using "faith" by itself to designate the soteriological reality which, with and like Christ, "comes." We may refer to this "faith" accordingly as "Christ-Faith."

---

[36]Note Paul's own additions in other instances: Gal 2:16a and Rom 3:20 citing Ps 142:2; Gal 4:30 citing Gen 21:10.

It may well be that Habakkuk 2:4 enjoyed widespread recognition in the early church as a prophecy of the coming faith (of Jesus Christ) by which the just would live. As we have seen, it was interpreted eschatologically at Qumran to refer to those who have faith in the Teacher of Righteousness (1QpHab on Hab 2:4b). In any event, Paul probably made Habakkuk 2:4 a foundation text in his missionary preaching. It appears in Romans 1:16-17 as a Scripture proof for a summary of the gospel. More significantly, in Galatians 3:11 it is not prefaced by an introductory formula.[37] Paul expects his readers to recognize this sentence. Not only that, the way he speaks so facilely about faith "coming" in Galatians 3:23-25 suggests that the idea of faith as a metonymy for the gospel will not have come as a surprise to the Galatians.

When one considers Paul's use of Habakkuk 2:4 together with his statements about "faith" in 3:23-25, it is evident that the apostle read this prophetic text *eschatologically*. Habakkuk 2:4 speaks of the time of fulfillment now arrived with Jesus Christ. It speaks of the πίστις Χριστοῦ. Prior to believing in Christ Paul will have understood Habakkuk 2:4, with its promise of life "from faith," to speak of the faithfulness of the righteous to God's law. Or, if he followed the Septuagint, he will have thought of the life of the righteous as grounded in *God's* faithfulness: ἐκ πίστεώς μου. As Christ's apostle, however, Paul has come to understand "faith" in Habakkuk 2:4 in a fresh light. He now reads Habakkuk 2:4 as a messianic text and understands it to speak of eschatological Christ-Faith. No doubt the early-Christian missionary call to *faith* in the resurrection of Jesus led Paul to fix on this term as a metonymy for God's act in Jesus Christ seen as a whole and embracing both the opening up of an eschatological reality from the divine side ("the promise that comes from Jesus-Christ-Faith might be given") and the grasping of eschatological life in faith by believers ("to those who believe"). As such, it may also include the idea that Jesus' own faithfulness unto death is the prototype of believing faith (see 2:20). Nevertheless, it is not the existential but the eschatological nature of Christ-Faith that receives the stress in Galatians, and justification by

---

[37]Hab 2:4 is also cited in Heb 10:38, again without an introductory formula. But there it is understood not christologically but anthropologically.

Christ-Faith means God's eschatological action in Christ toward those
who believe.[38]

Paul clarifies his use of Habakkuk 2:4 by adducing a second text (Lev
18:5), which he prefaces with the words, "And the law is not of faith."
The implicit logic of the proof he constructs in 3:11-12 follows the second form of Aristotle's first figure: "If A is predicated in no way of B
and B of all C, it follows that A belongs in no way to C" (*Prior Ana-
lytics* 25b40–26a2). Thus, if (A) the law [hence the person "in the law"]
is not of (B) faith [support: Lev 18:5] and (C) the just shall live by (B)
faith [Hab 2:4], then (A) those in the law will not be found among (C)
the just: "in the law no one is just." Of course, the proof is valid only
if, as Paul says, "the law is not of faith." But this statement almost goes
without saying, if the term "faith" refers here to eschatological Christ-
Faith, as Paul's appeal to Habakkuk 2:4 suggests. The law may indeed
call for faith as obedient trust, but in its narrow sense as "works of the
law" (halakah and *not* haggadah) one could not say that it calls for *faith
in Christ.* In view of Romans 4, we might have expected Paul to secure
his point by appealing to Abraham, who believed in "the God who raised
the Lord Jesus from the dead" before he was even circumcised. But instead Paul cites a law text that seems to send the argument in an unex-
pected direction. He quotes the words of Leviticus 18:5, which links up
thematically with Habakkuk 2:4 not by stating an alternative way to be
righteous but by proposing an alternative way to *live.*

Now if Leviticus 18:5 is to support the argument in progress ("no
one in the law is righteous"), Paul must assume that "to live" includes
"being righteous." That certainly holds true for his understanding of
Habakkuk 2:4, where the living in question is eschatological life. It also
goes for his understanding of Leviticus 18:5 as he uses this text in Romans 10:5. There he says explicitly: "Moses writes about the righteousness from the law that 'the one who does them shall live by them.' "

---

[38]According to Williams, "When Paul speaks of *pistis Christou,* he has in mind that
faith which is given its distinctive character by the absolute trust and unwavering obedience of Jesus, who created, in the last days, this mode of being human in the world"
("Again *Pistis Christou,*" 446). But nowhere in Galatians does Paul in any way make
explicit much less emphasize that "Christ-faith" is a particular form of obedience or
faithfulness. The aspect of Christ-Faith that Paul stresses in Galatians is its eschatological character, as Williams himself rightly observes.

And there as well, in a context dominated by the question of how righteousness is acquired (9:30–10:13), Paul virtually equates being righteous and having life. But does he make the same equation in Galatians 3:12? In order to answer this question we will have to examine more closely the contrast between Habakkuk 2:4 and Leviticus 18:5.

The words of Leviticus 18:5 had become by Paul's day a common sentence-summary of the law,[39] and the version of it in Galatians 3:12 has a sententiary, even slogan-like, ring. Furthermore, although Paul introduces Leviticus 18:5 as a word of Moses in Romans 10:5, he does not employ any introductory formula here. He expects his readers to recognize these words, just as they are to recognize the fundamental article of the gospel that he has taught them, namely, Habakkuk 2:4. Taken together, these observations suggest that Leviticus 18:5 is a Scripture slogan of the agitators, a text that *they* have taught the Galatians. That being the case, Leviticus 18:5 carries a very precise meaning in Galatians. It represents the agitators' claim that the one who does the law shall live by the Spirit. At a latter juncture in this study we will consider the value of this insight for reconstructing the agitators' theology (see chapter 3). At this point, however, we will treat only Paul's use of the sentence in the argument at hand.

Since Paul is concerned in Galatians 3:1-14 to show that doing the law does not promote the powerful presence of the Spirit, the thought lies near at hand that Leviticus 18:5 serves here to express what he takes to be the opposing point of view, whether the agitators have used this text or not. Paul himself speaks in 5:25 of "living by the Spirit" and then goes on to urge the Galatians toward righteous behavior ("walking by the Spirit"), which he understands to be an essential *aspect* of living by the Spirit. Furthermore, as we have observed, the apostle does not end his larger argument in 3:1-14 by making a point about righteousness. He speaks about the "blessing" coming upon the Gentiles (who are outside the law) and of receiving the promise of the Spirit by faith (v. 14). It would appear, therefore, that in the terminology of Galatians

---

[39]The thought or wording of Lev 18:5 is found, for example, in Neh 9:29; Ez 20:13; Luke 10:28; CD 3:16; and *Pss. Sol.* 14:3. In none of these instances is it introduced by any citation formula. That is true of its use in Gal 3:12 as well. Paul apparently assumes that his readers will recognize the statement. See further below, chapter 3.

"living by the Spirit" designates a larger reality than "being righteous," even if it includes "being righteous." We shall see that this insight goes a long way toward explaining texts like 2:21 ("if righteousness were from the law, then Christ died for nothing") and 3:21 ("if a law had been given that was able to make alive, then righteousness would really have been from the law"). For now it suffices to observe how the contrast of Habakkuk 2:4 and Leviticus 18:5 confuses the line of thought in 3:10-12 by all but leaving behind the theme of verse 11 ("no one in the law is righteous") in order to distinguish sharply two alternative ways of getting "life." The distinction is itself the argument, for unless Paul can assume that the Galatians will affirm the truth of Habakkuk 2:4 as a basic article of the gospel, there is no point in arguing. But if they do affirm it, they will have to acknowledge that "life," which they know concretely as life in the Spirit, comes from Christ-Faith and therefore cannot be said to come from doing the law.

From what has just been said, it appears that 3:12 is a kind of parenthetical excursus in the argument. Either Paul digresses or he gets ahead of himself, depending upon how one looks at it—the same point is made in 3:5; 3:9; and 3:14. One way to test whether 3:12 is an aside is to consider the flow of the argument without it:

> All who are from works of the law are under a curse, for it is written: "Cursed is anyone who does not remain in all the things written in the book of the law to do them." And that no one is righteous in the law [the curse indeed applies to everyone in the law] is evident [to us "Christians"], for [we know that] "the righteous shall live by faith [by Christ-Faith]." Christ redeemed us from the curse of the law by becoming a curse for us. . . .

The argument is now much more straightforward, which leads one to suspect that the introduction of Leviticus 18:5 was prompted by the fact that Habakkuk 2:4 speaks not only of "faith" and "righteousness" but also of "faith" and "living."[40]

---

[40]Although one may interpret the wording of Hab 2:4 (LXX) as Paul reproduces it to mean "the just from faith shall live," the ἐκ πίστεως is taken more naturally with the verb, and this best fits Paul's argument. On the problem, see H. C. C. Cavallin, " 'The Righteous Shall Live By Faith': A Decisive Argument for the Traditional In-

The just shall live (ζήσεται) by faith.

The one who does them shall live (ζήσεται) by them.

Now if Leviticus 18:5 is the slogan of the agitators, then it is not surprising that the moment Paul makes use of Habakkuk 2:4, he thinks immediately of Leviticus 18:5. But it is also not surprising in view of the interrelation of the themes of righteousness and life. In the end what we have identified as two directions in the argument of 3:10-12 do in fact cohere. Since Paul's apocalyptic worldview does not allow any middle ground between ''blessing'' and ''curse,'' his argument about the curse is itself an argument that the law does not mediate the blessing, and his argument that Leviticus 18:5 does not hold true eschatologically (because *Hab 2:4* does) is at the same time an argument in support of the assertion that those who depend on the law are under a curse. That is why the apostle can argue that to be redeemed from the curse is to come into the blessing (3:13-14), without making any step in between. Righteousness is not itself the blessing of the Spirit, but where eschatological righteousness appears, there the eschatological Spirit is also to be found (Isa 32:15-17; Gal 5:5).

The Line of Thought in 3:15–4:30

We return now to our examination of Galatians 3–4 as a whole. Having identified the primary aim of Paul's argumentation in these chapters, we will now trace more closely the line of thought in 3:15–4:30(31). This extended discussion is unified thematically by its treatment of the law, sonship (Abraham's seed), the promise, slavery (as the opposing state to sonship), and heirship. The last two terms (slavery and heirship) are new to the discussion.

Christ as the Sole Heir of the Spirit (3:15-18)

Paul introduces the theme of heirship with an argument from testamentary law (3:15-18). His introductory words, ''I speak like a man''

---

terpretation,'' *Studia Theologica* 32 (1978): 33-43; also D. Moody Smith, ''Ο ΔΕ ΔΙΚΑΙΟΣ ΕΚ ΠΙΣΤΕΩΣ ΖΗΣΕΤΑΙ,'' in *Studies in the History of the Text of the New Testament in Honor of Kenneth Willis Clark,* ed. B. Daniels and M. Jack Suggs (Salt Lake City: University of Utah Press, 1967) 13-25.

(κατὰ ἄνθρωπον λέγω) qualify not the example but the *argument* as "human." Although most interpreters think that the sentence means something like, "I offer an example from everyday life," no example of such a usage has yet been adduced. Furthermore, the evidence from Paul himself suggests that the phrase may serve as a kind of apology for even putting into words a blasphemous thought that the apostle himself rejects out of hand (see Rom 3:5). In Greek the phrase κατὰ ἄνθρωπον (as distinct from κατὰ ἀνθρώπους), typically conveys the sense of the "merely human," a diminuation that takes on markedly theological significance in Galatians 1:11, where Paul declares that his gospel is not κατὰ ἄνθρωπον.[41]Thus, when Paul says "I am arguing like a mere human being" he prepares his readers in advance for something in his argument that is not κατὰ θεόν ("according to God").

A close examination of the passage accounts for Paul's qualification in verse 15. The argument contains a blasphemous *premise* at the point where it treats the giving of the law as an attempt to cancel the promise (v. 17). According to Paul's logic, a cancellation of the promise is impossible not because it is unconventional but because it is *illegal.*[42] The apostle never disputes that the law is God's law, hence the argument of verse 17 implies that by giving the law God tried to renege on his promise. The point is not what God would or would not do but the fact that he is legally bound to his "previously ratified covenant" with Abraham. To be sure, neither the Galatians nor the agitators will have rep-

---

[41]Compare Philo *Virt.* 217; *Spec.* 1.116; *Leg. Gai.* 76; also Xenophon *Cyr.* 8.7.2; *HG* 3.3.1; *Mem.* 4.4.24; Aeschylus *Th.* 425; Sophocles *Ajax* 761; *Ajax* 777; *OC* 598; Athenaeus *Deip.* 10.444 B; Diodorus Siculus 16.11.2; Porphyry *De abst.* 2.2.; *Ox. Pap.* 1381.118; Ignatius *Trall.* 2.1; Origen *In Gen III.12* (*Philoc.* 23.19) quoting *Oratio Joseph*. See Cosgrove, "Arguing Like a Mere Human Being: Gal 3.15-18 in Rhetorical Perspective," *NTS* 34 (1988): 536-49.

[42]It is not certain which legal instrument Paul has in mind. The only example known from the ancient Mediterranean world of a disposition for the transfer of property that could not be changed even while the testator was alive is the *mattenat bari'*, to which Ernst Bammel has drawn attention. See "Gottes ΔΙΑΘΗΚΗ (Gal. III 15-17) und das jüdische Rechtsdenken," *NTS* 6 (1959–1960): 313-19. On the geographical distribution of this form of disposition, see Betz, *Galatians,* 155 n. 23. The difficulty with Bammel's suggestion is that Paul appears to be thinking throughout Gal 3:15-4:7 in terms of *inheritance* law, which allowed for amendment up until the time when the inheritance was finally transferred to the heir.

resented the law as an attempt to undo the promise. It is Paul who discerns in their claims about the law the implication that the law competes with the Abrahamic covenant, and it is this implication that serves as the blasphemous premise of his highly ironic argument and thus calls for the disclaimer, "I speak like a man." Paul defends his interpretation of their position by explaining (γάρ): "For if the inheritance is from the law (as you say), it is no longer from (the) promise—but God gave it to Abraham by promise" (v. 18).

The point of the argument is not that the reception of the promise is by faith rather than by the fulfillment of certain ethical conditions, as if Paul were speaking here directly about how one might qualify for the inheritance.[43] One does indeed qualify by faith, as Paul has argued in the preceding (3:1-14), but nothing is said here of qualifications which are to be met. The point is that the promise was made to only two persons, Abraham and his seed Christ (v. 16). It is the extension of the inheritance to others on the basis of another arrangement (the law) that Paul rejects as illegal. The inheritance is not from the law (or for law-keepers) because it was promised to *Christ alone*. Throughout the ensuing discussion Paul keeps this reduction of Abraham's seed to Christ in view. In 3:19 he speaks of "the seed to whom it had been promised" (τὸ σπέρμα ᾧ ἐπήγγελται), and in 3:29 believers qualify as "seed of Abraham" only by virtue of "having put on Christ" (3:27), of being "in Christ" (3:28), or of belonging to Christ (3:29).

The restriction of the promise to (Abraham and) Christ in 3:15-18 reinforces the preceding argument by disconnecting what the agitators must surely have kept together, the promise to Abraham and God's covenant with Moses. In 3:6-14 Paul does not argue for but *takes for granted* the equation of the Spirit with the Abrahamic blessing and promise. Paul's readers know that by "inheritance" he has in view "the promise of the Spirit" (v. 14) and not, as most interpreters assume, "justifica-

---

[43]The "gift-character" of the promise is not necessarily emphasized by κεχάρισ-ται. Ridderbos points out that "χαρίζομαι without the object is a technical term from the law of inheritance: make a grant, deed something by will" (Herman N. Ridderbos, *The Epistle of Paul to the Churches of Galatia*, trans. H. Zylstra [Grand Rapids MI: Eerdmans, 1953] 137 n. 13); see also the literature listed by Betz, *Galatians*, 160 n. 62.

tion by faith.''[44] The question that follows in verse 19 (''Why then the law?'') appears to introduce a fresh line of thought, as if the apostle had finished making his point that life in the Spirit does not depend on works of the law and were now turning to address the question of the law's proper role in salvation history. But in 3:19–4:30 the apostle is still mounting arguments that disengage life in the Spirit from lawkeeping, and his explanation of the law's role and purpose in God's economy serves this larger purpose. This section is therefore best understood as combining apology and polemic.

The questions, ''Why then the law?'' (3:19) and ''Is the law against the promises of God?'' (3:21), introduce apology for Paul's view of the law. Since Paul assumes throughout Galatians that the law is *God's* law, he must demonstrate that his understanding of the Torah preserves a meaningful place for it in the divine economy.[45] Hence his apology for the law takes the form of explanation and clarification. The statement that the law was given ''for transgressions'' (v. 19b) and the metaphor of the law as a παιδαγωγός (''slave guardian'') are ways of defending the law. But apologetic qualification serves at the same time as qualified polemic against what for Paul are inflated views of the law. Thus, in the course of defending his view of the law against misunderstanding, the apostle engages in pointed polemic ''against'' the law. The very statements that assign the law a meaningful purpose in salvation history severely restrict the law's soteriological potential: the law was given simply ''for transgressions'' and not ''for life.'' God's law is not against God's promises because God did not endow the law with the power to

---

[44]Becker, *Der Brief an die Galater,* 39; Schlier, *Der Brief an die Galater,* 150; cf. Bruce, *The Epistle to the Galatians,* 173. Paul never equates the inheritance with justification. And although the promise may be said to come ''through the righteousness of faith'' (Rom 4:13) or ''from the faith of Jesus Christ'' (Gal 3:22), it is never said to be received *as* ''justification by faith.''

[45]Schlier treats 3:21ff. as polemical, as if the question of v. 21a were provoked by the Judaizers' position and were not Paul's own: ''Der sündenerweckende, zeitlich-kosmische Charakter des Gesetzes macht deutlich, dass es die Verheissungen Gottes nicht stören kann. . . . '' (*Der Brief an die Galater,* 163). But the apostle inquires in v. 21 not whether the law is in a position to win out over the promises but whether the law is *against* the promises.

make alive (v. 21). Instead the law has served merely as our παιδαγωγός until Christ (vv. 24-25).

The Law Is Not against the Promises (3:19-22)

"Why then the law?" Paul answers this question in a rather general
and somewhat ambiguous fashion when he says that the law was given
τῶν παραβάσεων χάριν. This phrase probably means "because of
transgressions." The law was given to "deal with" transgression by
proscribing it and judging it. Here the old interpretation that sees the
law's function before Christ as one of inhibiting transgression[46] has some
place, inasmuch as deterrence goes hand in hand with proscription and
judgment. But Paul takes a dim view of the law's effectiveness in con-
taining sin's power. As far as he is concerned, the only final effect of
the law upon those "under the law" is to seal them under its curse (3:10-
13). Moreover, in Romans 7 the apostle even suggests that sin uses the
law against itself to provoke transgression, although there is no hint that
he has this idea in view in Galatians. In any event, Paul is far more interested in marking the end of the law with the coming of Christ than in
spelling out the precise function of the law before Christ. Hence, he states
the positive aim of the law as briefly as possible and then goes on immediately to declare its end with the coming of the Seed (v. 19c). This
makes perfect sense if Paul's concern is not to debate the usefulness of
the law for ethics but to define the relationship of the law to the promise.

The participial construction (διαταγεὶς κ.τ.λ.) makes an additional statement about the giving of the law and prepares for the little
argument of verse 20. By mentioning the role of angels in the giving of
the law, Paul agrees for the sake of his apology with a piece of Jewish
folklore intended to glorify the law.[47] But the reference to angels leads

---

[46]Thus Chrysostom spoke of the law as "teaching," "training" and "hindering
transgression" (see *PG* 61.654). See further Schlier, who supplies both the text from
Chrysostom and a list of Greek commentators who took a similar view (*Der Brief an
die Galater,* 153 n. 1).

[47]See Acts 7:53; *Jub.* 1:27-2:1; Heb 2:2. See also Josephus *Ant.* 15.136, where the
Jews are said to have received their noblest doctrines and holiest laws δ' ἀγγέλων παρὰ
τοῦ θεοῦ. It is debated whether angels or human messengers are in view. See W. D.
Davies, "A Note on Josephus, Antiquities 15. 136," *HTR* 47 (1954): 135-40; R. F.
Walton, "The Messenger from God in Hecataeus of Abdera," *HTR* 48 (1955): 255-57.

him to the "mediator," whose role affords Paul the opportunity to make a qualifying statement about the law: "The mediator is not of one."[48] This is the second time that Paul has made a point about "oneness" in connection with the promise, the first being in verse 16. If we interpret 3:20a in the light of 3:16, the sense seems to be that Moses as the mediator of the many Israelites and not of "the one" seed (Christ) does not in any sense represent the one seed at the giving of the law. And if he does not represent the one seed, then the giving of the law does not in fact have anything to do with the prior Abrahamic covenant. Seen in this light, verses 19-20 constitute an immediate continuation of the argument of 3:15ff., contributing an explicit rejection of the false premise adopted in verse 17 that the law amounts to an amendment of the Abrahamic covenant. Paul follows his statement that the mediator is not "of one" with a basic article of Jewish faith: "God is one" (3:20b). H. D. Betz may well be right when he suggests that the ancient axiom "like is the friend of like" (τὸ ὅμοιον τῷ ὁμοίῳ φίλον) informs the argument,[49] but the text remains nonetheless enigmatic, and we will not attempt to penetrate its opaque logic any further here.[50]

"Is the law, then, against the promises of God?" (3:21). This question has been in the air since 3:15-18, and 3:19-20 is already a partial answer. If "the mediator is not of the one," then the law is not against the promises by virtue of the fact that it has nothing to do with the promise. The promise was made to Abraham and his one seed (Christ), while the law was given to the people, who are many. But since the curse of the law blocks the flow of the promise (3:10-14), the question arises

---

[48]The definite article with μεσίτης ("mediator") may be taken as particularizing or generic. Since a mediator may well represent *one party* to another, the article is probably anaphoric (hence particularizing): "Now this mediator is not of one."

[49]See Betz, *Galatians,* 171-73. Betz applies the axiom to the text at hand by suggesting that for Paul any conception of the process of divine redemption must conform to the oneness of God. Thus, the law, which required a mediator who represented a plurality, does not conform to God's oneness and therefore cannot be incorporated positively into the scheme of redemption.

[50]On the numerous attempts to divine the logic of 3:19-20, see (in addition to the commentators) Terrance Callan, "The Law and the Mediator: Gal 3:19b-20" (Ph.D. diss., Yale University, 1976); idem, "Pauline Midrash: The Exegetical Background of Gal. 3:19b," *JBL* 99 (1980): 549-67.

whether it thwarts the aims of the Abrahamic covenant. Paul's answer is that sin is ultimately responsible for the cosmic situation in which the law's curse blocks the promise, and he "excuses" the law by stressing its impotence:

> For if a law had been given that was able to make alive, then righteousness would indeed have been from the law. But Scripture consigned all things under sin, that the promise might be given to believers from the faith of Jesus Christ. (3:21b-22)

The fact that righteousness was not "from the law" (a fact that Paul treats here as self-evident) is proof that the law was not endowed with the power to make alive. Thus, the construction conforms rhetorically to Paul's uses of unreal conditions elsewhere. The apodosis states what is known as proof of what the protasis aims to point out.[51] Paul does not imply that under "different cosmic conditions" the promise would have flowed "from" the Torah covenant. He says only that if the law had been able to overcome the power of sin, "righteousness" would have been "from the law," in which case the curse of the law would not have gone into effect to stop the flow of the promise. Of course, this is all hypothetical in the extreme for Paul, hence he does not reflect on what consequences this line of thinking might have for his contention that the promise was made to Christ alone (3:16). It is presumably the agitators who, quite understandably, take sentences from the Torah such as Leviticus 18:5 and Deuteronomy 30:15-20 to mean that the eschatological promise of life in the Spirit depends on lawkeeping (see below chapter 3). But as far as Paul is concerned, the Torah bears only a negative relation to the promise. It is endowed with a kind of veto power, inasmuch as "righteousness" ("justification") is a prerequisite of sharing in the inheritance (life in the Spirit). Therefore, although the law does not contain the promise (v. 18), it is able to disqualify persons from receiving the promise by pronouncing its verdict upon them as unrighteous. It is not for that reason "against" the promise, for it is sin and not the law that is responsible for unrighteousness.

---

[51] See Michael Winger, "Unreal Conditions in the Letters of Paul," *JBL* 105 (1986): 112.

By contrast with the interpretation just advanced, most interpreters have assumed that the apostle's point in 3:21 is that a person cannot acquire righteousness from the law.[52] But we are operating with the assumption that the issue in Galatians is how one "receives the Spirit" (promotes ongoing life in the Spirit). Hence, we are led to conclude that what Paul says about righteousness serves as common ground in the argument. We find support for this conclusion elsewhere in Galatians. In 2:16 Paul introduces the affirmation that justification is by "the faith of Jesus Christ" as common ground with Jewish Christians (εἰδότες . . . ἡμεῖς). And in 3:7, having quoted the words of Genesis 15:6 without any formulaic introduction (as if his readers knew the text by heart), Paul does not argue but reminds the Galatians, "You know,[53] then, that those from faith, these are sons of Abraham." As we have seen, this reminder is not itself the apostle's main point but serves as a step on the way to his point (v. 9). The same goes for 3:11-12, where Paul quotes Habakkuk 2:4, without any introductory formula, as a self-evident proof for believers (ὅτι . . . δῆλον) that "in the law no one is righteous before God" (v. 11), in order to make the point that *the Spirit is not from the law but from faith* (3:14). Therefore, it is not surprising that in 3:21 he uses the "accepted fact" that righteousness did not come from the law to prove that the law is not able to make alive. Concretely, Paul is relying on the Galatians' recognition that all who turn to Christ, *including the Torah-faithful*, acknowledge in so doing that apart from faith in Christ they are not "just" before God. Of course, common ground essential to an argument can always use reinforcing. Therefore, if some need to be reminded that there is no righteousness outside Christ, Paul explains in the next breath, "For Scripture shut up all things under sin that the promise might be given to believers from the faith of Jesus Christ" (3:22). Paul had already pointed out this "faith-datum" in the episto-

---

[52]Oepke states explicitly what most commentators seem to take for granted, namely, that "righteousness" and "life" are practically synonyms (*Der Brief des Paulus an die Galater,* 119).

[53]See the use of γινώσκειν in Rom 6:6; 2 Cor 8:9; Phil 2:22. Cf. the use of ἰδεῖν in Rom 2:2; 3:19; 5:3; 6:9; 7:14; 8:22; 8:28; 1 Cor 8:1, 4; 12:2; 16:15; 2 Cor 4:14; 5:1; Gal 2:16; 4:13; Phil 4:15). See further 1 Cor 8:4 (with οἴδαμεν). Although Betz is able to give some examples outside Paul of the rhetorical ("didactic") imperative (*Galatians,* 141 n. 23), most of the Greek fathers "heard" the indicative mood in Gal 3:7.

lary prescript: "Jesus Christ, who gave himself for our sins to deliver us from the present evil age" (1:4). This traditional[54] statement is itself an argument against the law's ability to mediate the Spirit. For to believe in Christ is to believe that Christ delivers "us" from bondage in the present evil age, and if that holds for lawkeepers and nonlawkeepers alike, then it is evident that doing the law does not bring life, deliverance, or the Spirit.

"Being under the Law" as Non-Access to the Spirit (Inheritance) (3:23–4:11)

Paul elaborates the idea of the law's impotence (v. 22) by means of a metaphor drawn from the field of *paideia* (3:23-29), which he follows up with an illustration drawn from inheritance law (4:1-7). The closing paragraph (4:8-11) belongs with the verses preceding it and serves as a concrete warning to the Galatians that coming "under the law" puts one "under the cosmic 'elements' " (ὑπὸ τὰ στοιχεῖα τοῦ κόσμου). The two sections, 3:23-29 and 4:1-7 (with vv. 8-11), exhibit parallel structures. Both treat first and essentially the situation of the Jew under the law (3:23-25; 4:3). Both go on to speak of how the coming of Christ changes this situation (3:26-27; 4:4-5) and do so by drawing upon traditional language and formulae. Both extend the benefits of God's act in Christ to Gentile believers (the Galatians), implying that the situation of the Gentile apart from Christ is analogous to that of the Jew under the law. In both sections an implication for Paul's readers is that a move "under the law" amounts to a return to their pre–Christian situation, a thought spelled out explicitly in 4:8-11. Further, both discussions speak of "sonship" as the new status given to those who believe in Christ and conclude by inferring from this new status the automatic benefit of "realized heirship" for the believer (3:26-29; 4:5-7).

There remain, however, differences between the two sections. The first discussion utilizes for its key metaphor an institution of Graeco-Roman education: the παιδαγωγός. The second develops an analogy from the realm of inheritance law. The two sections also differ in the

---

[54]For a discussion of this sentence as a traditional formula, see Klaus Wengst, *Christologische Formeln und Lieder des Urchristentums*, StNT 7 (Gütersloh: G. Mohn, 1972) 56-57, 61.

aspects under which they consider the situation prior to faith. In 3:23-29 Paul characterizes the situation of the Jew under the law as *imprisonment* (under sin), while in 4:1-7 he regards the situation prior to faith primarily as *non-access* to the inheritance. But it turns out that these two ways of describing existence under the law are in fact related, inasmuch as Paul develops the second as a clarification of the first (λέγω δέ, 4:1) by stressing more pointedly the position of those "under the law" vis-à-vis the promise: To be under the law is to be no better than a slave, without rights of disposal over the goods of the estate. This is the thrust of 3:23–4:11 as a whole. To translate the metaphor into the concrete language of the Galatians debate, being under the law does not increase one's access to the Spirit, it cuts one off from the Spirit (as the content of the inheritance).

Having considered the general structure and content of 3:23–4:11, we will now trace more closely its line of thought. When Paul says in verse 23 that "before Faith came, we (Jews) were being guarded under the law, being locked up until this coming faith should be revealed," he applies the universal statement of 3:22 to the situation of the Jew under the law. Since the redemption of those under the law (see 4:5) is none other than redemption from the curse of the law (3:13), it follows that the law "guards" the Jew by means of its curse. To that extent there is nothing "demonic" about the law in its capacity as "guard," since it performs this role by speaking a word of divine judgment upon the unrighteous. Moreover, the apostle immediately introduces a metaphor that protects the law from demonic caricature and at the same time defines the law and existence under the law as strictly penultimate: "The law became our guardian until Christ" (v. 24).

The "guardian" of which Paul speaks was a slave charged with custody of a youth until the latter's maturity. The Greeks called him παιδαγωγός, a term the Romans transliterated into Latin as *paedagogus*. In old Athens he was invariably a barbarian (a non-Greek). In Roman times, however, he was typically Greek, since among his various duties he was expected to help the boy with his learning of the Greek language. He accompanied the youth to school, carrying his books and other materials, attended his classes with him, guarded him from harm and bad influences on the streets, taught him manners, and shared informally in imparting moral education to him.[55] Hence, the law as *paedagogus* may be understood as a kind of moral guardian whose aim is to keep his charges *from* sin, even if his final say over them must take the form of a death-dealing curse.[56] Paul indicates that the law's function in this capacity is temporally limited, the metaphor itself suggesting that the law's rights over its charges falls to the time of their "minority." The point, however, of assigning the law to the past is not to suggest its obsolescence,[57] but to express its *disconnection from the promise:* (1) "given until the seed should come to whom the promises had been made" (3:19), (2) "thus the law became our *paedagogus* until Christ, that we might become just by Faith" (3:24), (3) "This is what I mean: the heir as long as he is a child is no better than a slave, though lord of all" (4:1).

It should not be overlooked that the *paedagogus* in Roman antiquity was typically a slave himself. Verse 22 already prepares for this aspect of the metaphor when it speaks not simply of all persons (cf. τοὺς πάντας in Rom 11:32) but of all things, the entire cosmos (τὰ πάντα), being shut up "under sin." The law is by definition included. The thought of the Torah's own "slavery" is developed even more explicitly in 4:21-31, where Paul takes up again the concept of existence "under the law" (4:21). There as well images of slavery and freedom provide the ruling motifs, and the logic of Paul's allegorical interpretation implies that the law (as Mt. Sinai/Hagar) bears children for slavery (4:24) precisely because it is itself a slave (cf. what v. 25 says about Jerusalem). Hagar, who represents the covenant from Mt. Sinai, is, after all, the "slave woman" (vv. 22-24).

---

[55]See E. Schuppe, "Paidagogos," in *Paulys Real-Encyclopädie der classischen Altertumswissenschaft,* vol. 18/1, reedited by Georg Wissowa (Stuttgart: J. B. Metzlerische Verlagsbuchhandlung, 1942) 2375-85; David J. Lull, " 'The Law Was Our Pedagogue': A Study in Galatians 3:19-25," *JBL* 105 (1986): 481-98; Norman H. Young, "*Paidagogos:* The Social Setting of a Pauline Metaphor," *NovT* 29 (1987): 150-76.

[56]Lull develops this point with great care, even if he fails to attend sufficiently to the negative aspect of the law's guardianship, namely, its death-dealing curse upon those under the power of Sin. See " 'The Law Was Our Paidagogos': A Study in Galatians 3:19-25."

[57]So Joseph B. Tyson, " 'Works of the Law' in Galatians," *JBL* 92 (1973): 423-31 (430-31).

In Galatians Paul does not develop that sophisticated reflection on sin's misuse of the law that we meet in Romans 7. The point of the *paedagogus* metaphor is not the law's pliability as sin's slave but the nature of the situation under the law. To be under the law is to be in slavery, and 4:1-7 clarifies what that means. The child, for whom disposal over the estate will come only with maturity,[58] is in effect no different from a mere slave. He is sociopolitically, and in the transferred sense spiritually, powerless, cut off from the Spirit as the content of the inheritance. The metaphor of the law as *paedagogus* does not dispute the law's *authoritative power,* by which it effects the curse, but its *dynamic power,* for lack of which it fails to produce life. Only this distinction explains how the apostle can move immediately from a statement on the law's impotence (3:22) to an image of its authority (3:23).

The thematic movement of the argument in its positive direction (24-29) matches exactly the thematic logic of 3:6-14. Paul begins with "justification by faith" (3:6; 3:24), moves to "sonship" (3:7; 3:26-29a), and concludes with a statement about the benefits of being sons (or "seed") of Abraham (3:9; 3:29b). The two arguments differ, however, in the way in which they establish the sonship of believers. In 3:7 Paul derives "sonship by faith" from the justification of Abraham. But by 3:24-29 he has already made a great point of restricting the seed of Abraham to a single individual, Christ (3:16; cf. 3:19). It is this one seed alone who is to inherit the promise, and Paul's task is to show how the singular "seedship" of Christ benefits believers. He has no difficulty doing this, since believers understand themselves already, by virtue of the baptismal tradition that Paul mentions in 3:27, as being "in Christ." And Paul even manages to preserve the singularity of this multiplicity of "sons

---

[58]See Betz, *Galatians,* 202-204. Betz also points out the difficulties that interpreters face in trying to correlate what Paul says with Roman law. In this connection we may note a recent article by Linda Belleville, who adduces two papyri texts which indicate that in the second century C.E. a father did enjoy the right of some discretion over when his sons should obtain their majority and thus gain access to their inheritance (*Ox. Pap.* 491 and 495). See " 'Under Law': Structural Analysis and the Pauline Concept of Law in Galatians 3:21–4:11," *JSNT* 26 (1986): 62. For general treatments of the relevant legal material, see Raphael Taubenschlag, *The Law of Greco-Roman Egypt in the Light of the Papyri,* 2nd ed. (Warsaw: Panstwowe Wydawnictwo Naukowe, 1955) and Fritz Schulz, *Classical Roman Law* (Oxford: Clarendon Press, 1954).

of God in Christ'' (v. 26) by citing another sentence from the baptismal formula: "There is neither Jew nor Greek, there is neither slave nor free, there is neither male nor female'' (v. 28).[59] Interpreters have tended to locate the significance of verse 28 for Paul's argument in its declaration that the Jew/Gentile distinction no longer holds,[60] but that is not where the emphasis lies. In fact, the formula would have served Paul's purposes equally well even if it had not included any reference to the end of the Jew/Gentile distinction. The contribution of the formula to the argument at hand is found in the words that immediately follow and thus interpret the negative half of the formula, words that probably belong themselves to the formula: "For you are all *one* in Christ Jesus.'' Paul quotes the formula to make the point that believers are "one'' in Christ and therefore count as Abraham's "one'' seed (τοῦ ᾿Αβραὰμ σπέρμα), which is equivalent to saying that they are "heirs according to the promise'' (κατ᾿ ἐπαγγελίαν κληρονόμοι, v. 29). And what do they inherit simply by being in Christ? The Spirit. That is taken for granted in 3:29 but stated explicitly in the further explication that follows, to which we now turn.

We have already noted that 4:1-7 portrays the time prior to faith (the time under the law) as a period of non-access to the promise. The child-heir, not having received his inheritance, is no better off than a slave. Not only that, but he is set under "guardians and trustees'' to whom he is immediately answerable (4:2). Therefore, the "slave-like'' status of the child signifies his powerlessness in two respects. He has no property (he does not "possess'' the Spirit, cf. vv. 6-7), and he must submit to the will of those above him (he is in bondage to the powers of this age, v. 3). But since this twofold impotence belongs to one and the same situation, the position of the minor, Paul treats the two aspects together:

---

[59] On the traditional character and meaning of the formulations in Gal 3:27-28, see Wayne A. Meeks, "The Image of the Androgyne: Some Uses of a Symbol in Earliest Christianity,'' *HR* 13 (1974): 183-84.

[60] See, for example, Betz, *Galatians,* 182; Oepke, *Der Brief des Paulus an die Galater,* 126; T. L. Donaldson, "The 'Curse of the Law' and the Inclusion of the Gentiles: Galatians 3.13-14,'' *NTS* 32 (1986): 94, 98.

> This is what I mean. The heir, as long as he is a child, is no different
> from a slave, even though he is lord of all. But he is under guardians
> and stewards until the time set by the father.

Stewards (οἰκονόμοι) were slaves entrusted with financial duties.[61]
Perhaps the stewards mentioned here are persons charged with managing the estate until the child comes of age. That would explain why
Paul introduces them, even though "stewards" were not guardians. The
time set by the father corresponds to "the fullness of time" when God
sent his Son to redeem those under the law. This "redemption of slaves"
turns out to be also an "adoption," and now the restricted "we" of "we
Jews under the law" expands to encompass believers as such (vv. 4-5).
But when Paul finally draws his conclusion, he addresses the Galatians
directly (vv. 6-7; cf. 3:28-29). The use of direct address no less than the
logic of the argument and the fact that we are at the end of it marks what
he says as the point of the entire discussion:

> And because you are sons [premise], God has sent his Spirit into our
> hearts crying "Abba! Father!" So then, through God you are no longer
> a slave but a son, and if a son also an *heir*.

The closing statement shows that the issue is not sonship but heirship,
which means "realized heirship" in this context. Therefore we are to
take the two verses as parallel. The first argues that God has given the
Spirit to believers simply because he has adopted them as his sons,[62] the
implication being that God continues to supply the Spirit for the same
reason and not because of works of the law. Verse 7 makes the same

---

[61]See John Reumann, " 'Stewards of God'—Pre-Christian Religious Application
of OIKONOMOS in Greek," *JBL* 77 (1958): 339-49 (342-44); Gerd Theissen, "Soziale Schichtung in der korinthischen Gemeinde," *ZNW* 65 (1974): 237-41.

[62]Since reception of the Spirit and "sonship" are closely associated in early Christian thinking (especially in Paul's churches), the apostle can argue from the fact of one
to the reality of the other. In Rom 8:16 Paul points to the fact of the Spirit as evidence
that his readers count as "sons." In Gal 4:6 he moves in the other direction, from the
fact of the Galatians' sonship to their reception of the Spirit on that basis. The unity of
Rom 8:16 and Gal 4:6 lies not in their respective arguments but in their shared assumption that God gives his Spirit to his sons.

point: "If a son, then also an heir." Sonship is what affords access to the inheritance, which is the Spirit.

Works of the Law as Service to Impotent Cosmic Powers (4:1-11)

The interpretive development in 4:1-7 of the argument in 3:23-29, together with the warnings in 4:8-11, raises the question of the Torah's relation to "the cosmic elements" (τὰ στοιχεῖα τοῦ κόσμου, 4:3; 4:9). The στοιχεῖα are identified in 4:1-7 with the figures of the administrators (ἐπίτροποι) and the trustees (οἰκονόμοι) in Paul's illustration. Hence we must determine whether the law as *paedagogus* is numbered by the apostle among these overseers and whether the law represents one of the cosmic στοιχεῖα.

The illustration that Paul introduces in 4:1 has a primarily negative thrust, as is evident from the application in 4:3. The στοιχεῖα are hardly to be conceived as "trustees" of humanity's rightful inheritance in Christ! Furthermore, it is clear from the whole of Paul's apology in 3:21–4:11 that the existential contexts described by the phrases "under the law" and "under the cosmic elements" *coincide*. Moreover, in 4:9-11 doing the law (v. 10) is associated closely with serving the cosmic elements. Does Paul, then, regard the law as an enslaving cosmic power? An answer to this question requires an elucidation of the expression τὰ στοιχεῖα τοῦ κόσμου.

Paul employs the expression τὰ στοιχεῖα τοῦ κόσμου of beings which are *really* (φύσει) not gods. The term στοιχεῖον was not used, as far as we know, in application to "gods" of any sort prior to or during the time of Paul.[63] It was used typically of the basic physical elements by which the world is constituted (earth, wind, fire, air, and sometimes ether). The expression στοιχεῖα τοῦ κόσμου outside of Paul and those influenced by him is always used in this way, even in the

---

[63]See especially the exhaustive study by Josef Blinzler, "Lexikalisches zu dem Terminus τὰ στοιχεῖα τοῦ κόσμου bei Paulus," in *Studiorum Paulinorum Congressus Biblicus 1961*, vol. 2, Analecta Biblica 17-18 (Rome: Pontifical Biblical Institute, 1963) 429-43. See also: G. Delling, *TDNT*, 7.666-87, s.v. στοιχέω; A. J. Bandstra, *The Law and the Elements of the World: An Exegetical Study in Aspects of Paul's Teaching* (Kampen: J. H. Kok N. V., 1964); P. Vielhauer, "Gesetzesdienst und Stoicheiadienst im Galaterbrief," in *Oikodome: Aufsätze zum Neuen Testament*, vol. 2, TBNT 65 (Munich: Chr. Kaiser Verlag, 1979) 183-95.

second century. In fact, leaving aside those in Colossians and Galatians, all of the eleven known instances of this expression that have been gleaned thus far from the Greek literature of antiquity have the physical elements of the cosmos in view.[64] Further, where we meet the "elements" as cosmic powers in later literature, there is no association positively or negatively with the law (for example, *T.Sol.* 8:2). This suggests strongly that Paul uses the term in a novel way,[65] hence that he himself first introduces "the cosmic elements" into the discussion. This conclusion finds support in the confinement of this language to the immediate context of Galatians 4:1-11. Its limited use here and its conspicuous absence from the epistolary prescript, from the thanksgiving parody (1:6-9), and from the central offensive (3:1-18) speak against a borrowing from the Judaizers or the Galatians themselves.

Since στοιχεῖον in Galatians 4 does not represent an immediately recognizable term for cosmic beings, perhaps we have to do with a general characterization for the powers or rulers of this age under whatever names or conceptions they are to be found. Paul speaks in 1 Corinthians 2:6, 8 of "the rulers of this age," a phrase that must be interpreted in the light of 1 Corinthians 15:24 and its apocalyptic conceptuality (cf. also Rom 8:38 and 1 Cor 8:5). But if Paul already possesses language for speaking of "the powers" in general, why should he turn in Galatians 4 to a term that does not in conventional usage mean "powers?" Short of second-guessing the apostle's motivations, it may be observed that the application of the expression στοιχεῖα τοῦ κόσμου to "gods that are not really gods" has the effect of identifying them very closely with the cosmos itself. We do not have here the "many gods and many lords" of 1 Corinthians 8:5, which distinguishes itself from Galatians 4:8 in that it speaks of gods that have real existence *as cosmic powers,* even if it is idolatrous to worship them (hence Paul's qualification: λεγόμενοι θεοὶ). By contrast, the expression στοιχεῖα τοῦ κόσμου,

---

[64]These are *Sib. Or.* 2:206; 3:80-81; 8:337; Philo *Aet.* 109; *Her.* 134 and 140; Irenaeus *Adv. Haer.* 1.5.4; Clement of Alexandria *Exc. ex Theodoto* 48.3; Galen *Comm. on Hippocratis de nat. hom.* 1.39 (Mewaldt 50.6); Ps.-Lucian *Amores* 19; *Orphic Hymn* 5.4 (Quandt 5). See Blinzler, "Lexikalisches," 440-41.

[65]So Delling: "It seems that Paul himself contributed the phrase στοιχεῖα τοῦ κόσμου in both Gl. and Col." (*TDNT,* 7:685).

which denotes ordinarily the basic constituent elements of the physical world, suggests in its transferred sense that the "elements" do not stand over the world as its demonic subjugators but belong themselves to the world in its futility (cf. Rom 8:20). This would account for Paul's description of them as "weak and beggarly" (4:9). Since lawkeeping entails calendrical observances Paul can equate it with serving the "cosmic elements," inasmuch as the cosmic order is what determines the calendar. In fact, the language of 4:10 recalls Genesis 1:14 (LXX), a sentence from the Torah itself that grounds the calendar in creation:

> And God said, "Let there be lights in the firmament of the heaven . . . and let them be for signs and for seasons (καιροὺς) and for days (ἡμέρας) and for years (ἐνιαυτοὺς)."[66]

Now those who belong to the present (old) cosmos have no recourse but to order themselves to it. The Jew has the Torah for this purpose and the pagan his astrological chart. Paul does not regard ordering oneself to the cosmos according to the Torah calendar "sin" any more than he regards the law and the στοιχεῖα τοῦ κόσμου as demonic powers. The ruling idea is that of service to that which is impotent and impoverished (τὰ ἀσθενῆ καὶ πτωχὰ στοιχεῖα), a conception that fits well with the simile of "being no better off than a slave" (4:1) and one that by no means excludes the possibility that these elements of the cosmos might be mistaken for gods and idolatrously served as such. But under whatever forms or conceptions "serving the στοιχεῖα" appears, it represents activity fitted only to the present order rather than to that of the new creation in Christ (cf. Gal 6:14-15). And that is a way of saying that keeping the Torah may be valid as a way of managing existence in the old cosmos, but it is not effectual for Life in the new creation.

An Argument from Kinship (4:12-20)

Paul's appeal in 4:12-20 is for *loyalty*. The basis of this appeal is, accordingly, the relationship established between Paul and the community. H. D. Betz is apparently the first to have recognized this and

---

[66]See Dieter Lührmann, "Tage, Monate, Jahreszeiten, Jahre (Gal 4, 10)," in *Werden und Wirken des Alten Testaments: Festschrift für Claus Westermann* (Göttingen: Vandenhoeck & Ruprecht, 1980).

to have considered its rhetorical implications. In his judgment the passage is "a personal appeal to friendship,"[67] the theme of friendship representing a conventional *topos* at home in a wide variety of rhetorical contexts. But it is the familial mode of discourse that predominates, from the opening vocative ("brothers") to the closing address ("my children") and the maternal metaphor in verse 19. Paul's concluding language is especially important. For although the address in verse 12 (ἀδελφοί) suggests a relationship of equality, hence the obligations of reciprocity that belong to friendship or fraternal relationship, Paul soon reminds the community of the obligations they owe to him as their *apostle*. He does this first by referring to his foundation preaching (v. 13), reminding the Galatians that they received him "as an angel of God, as Christ Jesus" (v. 14). This last idea is not a rhetorical exaggeration but a traditional apostolic self-conception, familiar to us from a variety of gospel strata.[68] The apostle represents the one who sends him and is to be treated as if he were the sender. The final figure in the paragraph conveys Paul's apostolic identity as well. Paul represents himself as a mother in labor straining to give birth once again to the Galatians, an image that underscores his exclusive apostolic claims on the community. The phrase "until Christ be formed in you" suggests that Paul's "giving birth" is to be understood not as the reconversion of the community but as the goal of their maturation as believers, as if the mother-apostle envisions the outcome of his apostolic ministry as a giving birth to fully formed Christian communities as "bodies of Christ" (cf. 1 Cor 12:12; Rom 12:4), to be presented to God on the day of Christ.

In addition to reasserting his apostolic claims on the Galatians, Paul makes certain statements about the Galatians themselves and about the opponents. In recalling the Galatians' former treatment of him, he stresses how they accepted him as a suffering apostle, as one afflicted with "weakness" (4:13). This may be what Paul means when he says that they received him as Christ Jesus, whom Paul treats in Galatians

---

[67]See Betz, *Galatians,* 221.

[68]See Matt 10:40; John 13:20; Luke 10:16; Mark 9:37 (par. Matt 18:5; Luke 9:48). Although the expression is not employed by Paul in 2 Corinthians, the idea is present: If the Corinthians reject the (suffering) apostle, they reject Christ (crucified out of weakness, 2 Cor 13:4).

almost exclusively as the crucified Christ.[69] This would also fit well with Paul's characterization of himself in Galatians as one who bears on his body the marks of Jesus (6:17; cf. 6:12-16; 5:11). Now that the Galatians have submitted themselves to the agitators, they have in effect rejected Paul (v. 16). Does this mean that they have rejected the suffering Paul and failed to appreciate the suffering (crucifixion) of Christ? We will have occasion to explore this possibility more closely in chapter 6. Paul does not develop such an idea here. Instead he warns the Galatians that the agitators' "zeal" for them is "not good" and alleges that they wish to "exclude" the Galatians so that the community will "pay court to them" (v. 17).

The charges of verse 17 represent rhetorical polemic on Paul's part and cannot be taken at face value. The claim that the agitators wish to exclude the Galatians is especially puzzling since Paul does not say *from what* they wish to exclude the community. The context, dominated as it is by the theme of loyalty and betrayal, suggests that the agitators seek to drive a wedge between the Galatians and Paul.[70] In that case, they want to cut the Galatians off *from Paul*. But the sentence may refer to a threat by the agitators to the following effect: "You are excluded from Christ unless you listen to us."[71] Nevertheless, it is probably better to take "they wish" (θέλουσιν) as Paul's way of projecting inimical or impure motives upon the agitators, just as he does in 1:7 and 6:12-13 using the same verb (cf. also 4:9). Just as they "want" to pervert the gospel of Christ (1:7), so they "want" to cut the Galatians off from Christ (4:17). Paul projects the motive in view of the effect as he sees it.

---

[69]Paul refers to the death of Christ in 1:4; 2:19-20; 2:21; 3:1; 3:13; (4:5?); 5:11; (5:24); 6:12; 6:14; (6:17). The resurrection is mentioned only once, as part of a traditional formula (1:1). Paul names ἀσθένεια as a mark of his apostolic mode of being (as conformity to Christ) in 1 Cor 2:3 (cf. 1 Cor 1:23-25); 4:10; 2 Cor 10:10; 11:30; 12:5, 9-10. What Paul says of Christ in 2 Cor 13:4 he applies to himself as apostle: "he was crucified out of weakness, but he lives by the power of God."

[70]So Mussner, *Der Galaterbrief,* 311.

[71]So J. B. Lightfoot, *The Epistle of St. Paul to the Galatians,* 177. Exclusion from "the true Christian community," which Lagrange suggests as a possible interpretation, would amount to the same thing. See *Saint Paul, Épître aux Galates,* 2nd ed. (Paris: J. Gabalda, 1925) 116.

The Law Has Given Sarah No Children (4:21-30)

We arrive now at the final argument before the apostolic exhortation, the so-called "allegory" of Abraham's two wives and sons.[72] For purposes here we may leave aside the question of the extent to which Paul's use of this Abraham story represents allegorical interpretation in the classic Alexandrian sense. But there is one question of form that requires attention at the outset. How are we to conceive the structure of the passage? In verse 28 we meet a vocative: "Now you, brothers, are children of promise like Isaac." Is this a vocative of *applicatio* or does it mark instead a new beginning? There is widespread agreement that this statement applies the results of the preceding interpretation of the Abraham story to the Galatians, in which case verse 28 serves as a conclusion.[73] But the weak conjunction (δέ) hardly suggests a conclusion. The opening, "Now you brothers," sounds instead like a new start,[74] as if Paul now takes up a particular theme for further development.

If verse 28 does represent a new beginning, then the idea that the Galatians are children of the promise is not an end point but a starting point in a new argument. This suggestion agrees well with what we have observed thus far of the ancillary role played by the theme of "sonship" in Paul's argumentation. Paul reinforces the Galatians' self-understanding as "sons of Abraham" and "sons of God" by adducing familiar Scripture texts and Christian traditions. In so doing he brings to the discussion what he regards as essential common ground between himself and the community. And even if some of the elements that Paul introduces to reinforce the Galatians' identity as "sons" are new to them—perhaps the specific language of *Abrahamic sonship* in 3:7—the aim of

---

[72]For a more detailed exploration of this passage, see Cosgrove, "The Law Has Given Sarah No Children (Gal. 4:21-30)," *NovT* 29 (1987): 219-35.

[73]See Hans Lietzmann, *An die Galater*, HNT 10 (Tübingen: J. C. B. Mohr [Paul Siebeck], 1910) 253-54; Oepke, *Der Brief des Paulus an die Galater*, 152; Schlier, *Der Brief an die Galater*, 226; Betz, *Galatians*, 249; Mussner, *Der Galaterbrief*, 328 and 333.

[74]The form of address, ἀδελφοί with δέ, is common in Paul and always marks a new start, whether major or minor. There are no instances where the expression introduces a logical conclusion. When Paul introduces logical conclusions with the appeal ἀδελφοί, he regularly uses ἄρα οὖν or ὥστε.

all this talk about sonship is to show that the Spirit is given to God's sons because they *are* his sons and for no other reason, certainly not because they keep the law.

C. K. Barrett, in what has become a highly influential essay, maintains that the Abraham story's "plain, surface meaning supports not Paul but the Judaizers,"[75] and he suggests that the apostle takes up the account only because the agitators have forced him to it by using the story to make their own case. Barrett envisions the Judaizers arguing that the Gentile Galatians need to get circumcised and thus join the right branch of Abraham's family. Only then will they count as "righteous" in God's sight and as authentic members of God's people. But leaving aside the question of who first interposes this particular Abraham story into the debate, it must be asked whether Paul's *point* in using the story is to align Gentile believers with Sarah, Isaac, and the heavenly Jerusalem. A close examination of the way in which Paul presents the dual alignments in his allegorical interpretation reveals that his attention is focused on the Hagar line. After the introductory statement in verse 24 ("These are two convenants"), Paul itemizes the allegorical significations that he finds on the "Hagar side":

> The one is from Mount Sinai bearing children for slavery; it is Hagar. (For) she (Hagar) is Mount Sinai in Arabia, and she (Hagar) corresponds to the present Jerusalem, for she (Jerusalem) is in slavery with her children.[76]

By contrast, although the formulation "Now one . . . " (μία μὲν κ.τ.λ.) leads one to expect a complementary "The other . . . " (ἡ ἑτέρα δέ κ.τ.λ.),[77] Paul never gets around to filling in the details of

---

[75]"The Allegory of Abraham, Sarah, and Hagar in the Argument of Galatians," in *Rechtfertigung: Festschrift für Ernst Käsemann,* ed. J. Friedrich et al. (Tübingen: J. C. B. Mohr [Paul Siebeck], 1976) 10.

[76]The text tradition is confused. My translation suggests that (1) whether we read δέ or γάρ, we have some kind of proof in v. 25 for the statement about the Sinai covenant in v. 24, and (2) whether we read Ἁγάρ or not, she is in any event the subject of the sentence in v. 25a. Hence, I have treated her as the subject of v. 25b as well. But the nearest antecedent to αὐτῆς (v. 25c) is "Jerusalem."

[77]See Theodor Zahn, *Der Brief des Paulus an die Galater,* 2nd ed., KNT 9 (A. Deichert, 1907) 230.

the Sarah line, which shows up only in the reference to the "Jerusalem above" (vv. 26-27).

Interpreters have not hesitated to *supply* the implied alignments on the "Sarah side" of the allegory. But such reconstructions lead to a distortion of Paul's argument when they are treated as the basis of interpretation, as if the difference between what Paul says and the contrasting allegorical alignments that interpreters are able to reconstruct is "only that Paul does not set the series [implied by the allegory] cleanly over against each other but introduces particular elements out of order in an incomplete fashion."[78] The words are Lietzmann's, who goes on to argue that the point of the allegory is the implied association of the Gentile Galatians with Sarah and the Jerusalem above:

> In v. 28 Paul draws formally a conclusion given in substance already in v. 26, "You are the true sons of Abraham according to the promise, corresponding to your prototype Isaac."[79]

But the weight of Paul's allegorical interpretation falls in fact on the Hagar side, which he articulates explicitly (vv. 24-25). Not only that, when Paul does turn to the Sarah side by speaking of the Jerusalem above, his argument serves to reinforce the *thesis* of verses 24-25 that the law is a slave bearing children for slavery. That is, he continues to defend what he has said about the "identity" of Hagar. That is the point of the proof from Isaiah 54:1, "Rejoice O barren one who did not bear. . . . " Paul chooses an "eschatological" text to interpret Sarah's barrenness until the miraculous birth of the child of promise. At Qumran the proclamation of Isaiah 54:1 about the widowed city Jerusalem had already been applied to the elect community of the new age (4QSIs[d]).[80] And in *4 Bar.* 5:35 the "Jerusalem above" is at the same time the restored Jerusalem to come, as the following benediction pronounced on Abimelech by a certain old man reveals: "May God illumine your way

---

[78]*An die Galater*, 253.

[79]Ibid., 253-54. See also Schlier, *Der Brief an die Galater*, 221-26; Betz, *Galatians*, 245 and 249; Becker, *Der Brief an die Galater*, 55-57.

[80]See J. M. Allegro, "More Isaiah Commentaries from Qumran's Fourth Cave," *JBL* 77 (1958): 215-21. Cf. also the citation of Isa 54:16 in CD 6:8.

to the city above, Jerusalem.''[81] That is, the heavenly Jerusalem, like Isaac in Paul's allegory, represents the prototype and with that the hope of the "eschatological Jerusalem" to come. Hence, when Paul applies Isaiah 54:1 to Sarah, he suggests that Sarah has remained barren until the birth of her child Christ (the one seed) and with him her many children (believers). And in that case *the law has given Sarah no children,* a particularly effective way of saying that the children of the law are not in line for the promise, at least not *as* children of the law.

What follows in verses 28-30 is a further application of the Abraham story. Paul knows another sentence from the story that he can press into service as a strong warning to the Galatians, namely, what Sarah says to Abraham in Genesis 21:10. Paul edits the statement to bring out more sharply the contrast between slavery and freedom:

> Cast out the slave woman and her son, for the son of the slave woman shall not inherit with the son of the free woman.

But the application of this warning to the Galatians requires a certain rhetorical preparation. Until now the identity of the Galatians as "children of Sarah" has remained only implicit, even if they are clearly included in the "our" of verse 26. Hence, it is only natural that Paul should state what his exposition has all along implied in order to supply a smooth transition to the statement of verse 29, which prepares directly for the word of judgment itself:

> Now you, brothers, are children of the promise like Isaac. But just as at that time the one born according to the flesh persecuted the one born according to the Spirit, so it is now.

The statement about persecution refers to the church's experience of persecution at the hands of the synagogue and thus draws the ancient scriptural context for the word of judgment into the present. In this way it provides the necessary transition to Sarah's words, which serve as a judgment on the agitators and a warning to the Galatians (v. 30). Although some interpreters refer the "persecution" (διώκειν) of the

---

[81]Cited from *Paraleipomena Jeremiou,* ed. and trans. R. Kraft and E. Purintun (Missoula MT: Society of Biblical Literature, 1972).

present to what the agitators are doing to the Galatians, this verb is never used in the New Testament of internal strife. Not once does Paul employ it when describing the campaigns of his Christian opponents or detractors. In Acts, the word appears typically in contexts where the church's difficulties at the hands of the synagogue are narrated (7:52; 9:4-5; 22:4, 7-8; 26:11, 14-15; cf. Luke 21:12). Moreover, Paul describes his own campaign against the church as διώκειν (Gal 1:13, 23; Phil 3:6). The point of Paul's allusion to the conflict between the church and the synagogue in Galatians 4:29 is to suggest that the people of the law, far from finding the wellspring of the Spirit in the Torah, are antipathetic to the Spirit and thus persecute the people of the Spirit. The synagogue's campaign against the church is supposed to serve as further proof that the law has not given Sarah any children and that those who promise the Spirit from the law align themselves with the synagogue, which lives in fact only from the flesh. In so doing, Paul maintains, they fall under the word of judgment in Genesis 21:10 on the slave woman and her seed.

Since 4:31 virtually repeats the thought of verse 28, we can hardly construe it as a logical conclusion. Although the διό may be secondary, as Zahn argues,[82] its presence remains the *lectio difficilior*. In any event, verse 31 is a strong reinforcement of something Paul has told the Galatians already, namely that their "sonship" means "freedom." To that extent there is an implicit imperative here, an "admonition to the brothers that they remember what they are."[83] But the aspect of their identity that they are to remember is that they are children of a *free* woman, which means to recognize that they enjoy the promise of the Spirit because they have been *liberated* by Christ and united with the "world above." What they now possess does not derive in any way from the present order, hence nothing that belongs to this present world order can maintain it or enhance it. And the law, which belongs indeed to the present world order (4:8-11) has no power to mediate the life from above. On the contrary, the law is an impotent slave, bearing children for slavery. The

---

[82]*Der Brief des Paulus an die Galater,* 243 n. 56.

[83]Schlier, *Der Brief an die Galater,* 228. Ellicott characterized v. 31 as an "inferential exhortation." See Charles J. Ellicott, *A Critical and Grammatical Commentary on Paul's Epistle to the Galatians,* 2nd ed. (Boston: Draper and Holliday, 1867) 116.

charge of verse 31, then, is to penetrate the meaning of sonship, to see that it means liberation from the present world order and entrance into the future world "from above," whose power the believer now experiences as the Spirit. It is therefore to recognize the utterly transcendent character of sonship, so that one will not imagine that the benefits of sonship (realized heirship) can be gotten or increased through participation in any worldly reality, including that of the law.

Concluding Summary

The proposal that Paul's dispute with the Galatians turns on the question, "Does the one who supplies you with the Spirit and works miracles among you do so because of works of the law?" finds confirmation in the argumentation of the letter as it unfolds in Galatians 3 and 4. We meet a variety of themes in this middle section of the epistle: faith, the law (works of the law), righteousness/justification, sonship (versus slavery), blessing/curse, the promise, the inheritance/heirship, and the Spirit itself. An analysis of their relationships and respective functions in Paul's argument yields a number of important results. First, an alignment emerges among the themes of the Spirit, the promise, the blessing, and the inheritance (realized heirship), next to which the motif of justification (righteousness) remains distinct and subordinate. The theme of sonship serves as a mediating concept. To the extent that it defines a certain status, it belongs together with justification as an ancillary theme. To the degree that it implies "realized heirship" as "possession" of the Spirit, it passes over into the primary thematic field. And one of Paul's strategies in the letter is to get the Galatians to see that "sonship" in Christ implies heirship with Christ.

Furthermore, the terms promise, blessing, and inheritance, as formal biblical concepts, all have for their specific content (in Galatians) the gift of the Spirit, with which they are identified. This identification of the Spirit as eschatological gift with the content of the Abrahamic blessing, promise, and inheritance is an extremely important feature of the epistle's language. Paul never *argues* for the identification of the Spirit with these concepts. He assumes their equation, and we are in a position to recognize this operating assumption by comparing 3:9 with 3:14 (the blessing = the promise of the Spirit) and 3:6-14 with 3:15-18 (the promise = the inheritance). The terms that make up what we have designated the primary thematic field of Galatians (the blessing, the promise, and the inheritance) represent *formal* categories, to the extent that a Jew or a believer in Christ could fill them with varying contents. When used as terms for eschatological hopes their potential contents are absolutely expansive: everything that belongs to eschatological fulfill- ment may be brought under one or more of these rubrics. But the focus varies with context. Hence, one observes diversity in the use of such language within Paul's own writings. In Rom 4:13 the content of the promise to Abraham is "inheriting the world." In Galatians the content of the promise is "inheriting the Spirit."

We conclude, therefore, that for Paul the issue at Galatia is *not* (1) the conditions necessary for justification before God, (2) the question of what constitutes the basis for "ethics" in the eschatological com- munity, or (3) the matter of whether one has to come under the Torah (or "become a Jew") in order to enter God's people in Christ (or at least count as a "full" member of that people), to name those reconstruc- tions of the "problem" at Galatia that have proven most influential in the history of interpretation. Paul addresses the Galatians as if the prob- lem were the conditions for sustaining or promoting life in the Spirit, as if the agitators had said:

> Perform the works of the law and you will experience more of the Spirit and its power, for "the one who does them *shall live* by them."

CHAPTER 3

The Logic
of the Opposing
Theology

The one who does them shall live by them.

—Leviticus 18:5 as cited in Galatians 3:11

WE CONCLUDED from our investigation of Galatians 3–4 that Paul's argument proceeds as if his readers, under the influence of the agitators, made a positive connection between eschatological life in the Spirit and keeping the law. We have termed this "as if" the "epistolary perspective" and in so doing acknowledge that we do not know whether the agitators did in fact encourage the Galatians to keep the law as a means of promoting ongoing life in the Spirit or whether Paul simply assumes that they did. It may be that when the Galatians received Paul's letter, they were surprised at his interpretation of their interest in the law. For all we know, they may have felt that they had been misunderstood. But the exegetical starting point that we sought in the opening chapters of this study was a window not on the "historical Galatians" but on the "epistolary Galatians." Hence our reconstruction of the "problem at Galatia"—the word "problem" itself reflects Paul's standpoint—is a reconstruction of the Galatians as the letter implies them (or "projects" them) as readers. The primary purpose of the present chapter is to bolster the plausibility of this reconstruction by demonstrating how logical it would have been for a Jewish Christian to have arrived at the view of lawkeeping and the Spirit that Paul attacks in Galatians.

This "Jewish Christian"[1] whose theological background in Jewish Scripture and tradition we are about to explore stands for the agitators (and the Galatians, for that matter) as their views of the law and the Spirit have been informed by Jewish Scripture and tradition from the vantage of faith in Christ. It is therefore not essential to the present undertaking that the agitators be ethnically Jewish, even if this inference lies nearest at hand. Johannes Munck, for example, has advanced the thesis that the agitators were Gentile converts of Paul.[2] But even if that be the case, which seems unlikely, the "background" that best illumines the opposing theology is the Jewish (or "Jewish-Christian") one. Since Galatians can be understood only by persons who possess a fair grasp of Jewish Scripture and theology, either the agitators were well versed in Jewish thought or Paul reads a highly nuanced Jewish-Christian theology into what they were saying.

This last possibility, however, reveals that the "Jewish Christian" we have in mind here stands not only for the agitators but also, and perhaps especially, for Paul himself. For if Paul misinterprets the agitators' teaching about the law, he does so presumably out of his own knowledge of Judaism (and Jewish Christianity), that is, out of his own understanding of the logic of the views we are about to investigate.[3] Therefore, by considering the conditions under which Jewish Christians might have arrived at the conclusion that doing the law is positively related to the ongoing gift of the Spirit, we shall gain a better understanding of Paul's argument. Furthermore, to the degree that our reconstruction renders our identification of the "problem at Galatia" plausible from a Jewish-Christian standpoint, we will have strength-

---

[1]Although in many ways the labels "Jewish Christianity" and "Jewish Christian" are anachronistic when applied in the period under consideration, they will be employed here for convenience' sake when reference is made to the primal Jewish wing of the church.

[2]*Paul and the Salvation of Mankind* (Richmond: John Knox Press, 1959); also E. D. Hirsch, "Zwei Fragen zu Galater 6," *ZNW* 29 (1930): 192-97.

[3]One should always bear in mind that Paul was himself a Jewish Christian and that his disputes with other Jewish Christians were part of a heated "family quarrel."

ened our case, even if we remain unable to determine to what extent the specific viewpoint Paul attacks represents the express teaching of the so-called agitators.

It should be clear from what has just been said that our reconstruction of the opposing theology is not to be regarded in the first instance as a reconstruction of what the *historical* agitators, whom we shall now call the "teachers,"[4] were telling the Galatians. The distinction being made here may be defined more clearly if we conceive of historical-critical reconstruction of a text's original audience as entailing two steps. The first step is the act of interpretation that identifies the implied audience of the text.[5] The second step, which completes the historical-critical task, is to take the "implied audience" as a starting point for reconstructing the historical audience. Admittedly, it is not always possible to do this, especially when the data are scanty and limited to the very source in question. The reconstruction we are about to undertake represents the necessary prerequisite (first step) to any historical-critical reconstruction of "actual" opponents or ecclesial situations at Galatia. But it is not feasible to complete the second step of historical reconstruction, short of conjecture. Nevertheless, at the close of this chapter we shall use this reconstruction as a point of departure to speculate about the views of the historical teachers.

---

[4]In his own reconstruction of their views, J. L. Martyn prefers to call them "the Teachers," in order to indicate that their identity and teaching cannot be defined simply in terms of their opposition to Paul. See Martyn, "A Law-Observant Mission to Gentiles: The Background of Galatians," *Michigan Quarterly Review* 22 (1983): 226. In what follows I shall adopt this designation as well, for the present chapter is concerned primarily with the logic of what the teachers are saying and not with their *activities* or *strategies* as "opponents" or "agitators."

[5]The notion of the "implied audience" of a text is receiving increasing attention from New Testament scholars. See, for instance, William S. Kurz, "Narrative Approaches to Luke-Acts," *Bib* 68 (1987): 195-220. For a general discussion from the side of literary criticism, see Walter J. Ong, "The Writer's Audience Is Always a Fiction," in idem, *Interfaces of the Word: Studies in the Evolution of Consciousness and Culture* (Ithaca/London: Cornell University Press, 1977). Since the peculiar nature of the Pauline letter poses its own special problems for the reconstruction of its implied "epistolary audience," there is no attempt in this study to treat the question of the implied audience of Galatians in terms of current literary-critical models.

We shall begin our investigation by considering the ways in which the law was related to "life," "blessing," and "the (Abrahamic) promise" in ancient Judaism, for these are the themes with which Paul associates the "problem of the law" in Galatians. We will then turn to Jewish Christianity and attempt to conceive how Jews who came to faith in Jesus as the Messiah might have understood the relation of Torah-faithfulness to new life in the Spirit poured out on God's people in the last days. With this reconstruction we will have achieved our principle aim, namely, to demonstrate the generic Jewish-Christian logic of the position Paul opposes.

The Torah Is for Life

In Paul's day the idea that "the Torah is for life" was a truism.[6] The connection of life with the law is found explicitly in the Torah itself, and one thinks especially of Leviticus 18:5 and Deuteronomy 30:15 as *loci classici* for this idea. As the law acquired a more central and exalted position in the life and thought of the Jewish people, this connection was naturally strengthened. One could speak of "the law of life" (Sir 45:5; Bar 3:9; 4 Ezra 14:30)[7] or the "law (meant) for life" (*Pss. Sol.* 14:2; Bar 4:1; cf. Rom 7:10).[8] The words of Leviticus 18:5 ("the one who does them shall live by them") became axiomatic (Neh 9:29; Ez 20:13, 21),[9] which is especially significant in view of Paul's use of this saying in Galatians 3:12. We should also note *2 Bar.* 45:2, in which Baruch,

---

[6]This statement is meant in a different sense than James Sanders intends by the same formula when he speaks of the Torah (which is both *mythos* and *ethos, haggadah* and *halakah*) as "adaptable for life." See Sanders, "Adaptable for Life" in *Magnalia Dei: The Mighty Acts of God: Essays on the Bible and Archeology in Memory of G. Ernest Wright,* ed. F. M. Cross et al. (Garden City NY: Doubleday, 1976). In the examples cited below the Torah in its more limited sense as "law" and "commandments" is in view. To be sure, the truism held in the broad sense as well (see *Mek., Tractate Pischa* 16. 128), and Jesus could say, in effect, that the law is for life and mean that it is *for* and not against "doing good" or "saving life" (Mark 2:27-28; 3:4).

[7]Cf. *Pirqe' Abot* 2.8 ("more Torah, more life"); cf. 6.7.

[8]The formula, ὁ νόμος (ἡ ἐντολὴ) εἰς ζωήν, seems to have been inspired by Deut 30:15, as the contexts of *Pss. Sol.* 14:2 and Bar 4:1 suggest.

[9]Each of these texts adopts the words of Lev 18:5 without citing Lev 18:5 as such; cf. also *Pss. Sol.* 14:3; Bar 4:1; CD 3:16; 4 Ezra 7:21; Luke 10:28.

speaking in language reminiscent of Galatians 3:21 ("a law able to make alive"), tells the leaders of the people, "For when you instruct them [in the law], you shall make them alive."[10]

The meaning of "life" as the gift or aim of the law varies all the way from present material blessing to the future eschatological inheritance. The story of Tobit seeks to demonstrate that "almsgiving" (as commanded by the law) leads to prosperity (Tob 4:5-19; 12:8-10),[11] and Jesus promises "eternal life" to the one who fulfills the two great commandments (Luke 10:25-28). In the *Testament of Joseph* we find the statement, "If you walk in the Lord's commands, God will exalt you with good things forever" (18:1), and the Jewish-Christian epistle of James promises that the doer of the law ("the perfect law," "the law of liberty") shall be blessed in his doing" (1:25). In what follows we will focus on three ways in which the connection between the law and life could be conceived: the link between the law and blessing in general, the link between the law and the promise to Abraham, and the link between the law and the specific blessing of the Spirit. We will treat the first of these briefly by itself and then take up the other two together in a more extended discussion.

The Law and Blessing

Once justice had been defined as fidelity to God's law, the old wisdom maxim that the just man shall prosper came to be understood as a promise that the lawkeeper would be blessed.[12] Psalm 1 gives classic

---

[10]Compare the later rabbinic formulation to the same effect: "While Israel stood below engraving idols . . . God sat above engraving tablets that would give them life" (*Ex. Rab.* 41.1).

[11]On almsgiving as a commandment of the law, see Tob 1:8 (cf. 6:12; 7:12). Erich Zenger observes that in Tobit, as in Psalms 1, 19, and 119 (as well as in *Pss. Sol.* 4:23-25; 6; 10; 14) "die Tora als segenwirkende Kraft individueller jüdischer Existenz empfohlen wird." See "Die späte Weisheit und das Gesetz," in *Literatur und Religion des Früjudentums,* ed. J. Maier and J. Schreiner (Würzburg: Echter Verlag, 1973; Gütersloh: Gerd Mohn, 1973) 53. See further H. J. Kraus, "Freude an Gottes Gesetz: Ein Beitrag zur Auslegung der Psalmen 1; 19B und 119," *EvTh* 10 (1950/51): 337-51.

[12]Gerhard von Rad, *Wisdom in Israel* (London/Nashville/New York: Abingdon Press, 1972) 128-37 and 190-95. On the relationship between this tradition and the theme of the suffering righteous in Jewish thought, see the introduction to ch. 6 below.

expression to this new version of the axiom when it says of the righteous man, "His delight is in the law of the Lord. . . . In all that he does, he prospers." Moreover, in the Torah itself one reads:

> Behold I set before you this day a blessing and a curse: the blessing if you obey the commandments of the Lord your God, which I command you this day, and the curse, if you do not obey the commandments of the Lord your God. . . . (Deut 11:26-28, RSV; cf. Deut 30:15-20; Josh 1:8)

A prophetic expression of the Psalm 1 theology is found in Jeremiah 17:5-18 (see esp. vv. 7-8), an oracle that is followed by a summons to observe the Sabbath correctly. Even more striking is the famous word of the Lord in Malachi 3:6-12, particularly its central imperative:

> Bring the full tithes into the storehouse, that there may be food in my house; and thereby put me to the test, says the Lord of hosts, if I will not open the windows of heaven for you and pour down for you an overflowing blessing. (Mal 3:10, RSV)

This passage expresses the widespread notion that earthly blessing depends on proper maintenance of the temple cult.[13] Although the idea that there is a direct relationship between maintaining the cult and enjoying earthly prosperity probably owes something to a cosmology that places the temple at the center of the earth,[14] we should not forget that in Paul's day speculation about the Torah had led to the conviction that the *Torah itself* is "eternal" (Sir 24:9; Wis 18:4; Josephus *Ag. Ap.* 2.277; *Jub.* 2:33; 6:14; Bar 4:1; *1 Enoch* 99:2; Philo *Mos.* 2.14; 4 Ezra 9:37; *Ps.-Philo* 9.8; 11.5)[15] and that, as cosmic Wisdom, it expresses the hidden order or structure of the world. One finds this last view expressed in Sirach.

---

[13]Jacob Neusner, *Judaism in the Beginnings of Christianity* (Philadelphia: Fortress Press, 1984) 39. See further the literature cited in n. 14 below.

[14]On this idea in Judaism and in the larger history of religions, see B. W. Anderson, *Creation versus Chaos: The Reinterpretation of Mythical Symbolism in the Bible* (New York: Association Press, 1967) 64-68; also Mircea Eliade, *Cosmos and History: The Myth of the Eternal Return* (New York: Harper, 1954) 6-11.

[15]Among these texts only Sirach affirms not only the everlasting character of the law but also its preexistence: Sir 24:9 (a statement about Wisdom applied to the Torah in 24:23).

Wisdom sings her own praises in Sirach 24, but in verse 23 a clumsy later gloss identifies "all of the above" as "the book of the covenant of the most high God, the law which he commanded to us through Moses." This interpolation shows how Sirach was read in the Diaspora, all the associations between Wisdom and Torah now being treated as identifications. An association of the two is also present in Baruch 3:28–4:1 and in Wisdom of Solomon.[16] To these we may add also Philo, who thinks of the Torah as an expression of the cosmic Logos,[17] and Josephus, who affirms that "everything [in the law] has a disposition in harmony with the nature of the universe (πάντα γὰρ τῇ τῶν ὅλων φύσει σύμφωνον ἔχει τὴν διάθεσιν)."[18] We have already considered the significance of this idea for understanding Galatians 4:8-11, with its reference to "days, months, seasons, and years." But the cosmic significance of the Torah is not limited to the value of its calendar. In the *Testament of Issachar,* for example, we find the following promise:

> You do these [the two commandments to love the Lord and every human being] as well, my children, and every spirit of Beliar will flee from you, and no act of human evil will have power over you. Every wild creature you shall subdue, so long as you have the God of heaven with you and walk with mankind in sincerity of heart.[19] (7:7)

According to Issachar, the two comprehensive commandments mentioned in this passage represent the substance of the law (see esp. *T. Iss.* 5:1-2; 4:6), hence the one who is faithful to the law shall benefit from a created order that works to his advantage. For such a one the commandment of

---

[16]The way contrary to Wisdom is termed lawbreaking (Wis 2:12; 4:20; 6:4); in Wis 6:17 we hear that "the love of her means keeping her laws;" and in 18:4 we no doubt have a reference to the Torah as a common universal ethic: "your sons through whom the immortal light of the law was to be given to this age" (cf. τὸν τῆς θειότητος νόμον in 18:9).

[17]See Burton Lee Mack, *Logos und Sophia: Untersuchungen zur Weisheitstheologie im hellenistischen Judentum*, SUNT 10 (Göttingen: Vandenhoeck & Ruprecht, 1973) 148-49.

[18]Josephus *Ant.* 1.24; cf. *Ant.* 18:59 (ἡ σοφία τῶν νόμων); see also the *Letter of Aristeas* 31, 141-48 (cf. 161 and 168). As the rabbis would express this thought, "The world was created by means of the Torah" (*Pirqe' Abot* 3.19).

[19]*OTP* 1:804.

Genesis 1:28 shall go into effect as a promise ("fill the earth and subdue
it . . . have dominion over the fish of the sea and over the birds of the air
and over every living thing that moves upon the earth").

In the field of Jewish historiography one thinks of a work like 2
Maccabees, which suggests an almost "causal connection," as one interpreter puts it, between sin and suffering on one hand, righteousness
in the law and well-being on the other.[20] "Causal" is not really the appropriate word, since the author associates success with Torah-faithfulness not because that is the way the world happens to operate but
because the Lord grants victory to those whom he judges to be worthy
(15:21). We should read this promise in the light of the opening of the
book, where the author presents a "letter to Jews in Egypt" in which
the following benediction (epistolary προσκύνημα) is found:

> May God do good to you and remember his covenant to Abraham and Isaac
> and Jacob, his faithful servants. And may he grant you a heart to worship
> him in everything and to do his will with a great heart and a willing soul.
> And may he open your heart to his law and to his precepts. (2 Macc 1:2-
> 4)

The reference in this passage to God's covenant with the patriarchs raises
the question of the relationship between the *promise to Abraham* (as
"blessing") and Torah-faithfulness.

The Law, the Promise, and the Spirit

We may begin by considering the language of "promise" as it is
used in connection with Abraham. The Abrahamic covenant is not called
a "promise" in Genesis, but the relevant passages describe God speaking to Abraham in promissory ways. Moreover, Psalm 105:42 refers to
God's covenant with Abraham as "his holy word," and the Hebrew
Bible speaks elsewhere of the land God swore to Abraham. The terminology of divine "promise" (ἐπαγγελία, ἐπαγγέλω) is rare in the
Septuagint but conventional in certain Hellenistic-Jewish circles. The

---

[20]Jochen Gabriel Bunge, *Untersuchungen zum zweiten Makkabäerbuch* (diss. phil.,
Bonn, 1971) 327, as cited by Gerhard Delling, "Perspektiven der Erforschung des
hellenistischen Judentums," *HUCA* 45 (1974): 149.

first extant reference is found in 2 Maccabees 2:17-18, where the term "inheritance" (κληρονομία) is also employed. Although Philo does not use the terms ἐπαγγελία and ἐπαγγέλω in this way, we do meet a number of examples in Josephus[21] and one in the *Psalms of Solomon*. Hence, when we speak of the "promise to Abraham," we are following Paul (Gal 3:15-18; Rom 4:13-16), who, for his part, appears to be following current Hellenistic-Jewish usage.

In Genesis the promise to Abraham includes land, nations, and kings for descendants, and blessing for all the nations of the earth (Gen 17:1-8; 17:16; 18:18). Sirach rehearses this promise, including its extension to Isaac and Jacob, and describes it as "a blessing for humankind as a whole (εὐ-λογίαν πάντων ἀνθρώπων) and a covenant" (44:19-23). The *Prayer of Jacob* speaks of God's favor to Abraham in giving him a *kingdom* (*Pr. Jac.* 5). The *Testament of Abraham* (resc. A) interprets Genesis 22:17 in terms of wealth rather than descendants (1:5; 4:11; 8:5), although it does mention the multiplication of Abraham's seed (8:6). The *Testament of Joseph* speaks more generally of "the promises (τὰς ἐπαγγελίας)[22] made to your fathers" (20:1) and evidently has in view the promised land. The *Ladder of Jacob* restates the promise as a blessing through Abraham's seed for all the earth and those living on it at the end of time (1:11).

It is not difficult to discern the connection with the "original promise" that is present in each of these formulations. At the same time, one sees at work in the eschatological interpretation of the promise what Gerhard von Rad has characterized as Israel's tendency to "swell Yahweh's promises to an infinity."[23] Genesis 15:18-21 had specified the land from the Nile to the Euphrates. But Sirach speaks of an inheritance "from sea to sea, from the River to the ends of the earth" (44:21), and *Jubilees* has the Lord tell Jacob that he will give his seed "all of the land under heaven," a promise

---

[21]See Josephus *Ant.* 1.236, where the Abrahamic promises are in view; cf. the references to God's promises to Moses (*Ant.* 2.219; 2.275; 5.39), which appear to be extensions of the Abrahamic promise.

[22]Some mss. have the singular τὴν ἐπαγγελίαν and *d* reads τὴν γῆν τῆς ἐπαγγελίας. See H. W. Hollander and M. de Jonge, *The Testaments of the Twelve Patriarchs: A Commentary*, SVTP 8 (Leiden: E. J. Brill, 1985) 409. See n. 21 above.

[23]Gerhard von Rad, *Old Testament Theology*, 2 vols., trans. D. M. G. Stalker (New York: Harper & Row, 1962 and 1965) 2:320.

that appears to have the *eschaton* in view (32:18-19; cf. 22:14). Now it is true that the idea of "inheriting the world" (cf. Rom 4:13) was not always linked explicitly with the Abrahamic promise. Fourth Ezra, for example, inquires why, "if the world has indeed been *created* for us," we do not "possess our world as an inheritance" (6:59).[24] Daniel envisions Israel's ultimate ascendance to world dominance (7:27; cf. 2:44), without mentioning the promises to the fathers. And Josephus makes reference vaguely to "an ambiguous oracle found in their [the Jews'] sacred Scriptures" that a member of the Jewish nation would one day rule the world (ἄρξει τῆς οἰκουμένης, *J.W.* 6.312). This oracle was in fact known widely among both Jews and non-Jews (see Tacitus *Hist.* 5.13.2), but its identity remains obscure.[25] Nevertheless, one assumes that people thought of "the promises of God" as a unity. The "single" promise to Abraham, as the founding promise to the children of Abraham, is to this extent implicit as a matter of course in references to God's "promises," whatever specific terminology is employed. Paul himself offers evidence of this way of thinking when he shifts so "carelessly" from the singular "promise" to the plural "promises" in Galatians 3:19-22, suggesting that he views all the promises of God as being included fundamentally in the "one" promise to Abraham.

In light of this last consideration it seems fair to say that in some sense every eschatological hope could be viewed by a Jew in Paul's day as grounded in God's promises to the fathers. But, as the preceding examples show, even when the promise is conceived eschatologically, the tendency is to speak of it in geopolitical terms, without mentioning other elements and dimensions of eschatological hope. Hence it should come as no surprise that we do not find the *Spirit,* which was indeed anticipated as an eschatological blessing (Ez 39:29; Joel 2:28-32; Isa 44:3;

---

[24]*OTP,* 1:536. Cf. 4 Ezra 7:10-16; 7:96.

[25]For a brief discussion of this prophecy in its various forms, see Menahem Stern, *From Tacitus to Simplicius,* vol. 2 of *Greek and Latin Authors on Jews and Judaism,* (Jerusalem: The Israel Academy of Sciences and Humanities, 1980) 61-62. The passage in Tacitus states that "the majority [of the Jewish people at the time of the Jewish war] believed that their priestly writings contained the prophecy that this was the very time when the East should grow strong and that men starting from Judaea should possess the world" (ibid., 31). One thinks of the promise to Abraham and the Isaianic vision of the nations streaming to Zion (Isa 2:2-3; 60:1-14).

Zech 12:10; *T. Levi* 18:11; *T. Judah* 24; *Jub.* 1:21,23; IQS 4:20-21), linked explicitly with the patriarchal promises, even though both Luke and Paul speak of "the promise of the Spirit" as if it went without saying that the gift of the Spirit belongs among the promises to the fathers. Nevertheless, we do find associations between lawkeeping and the giving of the promise, between lawkeeping and the fulfillment of the promise or eschatological hopes, and between lawkeeping and the Spirit. Hence, we have the pieces that might make up the view that "the promise of the Spirit," as eschatological pledge to Abraham or eschatological hope of the prophets, depends on Torah-faithfulness. It is by considering these pieces of traditional Jewish thinking about the law, the promise, and the Spirit that we gain insight into the kind of reflection about the Torah that may have led a Jewish Christian to conclude that charismatic life in the Spirit depends on keeping the law.

According to Sirach, Abraham kept the law of the Most High (44:20), and *therefore* (διὰ τοῦτο) God made the promise to him (ἐν ὅρκῳ ἔστησεν αὐτῷ κ.τ.λ., v. 21). In *Jubilees,* a writing that goes to great pains to establish the presence of the law and fidelity to the law during the patriarchal period,[26] Isaac charges his sons "to perform righteousness and uprightness upon the earth so that the Lord will bring upon you everything which the Lord said he would do for Abraham and for his seed" (36:3).[27] The *Psalms of Solomon* refer to "the promises" (ἐπαγγελίαι) just once. The language occurs in a prayer that "the *holy* of the Lord *inherit* the *promises of the Lord*" (12:6), the holy being of course "those who walk in the righteousness of his commandments, in the law, which he commanded to us for our life" (14:2). Here the "connection" between the law and the promise almost goes without saying: the promise is to Abraham's *seed,* which comes to be equated with lawkeepers, the identity of Israel being fixed by the Torah. The same set of assumptions is evident in the *Testament of Dan,* where Dan can prophesy in one breath that his sons will depart from God's law, and that they will be alienated from their inheritance, from the race of Israel, and from their patrimony (*T. Dan* 7:3; cf. 4 Ezra 7:119). *Ps.-Philo* apparently op-

---

[26]Compare *Jub* 6:19; 13:25-27; 15:1-3; 16:20-31; 23:10; *2 Bar* 57:1-3.
[27]*OTP,* 2:124.

erates with similar presuppositions when he has God put the following question to Moses:

> Are the promises that I promised to your fathers when I said to them, *"To your seed I will give the land* in which you dwell"*—are they at an end? For behold the people have not even entered the land yet and now have the Law with them, and they have forsaken me.[28]

The implication of this question is that infidelity to the Torah blocks the fulfillment of the promise.[29]

It had in fact become common by Paul's day to explain the frustration of the promise, from the Babylonian exile to the present subjugation of the Jewish people under Roman rule, as a result of national infidelity to the Torah.[30] And this laid the groundwork for the eschatological view that faithfulness to the Torah would prepare the way for the new age, even hasten it. If Martin Hengel is correct, this idea informs the synergistic eschatology of certain Jewish revolutionaries,[31] about whom Josephus has this to say:

> [They said that] upon their joint resolve to succeed, the deity would eagerly join them, all the more so if they were determined in their hearts to do great things, not shrinking from the effort [or bloodshed] required. *Ant.* 18.5[32]

A precedent for this conviction is found in 1 Maccabees 2:64, where the dying Mattathias encourages his sons to join Judas Maccabaeus in re-

---

[28]*Ps.-Philo* 12:4 (*OTP,* 2:320).

[29]Paul also holds the view that infidelity to the law, which incurs the curse of the law, blocks the flow of the promise (3:10-14). See "The Law Is Not Against the Promises of God" in ch. 2 above, together with the introduction to ch. 6 below.

[30]See Josephus *Ant.* 1.14; Dan 9:8; Bar 3:10; 2 Macc 7:18, 32, 33 and 6:12-16. See further, Odil Hannes Steck, *Israel und das gewaltsame Geschick der Propheten,* WMANT 23 (Neukirchen-Vluyn: Neukirchener Verlag, 1967) passim; David M. Scholer, "Israel Murdered Its Prophets: The Origins and Development of the Tradition in the Old Testament and Judaism" (Th.D. diss., Harvard Divinity School, 1980).

[31]*Die Zeloten: Untersuchungen zur jüdischen Freiheitsbewegung in der Zeit von Herodes I. bis 70 n. Chr.* (Leiden/Köln: E. J. Brill, 1961).

[32]Translation mine. See further, Hengel, *Die Zeloten,* 79 and 127. Cf. Josephus *Life* 83, where Josephus affirms that God protects those who do their duty.

volt against Antiochus Epiphanes: "Children, take courage and be strong in the law, for in it you shall be glorified (ἐν αὐτῷ δοξασθήσεσθε)." If, as Hengel argues, the Jewish activists of which Josephus speaks were looking for the messianic kingdom and understood their radical response to Roman rule as itself a supreme instance of Maccabean-like Torah-faithfulness, then their conviction that God's aid depended upon their unflinching boldness amounts to the idea that militant fidelity to the Torah will hasten the kingdom.[33]

But there were also nonmilitant ways of "hastening" the kingdom through fidelity to the law. For example, at Qumran the prophecy of Isaiah 40:3 ("prepare a way in the desert for the Lord") was applied to the study and practice of the Torah in the Dead Sea community:

> And when these become members of the Community in Israel according to all these rules, they shall separate from the habitation of ungodly men and shall go into the wilderness to prepare the way of Him; as it is written, *Prepare in the wilderness the way of . . . make straight in the desert a path for our God* (Isa. xl,3). This (path) is the study of the Law which he commanded by the hand of Moses, that they may do according to all that has been revealed from age to age, and as the prophets have revealed by His Holy Spirit.[34] (1QS 8:13-16; cf. 9:19-20)

This understanding of Torah-faithfulness is especially significant for our study in view of the way the Essenes related the Spirit to lawkeeping. According to 1QS 9:3, "When all these things happen in Israel [the establishment and ordering of the community] according to all these ordinances (it shall be) for the founding of the Holy Spirit in eternal truth."

---

[33]On the "messianic" character of such uprisings in Palestine, see Hengel, *Die Zeloten*, 235-318; also Richard A. Horsley and John S. Hanson, *Bandits, Prophets, and Messiahs: Popular Movements in the Time of Jesus* (Minneapolis/Chicago/New York: Winston Press, 1985). On "zeal for the Torah" among the motives of the Jewish revolt, see, e.g., Josephus *Life* 134-35, and further Hengel, *Die Zeloten*, 151-234. Horsley and Hanson rightly criticize Hengel, along with other previous interpreters of Jewish liberation movements, for attributing all militant activity in ancient Palestine to a so-called "Zealot party," thus obscuring the diversity and pervasiveness of popular liberation movements in the time of Jesus.

[34]Cited from Geza Vermes, *The Dead Sea Scrolls in English,* 2nd ed. (New York: Penguin Books, 1975) 85-86.

This passage has in view the establishment of the community in fidelity
to the Torah (the "preparation of the way in the wilderness," 8:13-16)
and the "digging of the well" (CD 6:3-11) as a present "founding of
the Spirit" in anticipation of God's future universal purification of the
world through the Spirit (1QS 4:20-21). Now Isaiah closely associates
the wilderness context with the eschatological outpouring of the Spirit
(Isa 44:2-3; 32:15). Thus the desert sectarians at Qumran understood
their correct interpretation and observance of the Torah as a preparation
for God's eschatological purification of Israel and humanity through the
Spirit, a purification in which they understood themselves to participate
already, as members of the eschatological community (1QS 3:6-12)
joined with the Sons of Heaven (1QS 11:8; 1QSa 2:8-9).

   The idea that obedience to the law prepares for the eschaton and the
pouring out of the Spirit is also found in the *Testament of Judah*. According to *T. Judah* 23–24, when God's people return to him and live
"according to all the Lord's commands" (23:5), then he will liberate
them from captivity, send the Messiah and pour out the Spirit. Although
24:2a ("And the heavens will be opened upon him to pour out a blessing
of the Holy Father"), sounds like a (Jewish-)Christian interpolation, recalling as it does the descent of the Spirit at Jesus' baptism, verses 2b-
3 are probably original to the underlying Jewish text: "And he will pour
the Spirit of grace upon you. And you shall be sons in truth, and you
will walk in his first and final decrees."[35] In favor of taking these sentences as original are the following considerations. The reference in verse
2a to the pouring out of the Spirit on the messianic figure himself creates
confusion in what follows about the subject of the pronouns (αὐτός in
2b, αὐτῷ and αὐτοῦ in v. 3). As the text stands, the subject must be
the Messiah, which seems unnatural in the light of the content of verses
2b-3. But if we delete verse 2a, not only does this awkwardness vanish,
but we can also explain why the Christian interpolator should have
thought of Jesus' baptism at precisely this point. The text before him
had already juxtaposed the advent of the Star of Jacob and the pouring
out of the Spirit. As for the statement in verse 3 ("And you shall be sons
in truth, and you shall walk in his first and final decrees"), it sounds
like something one would read in the writings from Qumran, where the

---

[35]Cited from *OTP*, 1:801.

members of the community are called "the sons of the truth" (1QS 4:5-6) and where "first and final decrees" represents a technical expression (CD 20:8-9; cf. 20:30 and 1QS 9:10).

Before turning to Jewish Christianity, we may consider briefly certain *noneschatological* connections between the law and the Spirit among the rabbis, although we cannot assume that these traditions were current in Paul's day. The oldest instance, as far as one may venture to date the materials, occurs in the *Mekilta* in a comment on Exodus 14:3 and 15:1.

> Great indeed is faith before Him who spoke and the world came into being. For as a reward for the faith with which Israel believed in God, the Holy Spirit rested upon them and they uttered the song, as it is said: "And they believed in the Lord . . . then sang Moses and the Children of Israel" (Ex. 14.3; 15.1). R. Nehemiah says: "Whence can you prove that whosoever accepts even one single commandment with true faith is deserving of having the Holy Spirit rest upon him? We find this to have been the case with our fathers. . . . "[36]

Along with this text and its parallels, Peter Schäfer has adduced additional passages from the rabbis as evidence of a relatively widespread tradition running counter to the prevailing opinion that the Spirit fell silent after the last of the biblical prophets.[37] We cannot assume that these rabbinic traditions connecting the law and the Spirit were current in Paul's day, but one does receive the impression that a rabbi who affirmed the postbiblical, premessianic accessibility of the Holy Spirit to God's people would have linked the presence of the Spirit with Torah-faithfulness.

The Law and the Spirit in Primitive Christianity

When Paul speaks of the "powerlessness of the law" in Romans 8:3, he has in view the law's impotence against the power of sin, as he has described it in Romans 7:7-25. This impotence is one facet of the law's

---

[36]Cited from Jacob Z. Lauterbach, *Mekilta de-Rabbi Ishmael,* 3 vols. (Philadelphia: The Jewish Publication Society of America, 1933) 1:252.

[37]*Die Vorstellung vom heiligen Geist in der rabbinischen Literatur,* SANT 28 (Munich: Kösel-Verlag, 1972) 127-33; see also W. D. Davies, *Paul and Rabbinic Judaism: Some Rabbinic Elements in Paul's Theology,* 4th ed. (Philadelphia: Fortress Press, 1980) 209.

inability to give life (Gal 3:21), an idea that the apostle can otherwise express as the law's *power* of death: "The commandment meant for life turned out to be death for me" (Rom 7:10). Or, as 1 Corinthians 15:56 puts it: "the sting of death is sin, and the power of sin is the law." Both the powerlessness and the power of the law are accidental to it. The law's impotence is a result of its "becoming weak through the flesh" (Rom 8:3), and its power for death is a consequence of the sin-dominated cosmos in which the law finds itself ("But the Scripture shut up all things under sin . . . " Gal 3:22). These two aspects, the power and the powerlessness of the law, are closely interrelated. The impotence of the law to give life *is* the law's power of death made effective by Sin. For the law's power is a derived power—better, a power exercised under coercion. That is, the powerless law becomes the power of sin by virtue of the law's weakness. At least that is how Paul conceives the relationship between sin and the law in Romans:

> Sin taking opportunity in the commandment deceived me and through the commandment killed me. . . . Sin, in order that it might appear as sin, worked death in me through the good (law). (Rom 7:11-13)

While Romans treats the inability of the law to give life from the standpoint of the law's impotence as a moral power, Galatians treats the inability of the law to make alive (3:21) from the standpoint of the law's inability to grant life in the Spirit. In view of Rom 8:1-4, we may conclude that the two are intimately related for Paul. Were the law able to mediate the Spirit, it would have produced life and righteousness. But Galatians does not take up directly the problem of the law's impotence as a "moral power," even if Paul's radical disconnection of the Spirit and the law implies it, given his own theological assumptions about the world's bondage to sin. Hence, in turning to the question of how early Christians viewed the law in its relation to "life," we will restrict ourselves to the second issue, the relation of the law to the Spirit.[38]

Primitive Jewish Christianity will have had no choice but to reflect on the relation of life in the Spirit to lawkeeping. From its very beginnings the

---

[38] I explore these questions of the law and moral power in detail in a forthcoming article, "The Law and Moral Power in Paul and Ancient Judaism."

Jesus movement understood itself as blessed and empowered by the Spirit,[39] and the decisive role *reflection on the experience of the Spirit*[40] must have played in the early church can hardly be overestimated. We may assume, then, that just as Jewish Christians were compelled by internal and external circumstances to consider the relation of the law to Christ and of lawkeeping to faith in Christ, so they had to think through the relation of the law to the Spirit and of lawkeeping to life in the Spirit.

Jewish Christians had essentially three avenues open to them for relating the Torah and the Spirit. Although the three are distinct, they are not in principle incompatible and could be combined in various ways. One was to take the view that eschatological life in the Spirit obviates lawkeeping, an idea that could be defended by the argument that life in the Spirit, as a kind of transearthly existence, renders conventional ethics obsolete. One thinks, for example, of the charismatics identified by Eduard Schweizer as objects of the polemic in Matthew 7:15-23.[41] A second possibility was to maintain that the power of the Spirit enables authentic lawkeeping, a view especially serviceable in debates with the synagogue. The expectation that the Spirit would one day create a people obedient from the heart to God's law is found in Ezekiel 36:26-27 (cf. 11:19-20), as well as in a variety of other Jewish texts (*Jub.* 1:21; *T. Levi* 18:11; *T. Job* 48:2-3; 1QS 4:20-21). In Romans 8:3-4 Paul expresses his own understanding of how this promise is being fulfilled in Christ, although he also affirms a version of the eschatological alternative already mentioned. Finally, Jewish Christians could argue that lawkeeping is a necessary condition for life in the Spirit, a view

---

[39]See especially Jacob Jervell, "Das Volk des Geistes," in *God's Christ and His People: Studies in Honour of Nils Alstrup Dahl,* ed. J. Jervell and W. Meeks (Oslo/Bergen/Tromsö: Universitetsforlaget, 1977). See further the classic treatment of early Christian views of the Spirit by Hermann Gunkel, *Die Wirkungen des heiligen Geistes nach populären Anschauung der apostolischen Zeit und der Lehre des Apostels Paulus* (Göttingen: Vandenhoeck & Ruprecht, 1888; ET: *The Influence of the Holy Spirit,* trans. Roy A. Harrisville and Philip A Quanbeck [Philadelphia: Fortress Press, 1979]); also James D. G. Dunn, *Baptism in the Holy Spirit,* SBTMS 15 (London: SCM Press, 1970).

[40]See also J. D. G. Dunn, "I Corinthians 15:45—Last Adam, Life-Giving Spirit," in *Christ and the Spirit in the New Testament, In Honour of C. F. D. Moule,* ed. B. Lindars and S. Smalley (Cambridge: Cambridge University Press, 1973) 132.

[41]"Observance of the Law and Charismatic Activity in Matthew," *NTS* 16 (1970): 213-30.

whose natural *Sitz im Leben* will have been intrachurch debate over the Gentile mission.

It is this third way of relating the Torah and the Spirit that interests us here, and we may sharpen the question before us by dividing our inquiry into three parts: (1) Under what assumptions might Jewish Christians have adopted this third alternative? (2) How are we to understand the contingency it affirms between lawkeeping and life in the Spirit? (3) What evidence is there in primitive Christianity (outside of Galatians) for the view that lawkeeping is a condition for sustaining life in the Spirit or a means of promoting the presence of the Spirit?

We will begin with the first question. The connection between the law and blessing found in the Jewish Scriptures and in other Jewish writings of the Second Temple period provides one conceivable basis upon which the case could have been made by Jewish Christians that the *blessing of the Spirit* depends in some way on keeping the law. This line of argument would have succeeded especially well if Jewish believers linked the law and the Spirit by means of a third term with which both are already traditionally joined, namely, "life." If the Torah is "for life" and the Spirit is the "Spirit of life,"[42] then Jewish Christians may have reinterpreted Leviticus 18:5 to mean that "the one who does them (the works of the law) shall live *in the Spirit* by them."

But Jewish Christians could also have defended the contention that life in the Spirit depends on lawkeeping by appealing to the unity of the Abrahamic and Mosaic covenants, in short, the unity of the promise and the law. It seems that the Galatians had already learned to identify the Spirit with the Abrahamic promise, since Paul takes this connection for granted in Galatians when he speaks of *the* blessing as *the* promise of the Spirit (3:14). But we may leave aside the question of whether it was

---

[42]God creates and sustains the world and especially living things by the (his) Spirit (see Gen 1:2; Ps 104:30; Philo *Op. Mundi* 30; *2 Bar.* 23:5; 2 Macc 14:46; Rev 11:11), and the hope of the coming Spirit probably depends in part on the thought pattern identified by Gunkel as basic to apocalyptic thinking: "Urzeit gleich Endzeit." See his seminal work, *Schöpfung und Chaos in Urzeit und Endzeit* (Göttingen: Vandenhoeck und Ruprecht, 1895). See also 1 Cor 15:45 ("The last Adam became a life-giving Spirit"), 2 Cor 3:6 ("The Spirit makes alive"), and John 6:63 ("The Spirit is what makes alive").

Paul or the teachers at Galatia[43] who taught the Galatians to make this equation and inquire simply after its logic.

The link between the Spirit and the promise to Abraham is eschatological. The early church counted the presence of the Spirit among them as a fulfillment of the eschatological hope that God would pour out his Spirit in the last days.[44] That is, the church viewed the presence of the Spirit among them as the fulfillment of a divine promise,[45] and in principle they could view all of God's promises as contained already in God's promise(s) to Abraham. According to Paul himself, who speaks as if the idea required no defense, Abraham was promised nothing less than that he should be "heir of the world" (Rom 4:13). Jewish Christians for whom the Spirit's presence in the church represented the powers of the coming kingdom (Matt 12:28)[46] or the presence of the age to come (Heb 6:4-5) could have viewed the "coming of the Spirit" as an initial fulfillment of God's promise to Abraham.

Evidence that there *were* Jewish Christians who viewed the Spirit's presence in the church as a fulfillment of God's promise to Abraham is found in Luke-Acts and Hebrews. Luke applies the expression "the promise" to the gift of the Spirit (Luke 24:49; Acts 1:4; 2:33, 39) and treats all the divine promises as extensions of the promise to Abraham (see Acts 7:17; cf. 13:32 and 26:6), a tendency that we have encountered already in Hellenistic Judaism. Acts 2:33 is of special interest, since

---

[43]Richard Hays seems to assume that Paul is the one who equates the Abrahamic promise with the Spirit, but the matter is more complex, since Paul does not defend this equation but takes it for granted. Nevertheless, Hays's suggestion that Isa 44:3 might have suggested a link between the promise and the Spirit is helpful. The passage runs as follows in the Septuagint: ἐπιθήσω τὸ πνεῦμα μου ἐπὶ τὸ σπέρμα σου καὶ τὰς εὐλογίας μου ἐπὶ τὰ τέκνα σου. See Hays, *The Faith of Jesus Christ: An Investigation of the Narrative Substructure of Galatians 3:1-4:11* (Chico CA: Scholars Press, 1983) 210-12.

[44]Acts 2:14-21; Gal 3:14; Heb 6:4-5; cf. Matt 3:11. See also Joel 2:28-29; Isa 32:15; 44:3; 1QS 4:21.

[45]See Jervell, "Das Volk des Geistes;" James D. G. Dunn, *Jesus and the Spirit* (Philadelphia: Westminster, 1975) 158-63.

[46]"But if I cast out demons by the Spirit of God, then the kingdom of God has come upon you." We apparently have here a recasting of a more primitive version of the logion (preserved in Luke 11:20) in the light of the church's experience of the Spirit.

it may preserve a very early traditional use of the terminology "the promise of the Spirit."

> Having been exalted to the right hand of God and having received the promise of the Holy Spirit from the Father, he has poured out this which you see and hear.

The idea that the resurrected Jesus receives the Spirit contradicts the Q tradition that Jesus was endowed with the Spirit at his baptism. Much closer to the theology of Acts 2:33 is the very old enthronement Christology preserved in Romans 1:3-4, which also associates the power of the Spirit with Jesus' coming into power. The evident antiquity of this tradition[47] suggests that Luke learned to speak about God's promises as he does from Jewish Christians. When we turn to Hebrews, a manifestly Jewish-Christian document, we find further evidence that Jewish believers in Christ came to identify the Spirit with "the promise." Hebrews makes this connection implicitly, but nonetheless unmistakably, by identifying the Spirit with "the heavenly gift" and "the powers of the age to come" as presently experienced ("tasted") by believers (6:4-5), apart from whom those faithful who have come before cannot receive "the promise" (11:39-40; cf. 10:36; 11:13).

We return now to our original question. How might the traditional (biblical) idea of the unity of the Abrahamic and Mosaic covenants have informed a Jewish-Christian theology of life in the Spirit through law-keeping? We have already seen that during the Second Temple period Jews tended to accentuate the contingency present already in the Torah itself between receiving the promise and faithfulness to the law. Jewish Christians who viewed the Spirit as (part of) the content of the Abrahamic promise could have argued on this basis that lawkeeping is a positive factor in promoting ongoing life in the Spirit. This conclusion would have found further confirmation from the traditional association of both the law and the Spirit with *life* as divine blessing. These converging lines of traditional logic make perfect sense on Jewish-Christian assump-

---

[47]For a survey of scholarly discussion concerning Acts 2:33, see J. Dupont, "Ascension du Christ et don de L'Esprit d'après Actes 2:33," in *Christ and the Spirit in the New Testament, In Honour of C. F. D. Moule,* ed. B. Lindars and S. Smalley (Cambridge: Cambridge University Press, 1973).

tions. Reception of the promise depends upon Torah-faithfulness, hence receiving the promise of the Spirit depends upon keeping the law. The law is *for life* ("The one who does them shall live by them"), hence the law must be *for the life of the Spirit*. The one who is righteous in God's law shall be blessed, hence the Torah-righteous shall be blessed in the last days with the Spirit. All of this becomes a genuine possibility with the arrival of the last days through God's Son Jesus Christ.

We turn now to discuss the particular ways in which this contingency between the law and the Spirit might have been conceived. Let us begin with Acts 7:1-53, where Stephen makes a speech in which he expresses what we now recognize as a widespread Jewish theology of history, according to which the frustration of the promise is attributable to national infidelity to the Torah. Observe especially the movement of Stephen's story from 7:17ff. ("As the time of the promise drew near, which God made to Abraham, the people grew and multiplied in Egypt . . . ") to 7:35ff. ("This Moses whom they rejected . . . [who] received living oracles to give to us, but our fathers refused to obey him . . . ") to 7:42-43 ("But God turned and gave them up to worship the host of heaven . . . " = the Babylonian captivity). Stephen concludes this speech with a strong word of judgment:

> Stiff-necked and uncircumcised in your hearts and ears, you always resist the Holy Spirit, as did your fathers before you! Which of the prophets did your fathers not persecute? And they killed those who announced the coming of the Righteous One, whose betrayer and murderer you have now become, you who received the law given by angels and did not keep it. (7:51-53)

No doubt we have here a typical example of Jewish-Christian polemic against the synagogue. The statement, "You always resist the Holy Spirit," describes Jewish rejection of the gospel. A Jewish Christian operating within the theological framework of this speech would probably have pointed to the "self-evident" absence of the Spirit from the synagogue[48] and would have attributed this absence to a "hard-heart-

---

[48]This point has been made effectively by Jervell, "Das Volk des Geistes." As Jervell emphasizes, the view that the Spirit is found only in the Christian community, not

edness'' manifest historically in failure to keep the law and evident now ultimately in rejection of God's Messiah Jesus. But this highly polemical way of conceiving the contingency between lawkeeping and life in the Spirit would have been inadequate to the *intra*church debate over the Gentile mission, where the self-evident presence of the Spirit among uncircumcised Gentile converts had to be confronted and interpreted.

In Galatians 2:7-9 Paul says that the ''pillar'' apostles ''saw'' (ἰδόντες) that God had entrusted him with the gospel to the uncircumcised and that they ''perceived the grace'' (γνόντες τὴν χάριν) given to him. This ''grace'' is God's effective activity through Paul among the Gentiles (v. 8). We may conclude from this that when Paul laid his gospel before the pillars (2:2), he told the story of the Spirit's manifest presence among the Gentiles; for the Spirit is the grace of God in action, and grace (χάρις) in Paul means power.[49]

Faced with the ''fact'' of the Spirit's presence among uncircumcised Gentile converts, Jewish Christians who were determined to defend the link between lawkeeping and life in the Spirit had at least three options open to them. (1) They could deny the authenticity of the Gentiles' experience of the Spirit. (2) They could interpret the presence of the Spirit among the Gentiles as provisional, maintaining that the Gentiles would lose the Spirit if they did not take up the Torah. Or (3) they could argue that lawkeeping increases or promotes life in the Spirit, since ''the law is for life.'' The first two possibilities distinguish themselves from the third in that they treat the reality of the Spirit in terms of a simple alternative: present or absent. This way of thinking about the Spirit has its home in baptismal theology. The person baptized into Jesus' name ''belongs'' to him, and the Spirit ''dwells'' in him.[50] In this model,

in the synagogue, pervades the New Testament and represents a judgment based on early Christian experience of the Spirit (87-88). This leads Jervell to the conclusion that the authors of the New Testament found no ''charismatic-prophetic life'' in the synagogues of their day. We should bear in mind that the contention, ''The Spirit is found in the church and not in the synagogue,'' is ''self-evident'' only on ''Christian'' terms and in the light of the church's ''charismatic'' experience of the Spirit.

[49]See Dunn, *Jesus and the Spirit,* 202-205; also John Nolland, ''Grace as Power,'' *NovT* 38 (1986): 26-31.

[50]See Rom 8:9, where the indwelling of the Spirit is attributed to both the community and the individual. For a thorough treatment of the Spirit and baptism (i.e., conversion/initiation), see Dunn, *Baptism in the Holy Spirit.*

"having" the Spirit and Christian identity are viewed as inseparable. But the early church also thought of participation in the Spirit as a repeated experience and characterized God accordingly as the one who "gives" or "supplies" the Spirit.[51] No doubt this way of thinking about the Spirit owes something to traditional Jewish conceptions of the Spirit as an occasional *charisma* rather than a personal "possession." One thinks especially of formulas such as, "The Spirit of the Lord came upon . . . " (Judg 3:10; 1 Sam 19:20) or "The Spirit of the Lord took possession of . . . " (2 Chr 24:20; Judg 6:34). But equally influential will have been the charismatic experiences themselves as occasioned by worship and varying in frequency and intensity of manifestation.[52] We should note that the early church did not regard these two models for conceiving its relation to the Spirit as mutually exclusive. Although Gunkel was right in his observation that the church soon came to view the Spirit as "an abiding, continuously indwelling power that appears on special occasions,"[53] these "appearances" could still be described as divine dispensations "from above." Thus Paul can employ language belonging to both types in the same context, speaking in the present tense to describe the ongoing work of God through the Spirit (1 Cor 12:6-11) and in the aorist tense to describe the community members' initiation into Christ and the Spirit (12:13; cf. Gal 3:5; 1 Thess 4:8; Luke 11:13).

The "experience of the Spirit," if conceived in terms of both models, could be interpreted by Jewish Christians as positively related to law-keeping in the following way. Although all believers "have" the Spirit, lawkeeping increases or promotes charismatic life in the Spirit. In applying this interpretation to the situation of uncircumcised Gentile Christians, Jewish believers could argue that lawkeeping promotes the manifestation of the Spirit in the life of the community, without disputing that the Gentiles in question "have" the Spirit. This argument might well have carried weight with Gentile believers, especially former "Godfearers." Paul characterizes the Corinthians as "zealous" for manifestations of the Spirit (1 Cor 14:12) and tells them to "strive for"

---

[51] 1 Thess 4:8; Gal 3:5; cf. Luke 11:13.

[52] See Hermann Gunkel, *The Influence of the Holy Spirit*, 42-44; Dunn, *Jesus and the Spirit*, passim.

[53] *The Influence of the Holy Spirit*, 43.

spiritual gifts (1 Cor 14:1; cf. 12:31). Evidently manifestations of the Spirit are to be sought. The apostle himself recommends that believers pray for the ability to interpret glossolalia (1 Cor 14:13), and Luke has Jesus assure his disciples that the Father will "give the Holy Spirit to those who ask him" (Luke 11:13). This last statement suggests that believers sometimes required encouragement about God's readiness to "give the Spirit," and one thinks of the saying found in John 3:8, which suggests the mysterious and incalculable way of the Spirit: "the Spirit blows where it wills." Paul echoes the same thought in 1 Cor 12:11 when he says that "the same Spirit distributes to each one as it wills."[54] How does one harness the wind? Are there conditions for receiving the Spirit? Can one actively promote the manifestation of the Spirit's power for exorcism or healing? It may be that fasting was practiced as a means of preparing oneself to be a vessel of the Spirit.[55] If there were indeed Jewish Christians who defended the views that Paul combats in Galatians, they will have argued as follows: If uncircumcised Gentile believers want to renew, sustain, or increase their ongoing life in the Spirit (whatever the case may be), they should submit themselves to God's law.

We turn now to our third question. As plausible as the foregoing reconstruction sounds and as neatly as it supplies the answering voice in the Galatian dialogue, what specific evidence is there, apart from Galatians itself, that anyone in the early church took the view that lawkeeping promotes life in the Spirit? We may begin by considering the Gospel of Matthew, since it reflects a type of Jewish-Christianity that understands fidelity to the Torah as an essential part of authentic life in the Spirit. Matthew teaches that the Spirit, speaking through inspired prophets, guides the flock of Jesus into understanding the law correctly

---

[54]The sentence τὸ πνεῦμα ὅπου θέλει πνεῖ sounds like a proverb, although I cannot adduce any other exact examples of it. But see Eccl 11:5 (also the "parallels" in J. Wettstein, *NTG*, 1:852).

[55]Gunkel thought Acts 13:2 was suggestive of this: "While they were worshipping the Lord and fasting, the Holy Spirit said . . . " (see *The Influence of the Holy Spirit*, 34). We may also note that exorcisms were probably often accomplished through fasting (as the text tradition for Mark 9:29 suggests), which is significant for the question at hand inasmuch as the early church apparently counted exorcism as a work of the Spirit (see Dunn, *Jesus and the Spirit*, 48, 210).

for the new eschatological situation.[56] But this is something altogether different from alleging that works of the law promote pneumatic life. Nor is there any indication that the apparently Torah-observant wonder-workers castigated in Matthew 7:15-23 related lawkeeping and spiritual power along such lines.[57]

Evidently, the *Hebraioi* (Ἑβραῖοι, 2 Cor 11:22) who caused Paul difficulties at Corinth were also law-observant Jewish-Christian pneumatics.[58] But there is no explicit evidence that they urged the Corinthians to keep the Torah. In 2 Corinthians Paul treats the law only in 3:1-18, which would be surprising if the "super-apostles" were advocating Judaizing practices at Corinth. Nevertheless, the sharp polemic against the law in 3:6, which seems almost out of place in view of the *a fortiori* logic by which Paul relates the two covenants in verses 7-11, suggests that real debates have shaped Paul's language: "For the letter kills, but the Spirit makes alive." Perhaps Paul, or a Jewish-Christian evangelist who shared his view of the law, coined this slogan originally in the context of debates between the church and the synagogue, as Jacob Kremer has argued.[59] That would explain why it does not quite fit its present context in 2 Corinthians 3. Kremer thinks the thrust of the formulation is that salvation is to be had "not from one's own powers but only through the Spirit of Jesus."[60] But it makes better sense to take the sen-

---

[56]See Ernst Käsemann, "Sentences of Holy Law in the New Testament," in *New Testament Questions of Today* (London: SCM; Philadelphia: Fortress, 1969) 66-81; also Schweizer, "Observance of the Law and Charismatic Activity in Matthew."

[57]See Schweizer, "Observance of the Law and Charismatic Activity in Matthew;" D. Hill, "False Prophets and Charismatics: Structure and Interpretation in Matthew 7, 7-23," *Bib* 57 (1976): 327-48. If these "false prophets" are characterized as "wolves in sheep's clothing," then they must conform at least outwardly to the Matthean community ethos.

[58]See E. Earle Ellis, *Prophecy and Hermeneutic in Early Christianity* (Grand Rapids: Eerdmans, 1978) 102-109.

[59]" 'Denn der Buchstabe tötet, der Geist aber macht lebendig': Methodologische und hermeneutische Erwägungen zu 2 Kor 3,6b," in *Begegnung mit dem Wort: FS für Heinrich Zimmermann*, ed. J. Konijewski and E. Nellessen, BBB 53 (Bonn: Peter Hanstein, 1980). According to Kremer, Paul depends on traditional formulations, which he has probably redacted, deriving from the missionary preaching of the early church (234-35).

[60]Ibid., 235.

tence as a Pauline sharpening of the early church's claim that the Spirit is to be found only in the Christian community, not in the synagogue.[61] If the life-giving Spirit does not have its home in the sphere of the Torah, then the synagogue must be subject to the death-dealing side of the Torah (see Deut 30:15). Of course, the synagogue in Paul's day may not have claimed that it "had" the Spirit (at least not as the early church understood having and manifesting the life of the Spirit) or that law-keeping as such unleashes the power of the Spirit among God's people. But the church-synagogue conflict helps to explain how Paul came to formulate his view of the Torah in sentences such as 2 Corinthians 3:6b or Galatians 3:21b ("If a law able to make alive had been given . . . ").

As a Christian Paul "knows" that a life of zeal for the Torah did not bring *him* into contact with the power of the Spirit. On the contrary, it led him to persecute the people of the Spirit (Gal 1:13-14). It is probably this autobiographical fact, and not simply his "exclusivistic soteriology,"[62] that determines Paul's view of the law from the start, and this may account in part for the difference in opinion between Paul and the teachers at Galatia. If the teachers were Jewish Christians whose relations with the Jesus movement had been more or less congenial from their first encounters with it,[63] then they will probably not have discerned any inherent antithesis between life in the Torah and life in the Spirit. They may have conceived of themselves and perhaps the majority of Jewish followers of "The Way" along the lines Luke delineates for the pious folk of his birth and infancy narratives, people who greet the births of John the Baptist and Jesus with joy (the parents together with Simeon and Anna), people whom Luke characterizes as ready vessels of the Spirit by virtue of their humble Torah-righteousness.

---

[61]Hence I agree with Jervell ("Das Volk des Geistes," 89) that the original *Sitz im Leben* of 2 Cor 3:6b is the church-synagogue conflict. The context in 2 Cor 3 supports this conclusion. Paul goes on to portray the synagogue service as devoid of the Spirit.

[62]So E. P. Sanders, *Paul, the Law, and the Jewish People* (Philadelphia: Fortress Press, 1983) 149-54. Cf. also Heikki Räisänen, *Paul and the Law*, WUNT 29 (Tübingen: J. C. B. Mohr [Paul Siebeck], 1983) 229-63.

[63]One thinks, e.g., of J. Louis Martyn's reconstruction of the earliest Johannine community "at home" in the synagogue. See Martyn, *The Gospel of John in Christian History* (New York/Ramsey/Toronto: Paulist Press, 1978) 93-102.

We have reason to believe that the stories we meet in Luke 1–2, together with similar stories about disciples of Jesus, and no doubt a variety of primitive "conversion" stories that celebrated the Spirit's "coming" upon Torah-faithful people, circulated widely in the early church.[64] Luke himself suggests throughout his two-volume work that Torah piety and receptiveness to the Spirit go hand in hand,[65] an idea that he probably did not invent. When Luke highlights this theme in his narration of the Jewish-Christian mission to the Gentiles (Acts 8:26-40; 10:1-48; 16:14-15; cf. Luke 7:1-10), he is probably only manipulating to his own ends a motif already present in the traditions at his disposal. After all, the typical Gentile convert in the Jewish-Christian mission to the uncircumcised was presumably a *Godfearer*,[66] a non-Jew in a generally anti-Semitic culture whose positive attitude toward the Jewish Torah prepared him, a Jewish Christian might argue, to receive God's Spirit by turning to the Messiah Jesus. Hence, the link between Torah piety and the Spirit is "there" for the Jewish Christian who wished to make something of it, and Luke tells a number of stories that are amenable to the view that God's Spirit characteristically falls upon those Gentiles who evidence Godfearing reverence for the law: the conversion of the Isaiah-reading Ethiopian (Acts 8:26-40), the conversion of the Godfearing Cornelius and his household (Acts 10:1-33), the healing of the Godfearing centurian's servant (Luke 7:1-10), and the conversion of the Godfearing Lydia (16:14-15). Moreover, it is but a short step from the contention that the Torah prepares the Godfearer to receive the message of Jesus to the conclusion that converted Gentiles might promote their ongoing life in the Spirit by putting themselves fully under the Torah. What

---

[64]Jervell has already made this case for stories about the "apostles." See "The Problem of Traditions in Acts," in Jervell, *Luke and the People of God: A New Look at Luke-Acts* (Minneapolis: Augsburg Publishing House, 1972) 19-39.

[65]See Acts 2:5-47, which gives the impression that the multitudes who witnessed Pentecost and believed in Jesus were "devout Jews" (2:5). Stephen describes his Jewish adversaries as people who "resist the Holy Spirit" (7:51) and "do not keep the law" (7:53).

[66]See, e.g., Heneke Gülzow, "Soziale Gegebenheiten der altkirchlichen Mission," in *Die Alte Kirche*, vol. 1 of *Kirchengeschichte als Missionsgeschichte* (Munich: Chr. Kaiser Verlag, 1974) 194-98. For a dissenting opinion, see A. Thomas Kraabel, "Traditional Christian Evidence for Diaspora Judaism: The Book of Acts," in *SBL Seminar Papers 1986*, ed. Kent Harold Richards (Atlanta: Scholars Press, 1986) 644-51.

better way of protecting the status of Torah-faithfulness from the Gentiles' Torah-free form of life in Christ (and "in the Spirit") that threatened it than by linking the manifestation of the Spirit to works of the law?

A Profile of the Teachers at Galatia

We shall now attempt a provisional reconstruction of the teachers. As a description of the *historical* teachers themselves this reconstruction is provisional in the sense that it synthesizes into a unified profile the various things that Paul says and implies about their teaching with minimal consideration of the ways in which what he says and implies argumentatively may misrepresent or distort their views.

The teachers are probably Greek-speaking Jewish Christians[67] pursuing a mission in the Diaspora. They believe in the Gentile mission, otherwise they would not trouble themselves over Paul's converts. They accept, either from conviction or out of strategic considerations, the Gentile Galatians as brothers and sisters in Christ, led by the Spirit as sons of God. We can deduce this last point from two observations about Paul's own argument in the letter. First, as we have seen, the status of the Galatians as members of God's people in Christ serves an ancillary role in Paul's argument. It functions as common ground with his readers, and this suggests that the teachers did not question the authenticity of the Galatians' share in Christ. Second, Paul nowhere seeks to defend the genuineness of the Galatians' experience of the Spirit. He simply takes for granted that the community does not doubt the reality of its initial reception of the Spirit (3:2), which suggests that the teachers do not dispute that the Spirit is among the Galatians. Instead, the teachers acknowledge the community's claim to "have" the Spirit and urge that the community come under the law in order to promote their life in the Spirit. They say that "works of the law" sustain or increase manifestations of the Spirit, and one suspects from the way Paul puts his question in 3:5 that the Galatians are practicing the law and celebrating a renewal of mighty evidences of the Spirit in their midst as a consequence, to their minds, of works of the law: "Does, therefore, the one who supplies the Spirit among you and works miracles among you do so in consequence of (ἐξ) works of the law . . . ?"

---

[67]See the introduction to this chapter.

In making their case, the teachers quote *Leviticus 18:5,* which explains why Paul can appeal to it in Galatians 3 without employing any introductory formula. They also stress the scriptural connection between the law and blessing (e.g., Deut 28:1-14; Pss 1; 119), maintaining that those who are righteous in the law will be blessed with the power of the Spirit. Paul provocatively counters this last thesis with Deuteronomy 27:26. Not the blessing of the law but its curse applies to lawkeepers (see above, chapter 2). The teachers also argue that the fulfillment of God's *promises* depends upon his people's fidelity to the Torah. If the Galatians wish to experience fully the promise of the Spirit, they should receive circumcision and thus become literal lawkeeping sons of Abraham, for "the inheritance is from the law" (Gal 3:18). The teachers develop this line of argument without questioning whether God has accepted believing Gentiles as his people or disputing the Galatians' status as "sons of God" in Christ. Paul responds by arguing that the Abrahamic promise was made to only *one* seed, Christ himself. Believers share in the inheritance by being "of Christ" ("one" in Christ), which is the only way that anyone gets "into" the single seed of Abraham and thus becomes an heir of the Spirit.

Our reconstruction of the debate relieves us from having to explain how the teachers could have gotten people who knew the presence of God's Spirit among them to doubt their identity as God's children. This problem has been altogether overlooked in studies on Galatians. Interpreters who assume that the debate concerns the Galatians' "status," or whether God "accepts" them, or whether they "belong" to God's people fail to explain how the teachers could have made a persuasive case for this in the face of the community's consciousness of "having" the Spirit. At the same time they fail to account for Paul's assumption that the Spirit works powerfully among the Galatians (3:5) and that the authenticity of these spiritual manifestations needs no defense. In this connection the experiential basis for early Christian identity as "sons of God," centered as it was in the "experience of the Spirit," is especially significant,[68] and it finds an analogy in contemporary charismatic ex-

---

[68]See Dunn, *Jesus and the Spirit,* 240-41.

perience.[69] To put the matter a bit differently, Paul hardly needs to *argue* from the Galatians' experience of the Spirit that they are "sons,"[70] although it makes perfect sense for him to argue from the intimate connection between "sonship" and the Spirit that being a son is the sufficient criterion for the ongoing experience of the Spirit. As we have seen, this is precisely the tenor of the argument in 4:6-7.

It is conceivable that Paul introduces the theme of the Galatians' filial relationship to God in order to counter the notion that believers are in a kind of "patron-client" relationship to God. First-century Mediterranean society depended heavily on the social institution of "benefaction," and people tended to think of God or the gods as benefactors who could be manipulated through appropriate and honoring forms of service.[71] By stressing the "sonship" of believers, Paul makes it clear that the One who supplies them with the Spirit and works powerfully among them is not a divine benefactor, whose gifts depend upon specific forms of service (such as "works of the law"), but a Father who gives them good gifts (the Spirit) because they are his sons (4:6-7).[72] Furthermore, the pervasive cultural value and institution of benefaction may also account in part for the Galatians' ready acceptance of the thought that the ongoing gift of God's Spirit could be promoted by "works of the law." That is, the idea of maintaining or increasing the flow of the Spirit through specific acts of service to God would have struck them as quite logical, even apart from arguments from the Jewish Scriptures.

It may be that in addition to advising the Galatians about how to promote eschatological experience in the present, the teachers also advo-

---

[69]See H. Newton Maloney and A. Adams Lovekin, *Glossolalia: Behavioral Science Perspectives on Speaking in Tongues* (New York/Oxford: Oxford University Press, 1985) 192-94.

[70]Dunn makes a similar point with regard to Rom 8:15-16, when he stresses that Paul does not treat "assurance" of sonship as something that is obtained through logical inference from the fact of the Spirit's presence. The *abba*-cry in the Spirit is already the expression of the believer's "sense of sonship" (*Jesus and the Spirit*, 240).

[71]See Bruce J. Malina, *The New Testament World: Insights from Cultural Anthropology* (Atlanta: John Knox Press, 1981) 71-93; Frederick W. Danker, *Benefactor: Epigraphic Study of a Graeco-Roman and New Testament Semantic Field* (St. Louis: Clayton Publishing House, 1982).

[72]Cf. Luke 11:11-13: "how much more shall your heavenly Father give the Holy Spirit to those who ask him."

cate lawkeeping as a means of hastening the future consummation. We can imagine them saying something to this effect:

> All the promises of God find their fulfillment in God's Messiah Jesus (cf. 2 Cor 1:20). But since the promises made to Abraham and his seed (cf. Gal 3:16) are linked with the Torah, they depend for their fulfillment upon the people of God's Messiah remaining faithful to the law. This means that the coming of the kingdom will be delayed until the Gentile churches embrace the Torah.

If the teachers held such a view, it explains why they took the trouble to dog Paul's steps on the Gentile mission field. On this theory, where Paul understands his mission to the uncircumcised as hastening the final consummation (Rom 11:11-32) and ''Peter'' summons the people of Israel to repentance and faith in Christ ''that times of refreshing may come from the presence of the Lord and that he may send the Christ appointed for you, Jesus . . . '' (Acts 3:19-21),[73] the teachers are convinced that the end cannot come until both wings of the church, the Jewish and the Gentile, submit to God's *law*. We have already observed that in certain Jewish circles the view prevailed that national fidelity to the Torah would advance the advent of the messianic kingdom. Nevertheless, if the teachers advocated a Christian version of this view, perhaps under the influence of the Isaianic vision of the Gentiles streaming to Zion (Isa 2:2-4), Paul gives no hint of it in Galatians.[74]

The introduction to this chapter stressed that the primary reconstruction undertaken here aims to clarify not the ''real'' views of the ''agitators'' but the views that Paul attacks. These may well represent Paul's own argumentative imposition upon them of certain ''implications'' or ''logical'' consequences of what they are saying, a projection based on his own understanding of the relevant themes (the law, the promise, blessing, life, the Spirit, and so forth) in Jewish Scripture and tradition.

---

[73]Acts 3:19-21 is striking in its use of a ''divine δεῖ'' in expressing what is an essentially *prophetic* conception of the future. See Cosgrove, ''The Divine Δεῖ in Luke-Acts: Investigations into the Lukan Understanding of Divine Providence,'' *NovT* 26 (1984): 186. Cf. Matt 23:39, ''You will not see me again until you say, 'Blessed is he who comes in the name of the Lord.' ''

[74]We shall speculate further about the strategy of the agitators in ch. 4.

If the foregoing reconstruction has rendered our initial identification of the ''problem at Galatia'' theologically plausible from a Jewish-Christian standpoint, we have strengthened our case, even if we remain uncertain about the extent to which the apostle projects the ''opposing theology'' onto the Galatians and the persons he calls ''agitators.''

The historical uncertainty mentioned in the last statement cannot be overcome, hence the concluding profile of the teachers must remain strictly provisional. Even the most compelling argument for concluding that the historical teachers do advocate in some form the view that law-keeping promotes life in the Spirit cannot be made sufficiently secure. To repeat this argument briefly, since Paul nowhere defends the authenticity of the Galatians' ongoing life in the Spirit, itself the most immediate and unshakeable evidence to the Galatians that they belong to Christ, the debate must concern the ''management'' of life in Christ rather than whether the Galatians ''count'' as God's people. Nevertheless, it is also conceivable that Paul does confront an explicit challenge by the agitators to the Galatians' very identity as members of God's people in Christ, but for rhetorical reasons treats the Galatians' being in Christ as beyond question and approaches the problem *as if* it concerned the ''maintenance'' or ''promotion'' of life in the Spirit. By the same token, the teachers may hold the view that circumcision is a basic requirement for joining God's people and yet, for tactical reasons of their own, suppress this opinion in view of the Galatians' manifest experience of the Spirit. Calculating that the Galatians probably cannot be persuaded that without circumcision they remain outside the circle of God's people, the agitators may recommend the law to the Galatians on other grounds. But putting all such speculation aside, what we are able to deduce from the letter is the ''opposing theology'' as Paul implies it in his argument, and we may sum up the substance and logic of that theology as follows. It advocates ''works of the law'' for the increase of life in the Spirit by applying an old and venerated dictum of the Torah to *the sphere of eschatological life in Christ*: ''the one who does them shall live by them.''

CHAPTER 4

The Apostolic Autobiography

But what counts most in deliberative oratory
is the authority of the speaker.

—Quintilian, *Institutio Oratoria* 3.8.12

I through the law died to the law
that I might live to God.

—Galatians 2:19

THE PRECEDING CHAPTERS have led us to the following conclusion. The "other gospel" (1:6) attacked by Paul in Galatians makes a positive connection between "works of the law" and ongoing life in the Spirit. According to the agitators, doing the law promotes the manifestation of the Spirit, a claim that the Galatians, at least those who have assumed the ways of the Torah, may well regard as now substantiated in their midst: since turning to the law the power of the Spirit has become more evident and effective among them. Assuming that this is "the problem at Galatia," as Paul sees it, how shall we understand the purpose of the apostolic autobiography (1:11–2:21)? In putting the question in this way, we remain methodologically faithful to the decision made above in chapter 1, to let the epistolary standpoint secured from Galatians 3:1-14 guide our reading of the letter as a whole. Therefore, we approach the material before us with a specific line of questioning in mind. What is the relevance of a given argument for the problem at

Galatia as we have reconstructed it? What does the introduction of a particular theme suggest in the light of the Galatian connection between the law and the Spirit? How are we to interpret Paul's use of certain key terms, such as "life" and "righteousness"?

Paul's autobiography is multivalent; the argument proceeds on a number of levels at once. Even the recognition that the narrative intertwines the themes of both "the gospel" and "the apostle"[1] does not go far enough in getting at the rhetorical polyvalence of the story. For the theme of the apostle serves not only to establish Paul's apostolic authority (*ethos*), but also to portray his solidarity with the Gentile cause, thus engaging the readers' emotions (*pathos*), and to present him as an exemplar of fidelity to the gospel in both thought and action (exemplary *ethos*).[2] Moreover, the theme of the gospel is woven into the presentation of all the characters in the story and not only that of the apostle. Therefore, rather than examine the narrative verse by verse, we shall treat the various rhetorical levels in the autobiography severally, without losing sight of the narrative progression of material, drawing the various threads of discussion into a unified whole at the end.

Paul's autobiography in Galatians 1:11–2:21 consists of a narrative and a "speech." Since the speech poses its own special problems, we will leave it aside for the moment and focus on the narrative in 1:11–2:14. There are two ways in which we can approach the story in 1:11–2:14. We can ask how the points Paul makes about himself and his gospel further his overall argument in the letter. Or we can speculate about

---

[1]E.g., J. Christiaan Beker, *Paul the Apostle: The Triumph of God in Life and Thought* (Philadelphia: Fortress Press, 1980) 44-47.

[2]Although I chart my own course through Paul's "rhetoric" in Gal 1–2, I am indebted to the basic insights of the following interpreters regarding Paul's rhetorical tactics in the autobiography: John Howard Schütz, *Paul and the Anatomy of Apostolic Authority*, SNTSMS 26 (Cambridge: Cambridge University Press, 1975); George Lyons, *Pauline Autobiography: Toward a New Understanding*, SBLDS 73 (Atlanta: Scholars Press, 1985); Steven John Kraftchick, *Ethos and Pathos Appeals in Galatians Five and Six: A Rhetorical Analysis* (Ph.D. diss., Emory University, 1985); B. R. Gaventa, "Galatians 1 and 2: Autobiography as Paradigm," *NovT* 28 (1986): 309-26; also George A. Kennedy, *New Testament Interpretation through Rhetorical Criticism* (Chapel Hill and London: University of North Carolina Press, 1984) 144-49.

what the agitators told the Galatians (regarding Paul and the gospel) that has elicited this particular autobiography from the apostle. We do best to keep these two lines of inquiry separate, since the first does not depend upon the tentative results of the second but can stand on its own. Therefore, our treatment of the history in 1:11–2:14a will proceed in two parts, after which we shall take up the speech (2:14b-21) as a relatively discrete unit.

The Narrative

The story Paul tells in 1:11–2:14a serves a variety of ends. It presents the uncircumcision gospel as a divine mandate. It establishes Paul's apostolic ethos (authority) as well as his personal ethos (loyalty to the Galatians and the Gentile cause). Finally, it defends Paul's apostolic independence from the Jerusalem apostles. We shall consider each of these in turn.

Paul claims that he received his gospel ("the gospel preached by me," 1:11) when he was commissioned by God as apostle to the Gentiles, a commissioning that took the form of divine revelation. We learn from the narrative of 1:11–2:14 that the gospel he received is "the gospel of uncircumcision" (2:7), that is, a gospel offered to the Gentiles without the demand that they submit to the Torah. Paul "proves" that his gospel is divine in origin by adducing three pieces of "evidence." First he stresses that he did not get his gospel from human beings but received it through divine revelation (1:12, 15). Second, he reminds his readers that he was completely indisposed toward any such gospel prior to his being commissioned (1:13-14), as if to say that the gospel he preaches was obviously not *his* idea! Third, he states that after receiving his revelation he did not "consult with flesh and blood," nor did he have any contact with the Jerusalem church for some three years (1:15-17; cf. 1:18). We will return to this last point when we attempt to reconstruct what the agitators may have been saying about Paul.

Paul's account of his reception of the gospel sets the stage for what follows. As Paul tells the story of the Jerusalem meeting (2:1-10), although he had reason to expect resistance from the church in Jerusalem (2:2; cf. 2:3-5), the "pillar" apostles recognized the divine origin of the gospel to the uncircumcised: "they saw that I had been entrusted with the gospel to the uncircumcised . . . they had perceived the grace that had been given to me'' (2:7-9). We should observe especially the use of the verb ''work'' (ἐνεργεῖν) in 2:8 and the phrase ''the grace given to me'' in verse 9 (τὴν χάριν τὴν δοθεῖσαν μοι). This is the language of God's powerful spiritual presence and activity. The description of God in verse 8 (''The one who worked in Peter . . . worked also in me'') should remind us of 3:5 (''The one who supplies the Spirit to you and works [ἐνεργῶν] miracles among you''). Thus Paul's description of the Jerusalem apostles' response to his gospel in effect lifts the question of the ''evidence'' for the divine origin of his gospel out of the purely private sphere of his own revelatory experience into the public sphere of community discernment. The divine origin of Paul's gospel is evident in Paul's mission, where God manifests his powerful presence among Gentiles who believe Paul's message.[3]

Now the Galatians should be able to hear their *own* story in Paul's description of God at work in his mission to the uncircumcised, and Paul encourages them to see the entire history, from his commission to the Jerusalem meeting, as having *them* in view all along: ''To these [the false brethren] we did not yield even for an instant, that the truth of the gospel might remain for you'' (2:5). The Galatians are to connect the story of Paul's commission with the ''facts'' of his Gentile mission and discern for themselves the divine origin of Paul's gospel to the uncircumcised. They are to recognize God's presence in their midst as the public confirmation of Paul's private commission. Thus Paul invites the Galatians to see themselves as occupying a privileged position from which to judge his gospel. This is an effective rhetorical move on Paul's part. He encourages his readers to adopt his own viewpoint by implicitly affirming the authenticity of *their* ''spiritual experience'' and suggesting that they are in a better position to know the truth of the gospel than the Jerusalem apostles, who have access only secondhand to the relevant ''evidence.''

---

[3]Paul's apostolic χάρις (2:9) is a χάρισμα. See H. von Lips, ''Der Apostolat des Paulus—ein Charisma? Semantische Aspekte zu χάρις-χάρισμα und anderen Wortpaaren im Sprachgebrauch des Paulus,'' *Bib* 66 (1985): 305-43. If the ''pillar'' apostles come to recognize the grace given to Paul (γνόντες τὴν χάριν κ.τ.λ.) as God working through him (ἐνήργησεν καὶ ἐμοί), when they hear him tell about the gospel he preaches (2:2), then one assumes that Paul told stories of the Spirit's powerful and evidential work in his mission among the Gentiles (cf. 2 Cor 12:12).

There is no "dialectic" in 1:11–2:21 "between [Paul's] being independent of and acknowledged by Jerusalem."[4] The Jerusalem apostles acknowledge the "truth of the gospel" and in so doing submit to the
authority of the gospel. As John Schütz puts it, Paul "patterns" the Jerusalem circle after his own conception of apostolic subordination to the
gospel.[5] But in so doing he indicates that the Jerusalem apostles must
submit themselves to the truth of the gospel as embodied in *Gentile* believers like the Galatians, who know firsthand "the grace given to Paul"
(2:9) as the effective presence of God among them.

Once the Galatians realize that no one is in a better position than they
to discern the truth of the "Torah-free" gospel preached by Paul, they
should draw the following conclusion. If the presence of the Spirit among
them (God effectively at work among them) is "public" divine confirmation of Paul's gospel to the uncircumcised, then it makes no sense to
imagine that the presence of the Spirit can be promoted by getting circumcised and keeping the law. This implication of Paul's narrative is
one of the principal contributions that the apostolic autobiography makes
to the larger argument of the letter. Paul does not state this implication
explicitly because the Jerusalem conference was not about the problem
of whether works of the law promote life in the Spirit. In fact, Paul does
not say *what* the Jerusalem conference was about, except to *imply* in 2:3
that it concerned the question of whether Gentile believers should be
circumcised. But for Paul's purposes in Galatians, proving that the gospel to the Gentiles explicitly excludes circumcision is sufficient for the
argument that God does not "give the Spirit" in consequence of works
of the law. In this way the autobiography prepares for the arguments to
come.

A second purpose of the autobiography is to establish at the outset
Paul's apostolic relation to the Galatians (cf. 1:1). If God has commissioned Paul as the apostle to the Gentiles, then the Gentile communities
established by him are obliged to listen to him. A number of those who
have analyzed the Galatian letter from the standpoint of Graeco-Roman

---

[4]Bengt Holmberg, *Paul and Power: The Structure of Authority in the Primitive
Church as Reflected in the Pauline Epistles*, CN/NTS 11 (Lund: CWK Gleerup, 1978)
15; see also Lyons, *Pauline Autobiography*, 160.

[5]*Paul and the Anatomy of Apostolic Authority*, 143.

rhetorical convention judge it to approximate most closely the style known as *deliberative rhetoric*,[6] a style of oratory that relies heavily on the authority of the speaker (Quintilian, *Inst. Or.* 3.8.12).[7] It is consistent with this view of the letter's general rhetorical style that throughout the epistle Paul speaks self-consciously as apostle. The letter begins in the apostolic voice, and the opening antithetical formulation anticipates the autobiography: "Paul, an apostle not from human beings or through them but through Jesus Christ." If a second function of the autobiography is to establish Paul's apostolic ethos in preparation for the central argumentation of the letter, then we need not assume, as many interpreters have in the past, that the stress on the divine origin of Paul's apostleship is occasioned by charges that have been levelled against Paul by the agitators.[8]

The autobiography reinforces not only Paul's apostolic relation to the community but also his personal solidarity with them. Paul portrays himself, in contrast to the various other characters in his narrative, as unfailing in his loyalty to *Gentile* believers and thus encourages the Galatians to see him as their ally. This aim of the autobiography is explicit in 2:5, where Paul declares, "To them we did not submit even for a moment, that the truth of the gospel might remain for you!" The "we" of this statement includes Paul, Barnabas (who will betray the cause at Antioch, 2:13), and the Greek Titus (2:3). Paul had already mentioned that when the party came to Jerusalem, Titus had not been pressured into getting circumcised, the implication being that his identification with Paul served as his protection: "But even Titus, who was with *me* (em-

---

[6]Evidently Nils Dahl was the first to suggest that Galatians, although evincing a rhetorically mixed style, approaches the deliberative style of oratory perhaps more closely than any other. Dahl's views are stated in an unpublished paper presented at the Society of Biblical Literature annual meeting in 1970. See Lyons (*Pauline Autobiography,* 119), who agrees with Dahl; also Kennedy, *New Testament Interpretation through Rhetorical Criticism,* 144-52.

[7]Quintilian's statement can be generalized for any attempt at rhetorical persuasion. See Kraftchick, "Ethos and Pathos Appeals in Galatians Five and Six," passim.

[8]The assumption that Paul's autobiography represents an apology for his apostleship is widespread. Schütz, however, has argued persuasively that, if anything, Paul is on the offensive rather than the defensive in Gal 1:11-2:21. See *Paul and the Anatomy of Apostolic Authority,* 114-58; see also Lyons, *Pauline Autobiography,* 75-176.

phatic ἐμοί), was not compelled to be circumcised, although he was Greek'' (2:3).[9]

But even more powerful rhetorically is Paul's expression of his loyalty to the Gentile cause at Antioch. We should bear in mind that when the Galatians hear the story of Antioch (2:11ff.), they will identify first of all not with Peter, Paul, or the party from James but with *the Gentiles* (2:12), and their openness to other characters in the story will be determined by this primary identification. Thus Paul's narrative is designed to reinforce the Galatians' trust in him, when they hear how none of the Jewish believers stood by the Gentiles at Antioch—*except Paul alone.* The "speech" that he delivers on their behalf ("before them all," v. 14) provides a dramatic instance of both Paul's loyalty to the gospel and his fidelity to the Gentile cause. Moreover, it serves as a model to the Galatians. They should stand up to the agitators just like Paul did to the Judaizers at Antioch.[10] It is instructive to observe that Paul alone provides this model in the Antioch story. Nowhere in 2:11-21 do the Gentile believers at Antioch join Paul in speaking out against the actions of Peter and the other Jewish Christians. The "we" of resistance in 2:5 is echoed by a solitary "I" in 2:11 and 2:14, an "I" speaking the truth of the gospel "before them all" (2:14). This fact alone suggests that Paul lost the debate at Antioch, a question that we will consider further below. At the same time, the picture evoked by 2:14 of Paul speaking as a minority of one to the whole church at Antioch prompts the question whether Paul regards his letter to the Galatians as another instance of the irony that he, the Jewish apostle to the Gentiles, remains faithful to the Gentile cause even when the Gentiles themselves betray that cause. Seen in this light, Paul's description of his solidarity with the Gentiles at Antioch, whose relation to him appears at best ambiguous, mirrors the situation in which the apostle finds himself vis-à-vis the Galatians.

---

[9]The clause is surely not concessive ("even though he was with *me*"), as some commentators seem to think. See e.g., Ernest De Witt Burton, *A Critical and Exegetical Commentary on the Epistle to the Galatians,* ICC (Edinburgh: T. & T. Clark, 1921) 75; Heinrich Schlier, *Der Brief an die Galater,* 5th ed., MeyerK 7/14 (Göttingen: Vandenhoeck & Ruprecht, 1971) 69.

[10]Lyons has emphasized the ways in which Paul's autobiography as a whole "serves as the paradigm of the behavior he persuades his readers to imitate" (*Pauline Autobiography,* 136). See also Gaventa, "Galatians 1 and 2: Autobiography as Paradigm."

We turn now to Paul's defense of his apostolic independence from Jerusalem. We shall explore this theme in connection with our attempt to reconstruct what the agitators may have been telling the Galatians about the events that Paul narrates in 1:11–2:14. The natural starting point for this line of inquiry is the one place in the narrative where Paul is surely on the defensive. In 1:20, after reporting his first visit to Jerusalem, Paul takes an oath: "In what I am writing, before God, I do not lie." The presence of this oath strongly suggests that in 1:16-20 Paul is engaged in countering something that the agitators have alleged about him.[11] Many interpreters imagine that throughout 1:16-24 Paul defends the claim, disputed by the agitators, that he did not receive the gospel from Jerusalem.[12] The debate over whether the verb (ἱστορῆσαι) in verse 18 means "inquire of" (that is, "with a view to gaining information") reflects this orientation to Paul's narrative.[13] But two considerations speak against the assumption that verses 16ff. have to do with the source of Paul's gospel. For one thing, even if the verb ἱστορεῖν can be used in the sense, "to see" or "to visit," it is extremely unlikely that Paul, in refuting the agitator's contention that he first learned the gospel in Jerusalem, would have expressed the purpose of his visit to

---

[11]Lyons (*Pauline Autobiography*, 160) and Gaventa ("Galatians 1 and 2," 316 n. 17) overstate their case for the paradigmatic, as opposed to apologetic, aims of the autobiography when they deny that Paul's oath in 1:20 indicates that he is rejecting something that the agitators have said about him. Moreover, neither gives any clear explanation of the function of this oath. On the significance of oath taking in first-century Mediterranean culture, see Bruce J. Malina, *The New Testament World: Insights from Cultural Anthropology* (Atlanta: John Knox Press, 1981) 37.

[12]See Burton, *The Epistle to the Galatians*, 53-55; F. F. Bruce, *The Epistle to the Galatians: A Commentary on the Greek Text*, NIGTC (Grand Rapids: Eerdmans, 1982) 95; H. D. Betz, *Galatians: A Commentary on Paul's Letter to the Churches of Galatia*, Hermeneia (Philadelphia: Fortress Press, 1979) 80; cf. Schlier, *Der Brief an die Galater*, 60.

[13]See G. D. Kilpatrick, "Galatians 1:18 ἹΣΤΟΡΗΣΑΙ ΚΗΦΑΝ," in *New Testament Essays: Studies in Memory of T. W. Manson*, ed. A. J. B. Higgins (Manchester: Manchester University Press, 1959) 144-49; James D. G. Dunn, "The Relationship Between Paul and Jerusalem according to Galatians 1 and 2," *NTS* 28 (1982): 461-78; Otfried Hofius, "Gal 1,18: ἱστορῆσαι Κηφᾶν," *ZNW* 75 (1984): 73-85; Dunn, "Once More—Gal 1,18: ἱστορῆσαι Κηφᾶν in Reply to Otfried Hofius," *ZNW* 76 (1985): 138-39.

Jerusalem with a verb that often does mean "to inquire of." [14] That is, ἱστορεῖν is simply not the verb one would choose in order to *stress* that one's purpose in going somewhere was *simply* to visit and *not* to inquire. Not only that, the gospel under consideration here is the gospel preached by Paul in distinction from the "gospel of the circumcision," which one would indeed learn in Jerusalem. That is, Paul certainly does not need to argue that he was in no position to receive "the gospel preached by me," namely, the *uncircumcision gospel*, from the apostles in Jerusalem! Hence, it makes better sense to construe verse 17 with what follows and to let verse 16b be sufficient for the point that, at the time of his revelation, he did not consult with human beings about its import. From verse 17 on, the question of where, or from whom, Paul "learned" the gospel is no longer in view.

But if not the garnering of information, what is at stake in 1:18ff.? Why does Paul take such pains to describe his contact with the Jerusalem apostles as being limited to Peter and—the afterthought in this context sounds contrived—James? Why does he find it necessary to take an oath (1:20)? The reference to preaching in 1:23 provides a clue. Here is the first reference to concrete evangelizing by Paul. One gets the impression that the apostle began his mission to the Gentiles, in accordance with the call of 1:16, *after* his first visit to Jerusalem. And the narrative of 1:17-24 makes good sense when viewed as a response to the agitators' argument that Paul was commissioned as an apostle by Jerusalem and therefore is obliged to abide by the "Jerusalem version" of the gospel (as they represent it). Seen in this light, the distancing from Jerusalem described in 1:17-24 must aim to demonstrate that, before embarking on his mission, Paul was party to no official meetings in Jerusalem. His contact with the Jerusalem church consisted of informal encounters with individual apostles, and with only two at that. There can be no talk of a "commission" by Jerusalem. [15]

---

[14] When employed with either a personal object (as in Gal 1:18) or an impersonal object, the idea of inquiry (the aim of getting information) is very often conveyed by this verb (Polybius 3.48.12; Plutarch *Mor.* 516c; Epictetus *Disc.* 3.7.1; Herodotus 2.19; 3.77; Josephus *Ant.* 8.46; see *LSJ* s.v. ἱστορέω).

[15] Holmberg rightly pinpoints Paul's aim as being "to quench any possible rumours or suspicions" that his mission in Syria and Cilicia was carried out under the auspices

In his account of the Jerusalem meeting (2:1-10) Paul continues to portray himself as independent of Jerusalem authority. As Paul tells it, he was not summoned to Jerusalem; he went up "according to revelation" (2:2). Jerusalem probably called the meeting in view of certain questions raised by Paul's noncircumcision gospel. But Paul carefully describes his attendance in such a way that he avoids giving any impression that he went in response to an authoritative summons from Jerusalem. He does not even suggest that he was sent by the *Antioch* church as an official delegate along with Barnabas. Moreover, there is no hint in 2:1-10 of any ecclesiastical certification of Paul and his message. Rather, the Jerusalem pillars are depicted as *perceiving the grace* given Paul by God (γνόντες τὴν χάριν κ.τ.λ., 2:9). Here, as in 1:24, Jerusalem acknowledges the validity of the gospel preached by Paul, but the authorization of his mission and his gospel belongs to God.[16]

If Paul defends his apostolic independence in the face of certain contentions by the agitators, we must ask how the agitators' assumption that Paul is subject to Jerusalem fits their strategy and program at Galatia. It has often been argued that the agitators, acting as an arm of the Jerusalem church or at least claiming to represent Jerusalem,[17] *require* circumcision of Gentile believers as a basic kingdom qualification. But no one in Paul's narrative says anything to this effect about Gentile believers. The "false brothers" (2:4) are spying on *Paul,* the party from James is concerned about *Jewish* believers in a mixed church, and the pillars *affirm* Paul's Gentile mission. Furthermore, as far as one can tell from Paul's account, Peter and the other Jewish believers at Antioch begin to Judaize without insisting that the Gentiles follow suit. Finally, the agitators themselves, to judge from Paul's argument in the letter, do

---

of Jerusalem (*Paul and Power,* 80). Franz Mussner identifies two distinct purposes in 1:15-17. On one hand Paul is said to deny that he got his gospel "from men," and on the other hand to dispute that he received his apostolic commission from Jerusalem. See Mussner, *Der Galaterbrief,* 4th ed., HTKNT 9 (Freiburg/Basel/Vienna: Herder, 1981) 89-91.

[16]See the fine discussion by Schütz, *Paul and the Anatomy of Apostolic Authority,* 138-50.

[17]For a discussion of the history of interpretation regarding this question, see Werner Georg Kümmel, *Introduction to the New Testament,* rev. English ed. (Nashville: Abingdon, 1975) 298-301.

not insist that Gentiles must get circumcised (come under the Torah) in order to qualify as members of God's eschatological people. They recommend the value of works of the law for the spiritual life of the Galatians on the assumption that the Galatians already belong to God's people and enjoy authentic life in the Spirit.[18]

Let us rehearse the facts before us. First, Paul's oath in 1:20 indicates that the agitators have indeed made something of Paul's relation to the Jerusalem apostles, and we have concluded that they represent Paul as dependent on Jerusalem for his authority as an apostle. Second, no one in Paul's narrative contends that Gentiles must get circumcised in order to belong to God's people, although Paul asks Peter how he can "compel" Gentiles to Judaize (2:14). Third, as far as we can reconstruct their views, the agitators accept the Galatians as brothers and sisters in Christ and invite them to increase their share in the Spirit by taking up the yoke of the Torah. The clue to what the agitators have been saying about Paul and Jerusalem probably lies somewhere in the connections that exist among these three facts. Let us begin with the second point and, in particular, the case of Peter. In Paul's own version of the episode at Antioch Peter does not compel Gentiles to Judaize, but Paul treats Peter's abandonment of the Gentile table as, in effect, "compelling Gentile believers to Judaize" (2:14). Now one may speculate that Paul viewed the rift in fellowship created by the Jewish-Christians withdrawing from the Gentiles as a kind of implicit pressure on the Gentiles to Judaize for the sake of preserving community. But the strong verb "compel"[19] would seem to be justified only if, as Paul writes Gala-

---

[18]The statement about the agitators "compelling" the Galatians to be circumcised (6:12) is no evidence to the contrary. The agitators are in a position to "compel" the Galatians only through *persuasion,* and one cannot tell from Paul's polemical use of the word ἀναγκάζειν what the agitators said that was so "compelling."

[19]According to George Howard, Peter not only broke fellowship with the Gentile table but began a circumcising campaign in Antioch. See Howard, *Paul, Crisis in Galatia: A Study in Early Christian Theology,* SNTSMS 35 (Cambridge: Cambridge University Press, 1979) 24-25. David R. Catchpole has also advocated taking the ἀναγκάζειν literally of Peter's behavior: "Paul, James and the Apostolic Decree," *NTS* 23 (1977): 441. But all Peter is depicted as doing in the narrative of 2:11-14b is "withdrawing and separating himself" (ὑπέστελλεν καὶ ἀφώριζεν ἑαυτὸν, 2:12). Hence, it would seem advisable to take the verb "compel" *seriously,* as Howard and Catchpole urge, but not *literally.*

tians, he can look back on Gentile Judaizing at Antioch as the *outcome in fact* of the events he reports in 2:11-13. In that case Paul lost the debate at Antioch, which would explain why he passes over the outcome of the controversy in silence.[20] If this is so, then the agitators might have related the story of Antioch to the Galatians along the following lines:

> A party from James came to Antioch and convinced the Jewish believers there not to forsake the law. Peter, Barnabas, and the other Jewish believers at Antioch returned to the Torah and the whole church was caught up in spiritual renewal. Even the Gentiles saw the value of a Torah-faithful life and united with their Jewish brethren in zeal for the law. Jerusalem was quite pleased with this outcome and now takes the official position that although circumcision is not to be required of Gentile believers, neither is it to be forbidden. As an apostle, Paul is obliged to abide by this Jerusalem decision.

Perhaps the agitators also told the Galatians that at Antioch God supplies the Spirit and works powerfully among the Gentile believers there as a result of their Torah-faithfulness.

If the agitators made something of the Jewish believers' return to the law at Antioch and the consequences this had for the Gentiles there, we should expect Paul to respond by saying that what the Jewish believers did at Antioch was in fact wrong. For by showing that *Jewish believers* should not Judaize in a mixed church, he would in effect be removing all grounds for celebrating any Gentile imitation of Jewish-Christian loyalty to the Torah. Paul makes precisely this point in describing the Antioch episode. While the Jewish believers were eating with the Gentiles, they were walking in accord with the truth of the gospel; when they abandoned the Gentile table, they betrayed the gospel. Furthermore, it is this position that Paul defends theologically in the first part of his speech at Antioch, to which we now turn.

---

[20]So also Howard, who doubts that Peter had abandoned his circumcising campaign, as he calls it, by the time of Galatians (*Paul, Crisis in Galatia*, 45, with n. 142); cf. Schütz, *Paul and the Anatomy of Apostolic Authority*, 150-52. On the conflict at Antioch and its outcome, see further the comprehensive considerations of C. K. Barrett, "Pauline Controversies in the Post-Pauline Period," *NTS* 20 (1974): 230-31.

Paul's Speech

There is a general consensus among interpreters that Paul, in the "report" of his speech at Antioch (Gal 2:14b-21), addresses Peter and the Antioch community formally, but the Galatians materially.[21] This judgment is generally correct, although one should not press it too far. Clearly Paul rehearses this speech for the Galatians' sake, and at points he seems to speak past the Antioch situation as described in 2:11-13 and toward the Galatian horizon as we know it from 3:1ff. This suggests that Paul projects the Galatian situation to some extent onto Antioch. Nevertheless, it would be a mistake to interpret the speech without reference to Antioch, which is certainly in view in the opening (v. 14b). Furthermore, one has to give some consideration to the possibility that where the speech appears to leave the Antioch episode behind it may in fact be addressing the agitators' interpretation of what happened there. Hence, our attempt to understand the passage is complicated by the possibility that Paul's speech presupposes not only his own but also the agitators' version of the Antioch affair (recall the preceding discussion). Faced with these difficulties, our only recourse is to think through Paul's address with an eye to its relevance for the Galatians, paying attention to those points where the speech keeps the facts narrated in 2:11-13 in view and where it does not.

The method we have adopted leads us immediately to the following observation. Although it is easy to read 2:14b-18 as a response to the events recounted in 2:11-13, granting Paul's interpretation of Peter's action as "compelling" the Gentiles to Judaize, 2:19-20 seems to transcend the Antioch horizon. The enigmatic statement in verse 19 ("I through the law died to the law") remains opaque apart from what follows in 3:1-14, and the idea of "eschatological life" ("living to God" in v. 19 and "Christ living in me" in v. 20) is a central theme of the

---

[21]Albrecht Oepke, *Der Brief des Paulus an die Galater*, 4th ed., ThHK 9 (Berlin: Evangelische Verlagsanstalt, 1979) 87; Burton, *The Epistle to the Galatians*, 117; J. B. Lightfoot, *The Epistle of St. Paul to the Galatians* (Grand Rapids: Zondervan, 1957; reprint of 1865 ed.) 113-14; Hans Lietzmann, *An die Galater*, HNT 10 (Tübingen: J. C. B. Mohr [Paul Siebeck], 1910) 238; Schlier, *Der Brief an die Galater*, 87-88; Jürgen Becker, *Der Brief an die Galater*, NTD 8 (Göttingen: Vandenhoeck & Ruprecht, 1981) 29; Mussner, *Der Galaterbrief*, 145-46.

discussions to follow. Not until verse 21 does Paul return to the theme of "righteousness" that dominates verses 14b-18. Moreover, even the style of 19-20 suggests that the discussion proceeds in these verses at a new level. Although verse 19a is introduced by γάρ, we meet no more subordinating conjunctions in verses 19-20, while the use of loose connecting δέ and asyndeton imparts a certain elevated tone to this part of the speech.

The Line of Thought in 2:14b-18

Paul's rhetorical question to Peter in verse 14b serves as a kind of topic sentence for the first part of the paragraph: "But if you, being a Jew, live like a Gentile and not like a Jew, how can you compel Gentiles to Judaize?"[22] Although Paul's question in verse 14b sets both Peter's "not living Jewishly" and his "compelling Gentiles to live as Jews" in the present tense, the narrative in 2:12 shows that the present tense aspect of "not living Jewishly" is not to be pressed strictly, as if Peter's withdrawal from the Gentile table were not precisely the opposite of not living as a Jew. Schlier brings out the sense well in describing Peter's "not living Jewishly" as his customary behavior, which his present actions astonishingly contradict.[23]

But perhaps we can do still better justice to the present tense in Paul's description by viewing it as a rhetorical means whereby Paul draws Peter, even in his complaint against him, onto his own side. In the light of Peter's characteristic behavior prior to the arrival of the party from James, Paul treats Peter as one who no longer lives "Jewishly."[24] Consequently, when Peter abandons table fellowship with the Gentiles, he betrays the truth as he knows it and has been living it out up to this point. As Paul puts it in 2:12, Peter acts not out of conviction but out of fear. Therefore, the point of Paul's question in verse 14b is not simply that

---

[22]Paul indicates that by "Judaize" he means "to live Jewishly" (2:14); see further below.

[23]*Der Brief an die Galater*, 86.

[24]Burton draws attention to what he terms the "general present" (tense), which describes "a habit or mental attitude which, being illustrated by a recent act, may itself be assumed to be still in force." He cites as examples Mark 2:7; Matt 12:26 ff.; Acts 22:7,8; 23:3,4; and Ps 89:42, 43 (LXX) (*The Epistle to the Galatians*, 112).

Peter behaves *inconsistently,* but that Peter, as one who no longer lives as a Jew, knows that Gentiles are not summoned by the gospel to live as Jews. But that is not all. The point is also that Peter knows that the gospel does not require *Jews* to ''live as Jews.'' Not only that, in a mixed church Jews are to give up the law insofar as it determines the scope of Judaizing, particularly the observance of dietary laws, which impedes fellowship between Jews and Gentiles. In the argument that follows (vv. 15-18) it is this second issue that Paul pursues. The concern dominating these verses is whether Jews who live in Christ ''as Gentiles'' count as sinners before God. That is, was the custom of Peter and the other Jewish Christians to eat with the uncircumcised Gentile believers *wrong?*

Having begun his argument with the ''traditional'' polarization of being a Jew versus being a Gentile sinner (v. 15), which is manifestly the assumption by which the party from James operates at least to some extent, Paul goes on to make an observation that decisively relativizes this conventional[25] antithesis: ''Even we have believed in Christ Jesus'' (v. 16b). This point derives its argumentative force from two corners. One is the self-understanding that Paul identifies as the motivation for Jews putting their faith in Christ. The other is the fact (implied in ''even we'') that in turning to Christ ''we Jews'' found exactly the same solution to ''our plight'' as the Gentiles did to theirs.

The Jewish self-understanding that informs believing in Christ is, according to Paul, ''knowing that a person is not justified by works of the law but only through the faith of Jesus Christ'' (v. 16a). Two things are to be marked about the function of this sentence in Paul's argument. First, it is not the main point but a supporting statement. Second, Paul introduces it as *common ground* with Jewish Christians in general.[26] Therefore, to suggest, as some interpreters have, that this sentence is

---

[25]See, e.g., Matt 3:7-9 and *Jub.* 23:23-24; also the Jewish parallels adduced by Günter Klein, ''Individualgeschichte und Weltgeschichte bei Paulus,'' in *Rekonstruktion und Interpretation: Gesammelte Aufsätze zum Neuen Testament,* BET 50 (Munich: Chr. Kaiser Verlag, 1969) 182.

[26]This point is made also by Betz, who calls ''justification by faith'' in this context a piece of Jewish-Christian theology (*Galatians,* 115-17). Paul himself says ''we (Jewish Christians) know,'' which is how he often introduces accepted or well-known ideas or traditional formulae (see Rom 2:2; 3:19; 5:3; 6:9; 7:14; 8:22?; 8:28; 1 Cor 3:16?; 5:6; 6:2-3; 6:9; 6:15?; 6:16?; 6:19?; 8:1; 8:4; 9:13; etc.).

itself a rejection of Judaizing is to misunderstand its role in the context of Paul's argument.[27]

In order to understand the statement, "no one is justified by works of the law," as an expression of common Jewish-Christian faith, we must attend closely to Paul's language.[28] We may begin by observing that Paul uses the prepositions ἐx and διά. The expression "not justified by works of the law" does not say that "works of the law" constitute the wrong standard or, if construed as a person's *own* works, an inadequate empirical basis for "justification" in God's sight. In short, Paul does not write "a person is not justified *on the basis of* (χατά with accusative or ἐπί with dative) works of the law." He says that a person is not justified *by means of* the works of the law. Now in the Septuagint, the passive verb "be justified" (διχαιοῦσθαι) regularly means "be or become just or righteous,"[29] and we should understand the verb in Paul's sentence accordingly, since it is not a "divine passive." This is evident from the parallel formulation in Romans 3:20, where Paul includes the words "in his sight" (cf. Ps 142:2 LXX; Gal 3:11). The agent of this justification is not God but the person who would become righteous by means of "works of the law." Nevertheless, these works are not a person's own particular works but "the works of the law" as such.[30] Likewise the mode or instrument that Paul contrasts with "works of the law" is not a person's own particular "faith" but "the faith of Jesus Christ."[31]

---

[27]See, e.g., Becker: "Müsste die Gemeinde von Antiochia ihre Gesetzesfreiheit—die ja eine Neuerung war—legitimieren, lag nichts näher, als es in solchen Sätzen zu tun" (*Der Brief an die Galater,* 27). The sentences Becker has in mind are all those in Paul which affirm, as does Gal 2:16a, justification in Christ alone and not by works of the law.

[28]For a more detailed treatment of this sentence, see Cosgrove, "Justification in Paul: A Linguistic and Theological Reflection," *JBL* 106 (1987): 653-70.

[29]See M.-J. Lagrange, *Saint Paul: Épître aux Romains* (Paris: J. Gabalda, 1950) 126; Cosgrove, "Justification in Paul," 662 n. 25.

[30]As Ernst Lohmeyer observes, Paul never formulates ἔργα (or πίστις) in διχαιοῦν-constructions with a *genetivus auctoris*. From this he concludes rightly that "in unsere Wendung die Frage der menschlichen Erfüllung oder Nichterfüllung gar nicht hineinspielt." See Lohmeyer, *Probleme paulinischer Theologie* (Stuttgart: W. Kohlhammer, n.d.) 71.

[31]Recall the discussion of this expression in ch. 2 above, where we termed it "an eschatological reality" ("Jesus-Christ-Faith").

Finally, the sentence is formulated in retrospect. As Paul has it, Jewish Christians confess that "no one becomes righteous by works of the law." In so doing they acknowledge that formerly, prior to baptism into Christ, they were unjust and impotent to become just. As far as their relation to the power of sin, they were indeed like Gentile sinners.

It is not surprising that the apostle represents his axiom as common ground with Jewish believers. The sentence in Galatians 2:16a does not dispute the righteousness of the law and its demands. It rejects the capacity of the law (or doing the law) to alter the situation of the sinner apart from Christ. Jewish Christians who were willing to affirm the statement in Gal 2:16a might still have maintained that those who have been renewed by the Spirit of Christ should do the works of the law. They may have argued that although the law cannot in itself make a person righteous (deliver one from the power of sin), it does define the ethic to which one is obligated to Christ.[32] Paul himself affirms a qualified version of this view in Romans 8:1-8, for which there are Old Testament and other Jewish antecedents (Ezek 36:26-27; *Jub.* 1:21; *T. Lev.* 18:11; *T. Job* 48:2-3; IQS 4:20-21). But he does not include practices entailed in Judaizing within the horizon of his Christian ethic. Moreover, he is able to argue against Judaizing *on the basis of* the axiom of Gal 2:16a, as we shall now see.

In order to understand Paul's attack on Judaizing in 2:14b-18 and the significance of this attack for the problem at Galatia, it is necessary to have a clear understanding of the word "Judaize" and its relation to keeping the Torah. From the relatively few instances of this word ('Ιουδαΐζειν) in extant Greek literature, one gets the impression that it is not an insider's term for lawkeeping but an outsider's designation for the practice or assumption of a Jewish lifestyle. Of the three known examples where Jews employ the term (Esther 8:17 LXX; Josephus *J. W.* 2.454 and 2.463), two concern an inauthentic, opportunistic adoption of Jewish practices. There is also an instance in one of Alexander Polyhistor's summaries of material from Theodotus, a Hellenistic Jew or Samaritan who composed a poem in epic style about the rape of Di-

---

[32]Cf. Betz: "In view of the controversy in Galatia, it should be noted that the denial does not imply that 'the works of the Torah' do not need to be done. Denied is only that they produce justification before God" (*Galatians,* 117).

nah and the sack of Shechem, but it is not clear whether the use of the term "Judaize" stems from Theodotus himself or Alexander (see Euseb. *Praep. ev.* 9.22.5). The only other examples derive from non-Jewish sources (Plutarch *Vita Ciceronis* 7.5; *The Acts of Pilate* A, 2.1; Ignatius *Magn.* 10.3).[33] "Judaizing" refers to those practices that a non-Jew regarded as distinguishing the Jew from other members of society (typically circumcision, keeping the Sabbath and the Jewish festivals, and observing the Jewish dietary laws). Non-Jews in general despised these practices, and Jews tended, in response, to accentuate them.[34]

With the understanding that "Judaizing" is first of all an *ethnic* label, we can do justice to Paul's logic in 2:15-16. The train of thought is as follows. If, "knowing that a person does not become righteous by works of the law," Jews have become righteous in the same way as the Gentiles, then the distinction between Jews and Gentiles expressed in verse 15 falls away. It is this reduction of Jews and Gentiles to the same level in Christ that constitutes the repudiation of Judaizing,[35] which in turn has consequences for how Jewish believers are to understand their relation to the law. Most interpreters, however, reverse the argument and view the obviation of Judaizing as dependent on a prior rejection of the law as binding on believers, as if Paul's argument ran as follows: All believers in Christ are free from the law, hence Judaizing is not an obligation for those in Christ.[36] But Paul's argument here does not yet

---

[33]See further, G. W. H. Lampe, *A Patristic Greek Lexicon* (Oxford: Clarendon Press, 1961) s.v. Ἰουδαΐζειν.

[34]See J. L. Daniel, "The Origins of Anti-Semitism in the Hellenistic-Roman Period," *JBL* 98 (1979): 45-65 (esp. 51-54); Bilhah Wardy, "Jewish Religion in Pagan Literature during the Late Republic and Early Empire," in *Aufstieg und Niedergang der römischen Welt,* ed. H. Temporini and W. Hanse, *Principat,* vol. 19/1: *Religion* (Berlin/New York: Walter de Gruyter, 1979) 592-613. Menahem Stern, "The Jews and Greeks in Greek and Latin Literature," in *The Jewish People in the First Century,* ed. S. Safrai and M. Stern, Compendia Rerum Iudaicarum ad Novum Testamentum 1/2 (Philadelphia: Fortress Press, 1976) 1101-59; Gutbrod, *TDNT* 4:1049. See also A. E. Harvey, "The Opposition to Paul," in *Studia Evangelica,* vol. 4, ed. F. L. Cross, TU 102 (Berlin: Akademie-Verlag, 1968) 319-32. Harvey stresses rightly that the term does not mean "hold Jewish beliefs" but "adopt Jewish observances" (p. 322).

[35]So also Klein, "Individualgeschichte und Weltgeschichte bei Paulus," 184-85.

[36]See for instance, Becker, *Der Brief an die Galater,* 29-30; and Ulrich Wilckens,

depend on the presupposition that believers are free from the law, an idea that has not yet been introduced. Moreover, since the conviction that no one shall be justified by works of the law does not in itself imply that these works should not be done, it cannot be said to obviate Judaizing by implying that believers are free from the law. To be sure, the apostle is about to speak of being in Christ as "death to the law" (2:19), which suggests that the Torah does not have any authority over those in Christ. Nevertheless, at this point in the argument it is the obviation of Judaizing through the gospel that implies freedom from the law for those in Christ and not the reverse, an observation that reinforces our initial impression that the speech in 2:14b-21 does not comprise a single line of argument but divides into two loosely connected halves as Paul turns in verse 19 away from the Antioch horizon to address the Galatian issue more directly.

Whether or not Jewish Christians in general would have found Paul's appeal to common ground (2:16a) compelling is an interesting question. But the argument depends rhetorically on whether the *Galatians* find it persuasive. Since our investigation indicates that the question of the Galatians' status in Christ is not itself at stake in the letter, we have every reason to believe that the Galatians will have applauded the opening words of Paul's speech. Thus Paul's initial remarks really serve to lay out what the apostle presumes is common ground between himself and the Galatians in preparation for what is to follow.

The foregoing interpretation of verses 14b-16 illumines verses 17-18. If Paul has proven from a "common" understanding of "justification in Christ" that it is right for Jewish Christians *not* to Judaize in mixed churches, then verse 17 is evidently a *reductio ad absurdum:* "If, by seeking to be righteous in Christ, we have become sinners, then is Christ a servant of sin?!" Paul does not accept the judgment that the Jewish Christians at Antioch made themselves sinners by eating with the Gentiles. In his view, their actions were informed by their correct understanding of the socioethical implications of being in Christ. Therefore—and here is the *reductio*—if they became sinners by seeking

---

"Was heisst bei Paulus: 'Aus Werken des Gesetzes wird kein Mensch gerecht'?" in *Vorarbeiten,* pamphlet 1, ed. E. Schweizer et al., EKK, (Neukirchen: Neukirchener Verlag, 1969; Zürich: Benziger Verlag, 1969) 59-62.

to be righteous in Christ, then is Christ a servant of sin?[37] The apostle finishes off this little argument with a conventional rhetorical flourish: "Let it not be!" (μὴ γένοιτο). Now it is true that elsewhere in Paul μὴ γένοιτο following a question does not reject the premise of the argument but only the false inference contained in the rhetorical question itself (for example, Rom 3:5-6; 6:1-2), and this may account in part for the many tortuous attempts to interpret the statement, "we are found to be sinners" (v. 17a), as something Paul affirms.[38] But Paul is not bound to use μὴ γένοιτο rhetorically always in the same way, and it is instructive to note that Epictetus, who customarily employs this expression exactly as Paul does, also shifts his use of it in just one case, where he too develops a *reductio ad absurdum* (*Disc.* 4.7.25-27).

The first line of argument in Paul's speech concludes with an explanatory parenthesis: "For if I build up (reinstate) the things I tore down (for example, dietary laws as regulative for the church), then I show myself to be a transgressor (sinner as lawbreaker)" (v. 18). This statement clarifies verse 17a by explaining that when Peter and the others separated themselves from the Gentiles, they were in effect treating their former table fellowship as transgression, "showing themselves to be" transgressors by reinstating the regulations they had rejected.[39]

So far we have treated verses 14b-18 primarily in terms of the confrontation at Antioch. We must now reflect on the significance of these verses for the Galatians. The key to understanding the import of 2:14b-18 for the Galatian situation is to recognize that Paul employs an argument against Judaizing that should appeal to the Gentile Galatians as

---

[37]The interpretation advocated here has certain affinities with that of Rudolf Bultmann, "Zur Auslegung von Gal. 2, 15-18," in idem, *Exegetica: Aufsätze zur Erforschung des Neuen Testaments*, ed. Erich Dinkler (Tübingen: J. C. B. Mohr [Paul Siebeck], 1967).

[38]See, e.g., Schlier, *Der Brief an die Galater*, 95-96; Becker, *Der Brief an die Galater*, 30.

[39]For other ways of interpreting v. 18, see W. Mundle, "Zur Auslegung von Gal 2, 17.18," *ZNW* 23 (1924): 152-53; Jan Lambrecht, "The Line of Thought in Gal. 2.14b-21," *NTS* 24 (1977–1978): 484-95; Robert C. Tannehill, *Dying and Rising with Christ: A Study in Pauline Theology*, BZNW 32 (Berlin: Alfred Töpelmann, 1966) 56-57. My interpretation of this sentence depends upon my understanding that v. 17 has the Antioch situation still concretely in view.

a way of making a case against lawkeeping, which is what they need to hear. If the Galatians assent to Paul's contention that the Jewish Christians at Antioch did the right thing before God in living "as Gentiles" among the Gentiles, then they will see how foolish it is for them to expect that God would "supply the Spirit and work wonders among them" because of practices that entail Judaizing.

A Focal Shift in 2:19-21

Having used the episode at Antioch to make his case against Judaizing (vv. 14-18), Paul begins to speak more directly (vv. 19ff.) to what we recognize as the Galatian horizon. The focus of the speech is now explicitly the conditions under which one participates in eschatological life, conditions which include "death to the law" for the Jewish-Christian Paul: "I, through the law, died to the law that I might live to God." As the reference in verse 20 to Christ's crucifixion shows, Paul is not speaking about a purely inward experience but about Christ's death, in which he participates. According to Paul's postscript, this death has eschatological dimensions (6:14-15). Death with the crucified Christ means death to the world, even the crucifixion of the world in a qualified sense. He had already spoken in a similar vein in the epistolary prescript when he described Christ's self-offering "for our sins to deliver us from the present evil age" (1:4). It is appropriate to speak of the eschatology implied in such statements as "apocalyptic"[40] as long as one recognizes that the realized aspect of this eschatology touches believers in the world but not yet the cosmos itself, except as the cosmos touches believers ("and by which the cosmos has been crucified to me"). Since Paul equates his "death to the law through the law" with "crucifixion with Christ," the logic of verse 19 must depend on the thought that *Christ* died to the law through the law. Now the instrumentality of the law (διὰ νόμου) in Christ's death is evident in 3:13, where Paul says that Christ took upon himself the "curse of the law."[41] The idea that in so doing Christ also "died to the law" derives from the convic-

---

[40]See J. Louis Martyn, "Apocalyptic Antinomies in Paul's Letter to the Galatians," *NTS* 31 (1985): 410-24. Cf. Albert Schweitzer, *Die Mystik des Apostels Paulus* (Tübingen: J. C. B. Mohr [Paul Siebeck], 1981; reprint of 1930 ed.) 186.

[41]See Tannehill, *Dying and Rising with Christ*, 56-57.

tion that in dying and being raised from the dead, Christ was released from the world and its powers, both good powers, such as the law (cf. Rom 7:1-6) and evil ones, such as sin and death (cf. Rom 6:9-10). Therefore, those who share in Christ's death also participate, at least provisionally, in his release from the world, and in so doing "live to God."

In Jewish and Christian literature, the idea of "living to God" (ζῆν θεῷ) often refers to resurrection life. Of particular interest is 4 Maccabees 7:19, which contains what represented for both Jews and early Christians a vital *theo*-logical statement: " . . . believing that to God they do not die (θεῷ οὐκ ἀποθνήσκουσιν), just as our patriarchs Abraham and Isaac and Jacob do not (die) but live to God (ζῶσιν τῷ θεῷ)." One thinks immediately of Luke 20:37-38, where Jesus points to the fact that Moses called the Lord "the God of Abraham, the God of Isaac, and the God of Jacob" and concludes from this that God "is not the God of the dead but of the living, for all live to him (πάντες γὰρ αὐτῷ ζῶσιν)." A version of the same tradition is found also in 4 Maccabees 16:25, where it is also introduced as a well-known conviction of faith (ταῦτα εἰδότες), and examples abound in *Hermas*.[42] In Romans 6:10 Paul applies the expression to the resurrected Jesus and in Romans 6:11 to believers, who have died with Christ and are now dead to sin and alive to God. In so doing he combines both the ethical use of the expression (typical of Philo) and the eschatological. His argument there shows that he regards ethical living to God to be dependent upon sharing in eschatological life through Christ. In Galatians 2:19, however, he is not speaking of "living to God" as a form of new ethical existence but is trying to make the point that eschatological life as such comes through crucifixion with Christ and death to the law.[43]

---

[42]See George W. E. Nickelsburg, *Resurrection, Immortality, and Eternal Life in Intertestamental Judaism*, HTS 26 (Cambridge: Harvard University Press, 1972) 111 and 160.

[43]Interpreters have long been inclined to read Gal 2:19-20 through the lens of Rom 6, as if the question that these verses address were "What then? Shall we sin because we are not under the law but under grace?" (Rom 6:15). So Schlier, *Der Brief an die Galater*, 98-101; Mussner, *Der Galaterbrief*, 82 (final comment on v. 19); cf. Burton, *The Epistle to the Galatians*, 137. But this sort of question is never raised in Gal 2:14b-21. Unlike Rom 6:15, no such objection is stated, and the formulations in vv. 19-20 are not strictly *ethical*.

The significance of what Paul says in 2:19-20 can be brought out by comparing his assertions with the claim that "the one who does the works of the law shall live in the Spirit by them." Paul the Jewish Christian confesses that he found eschatological life only by dying to the law through crucifixion with Christ. The emphatic 'I' (ἐγώ) is first of all the 'I' of testimony, but as such it also carries exemplary force. The Christological form of the argument leads Paul to speak of life in the Spirit as "living to God" and "Christ living in me," which is natural enough inasmuch as the Spirit of Christ is also the Spirit of resurrection life (cf. Rom 8:9-11). The christological form of the argument also leads him to make what appear to be declarations of an overly realized eschatology, as if everything that holds true of the risen Christ can be ascribed to believers as well. Nevertheless, in using the perfect form of the verb "crucified" in verse 19, Paul qualifies this realized eschatology in a decisive way, suggesting that participation in Christ's crucifixion is not left behind when the believer is transferred into the sphere of Christ's life but remains the enduring "occasion" of that life in the world.

Paul interprets the statement of verse 19 by declaring: "*I* no longer live, but Christ lives in *me*, and what I live in the flesh I live by the Faith of the Son of God, who loved me and gave himself for me." If we treat "the faith of the Son of God" as an alternate formulation for "Christ-Faith," as the genitive constructions suggest we should, we will understand the ground or instrument (ἐν) of eschatological life to be Christ-Faith as a new eschatological reality brought into the world by God through the gift of his Son "in the fulness of time" (4:4) "to deliver us from this present evil age" (1:4). This Faith, as a metonymy for the gospel of Christ, mediates life in the Spirit ("Christ lives in me"). But here Paul also suggests that participation in Christ-Faith means obedience unto death ("who loved me and gave himself for me"), which only goes to show that Paul includes Christ-like love and faithfulness as a matter of course in his conception of participation in Christ-Faith, although it would be a mistake to assume that Christ's own "faith" is always in view when Paul speaks of the "Faith of Christ."[44] In 2:20 the switch to the title "Son of God" and the explicit reference to the Son's love and self-giving draw this element into focus and reinforce the thought that

---

[44]See the discussion of "Christ-Faith" above in ch. 2.

in some way ongoing participation in Christ's crucifixion is the "locus" or "occasion" (ἐν πίστει κ.τ.λ.) of eschatological life in the world (ἐν σάρκι). We shall pursue this suggestion further in chapter 6.

In verse 21a Paul declares, "I do not nullify the grace of God." This sentence reaffirms what Paul has already said in verses 17-18. Jewish-Christian freedom from the law does not contradict the gospel. There is no need to infer a charge against Paul behind the negative formulation in verse 21a. It is just as natural to hear in Paul's first-person denial the suggestion that the Galatians will end up nullifying the "grace" (χάρις) of God and losing the charismatic grace of the Spirit, if they do not follow Paul's word and example. Paul reinforces (γάρ) his statement by restating its premise in the form of an argument from the "necessity" of Christ's death: "For if righteousness were through the law, then Christ died for nothing" (v. 21b). E. P. Sanders thinks that these words disclose the real *reason* (as opposed to just another "argument") for Paul's view of the law:

> In the midst of a somewhat bewildering series of arguments, quotations, and appeals there seem to be two sentences in Galatians in which Paul states unambiguously not only what his position is (which is never in doubt), but *why* he holds it. . . . Put in propositional terms, they say this: God sent Christ; he did so in order to offer righteousness; this would have been pointless if righteousness were already available by the law (2:21); the law was not given to bring righteousness (3:21). That the positive statement about righteousness through Christ grounds the negative one about the law seems to me self-evident.[45]

It is remarkable that Sanders finds the key to Paul's teaching about righteousness and the law in a sentence like Galatians 2:21b (which he calls "dogmatic"[46]) when so little of Paul's specific teaching about these themes is implied by this statement.[47] In fact, 2:21b sounds like just the kind of argument one would use to reinforce a basic point of agreement

---

[45]*Paul, the Law, and the Jewish People* (Philadelphia: Fortress Press, 1983) 27. Recall the discussion above in ch. 1 of Sanders's distinction between "reasons" and "arguments" in Paul.

[46]Ibid., 111.

[47]For one thing, 2:21b does not imply that the law should not be done any more than the formula in 2:16 does (see above).

with one's dialogue partner. A believer in Christ who could affirm that "no one is righteous except through Jesus Christ" (2:16a) should have little trouble agreeing with the logic of saying that if righteousness were through the law, then Christ died for nothing. Paul's statement sounds "dogmatic" because he has reached a point of common ground with his readers that needs no further defense. This point (whether righteousness came by the law) is not the issue in Galatians but an important sub-theme, which Paul stresses here because it implies the impotence of the law (cf. 3:21-22) and because he is about to take it up again in 3:6ff. as a building block in his argument that works of the law do not bring the Spirit (see chapter 2 above).

By closing off his speech with an argument from Christ's death, Paul also provides a thematic link with the opening sentence of address to the Galatians: "Oh foolish Galatians! Who has cast this spell over you, before whose very eyes Christ was publicly portrayed as crucified?" The death of Christ figures centrally in the argument of 3:1-14. The Spirit comes in consequence of Christ's death (vv. 13-14) "for us," which is exactly what Paul was driving at in 2:19-20. But now that we have seen the connection between 2:19-20 and 3:13-14, the theme of the "one seed (heir)" that runs through the argument from 3:15-29 appears in a new light. The one seed Christ is the *crucified* Christ. To be "one" in him and thus to share his inheritance means union with him as the Crucified. Since Christ's crucifixion brings the inheritance of the Spirit that belongs to the one seed alone, only those who participate in Christ's *crucifixion* ("I am crucified with Christ") receive the promise of the Spirit ("live to God"). Participation in the crucified seed is the sole "condition" for receiving the Spirit. It is therefore also the irreplaceable one. The implications of this link between the cross and the Spirit for Paul's theology are quite profound, and one thinks immediately of the ways in which the apostle joins the "death" and "life" of Jesus in 2 Corinthians. In chapter 6 we shall explore the theme of "life in the Spirit through participation in Christ's death" in greater detail by treating it within the larger context of Paul's thought.

Conclusion

We may gather up the various results of our examination of the apostolic autobiography by considering how it prepares the audience both theologically and emotionally for the central argumentation in Galatians 3–4. The autobiography may be viewed as a story of how various representative characters, among whom Paul looms most prominently, have "recognized" and "walked before" the "truth of the gospel." Jerusalem "pillars," Jewish believers, one of Paul's coworkers, and Gentile believers all make their appearances on a stage that is continually occupied by the apostle himself. And each character or group becomes the occasion for Paul to reinforce his view of the gospel, appeal emotionally to the Galatians in subtle ways, or press the question of fidelity to the gospel.

Paul tells the Galatians that his uncircumcision gospel rests on a divine mandate, and in the course of the argument in Galatians 1 and 2 it becomes clear that this gospel carries with it a mandate that Gentiles not be circumcised. As proofs of his uncircumcision gospel Paul reminds the Galatians of both the private revelation he received at the time of his commission and the "public" divine attestation that his gospel (or "apostolate") enjoys on the mission field. The pillar apostles in Jerusalem also "recognize" the truth of Paul's gospel, but the way in which Paul speaks about the basis of this recognition shows that their opinions are not to serve in and of themselves as confirmation of Paul's gospel in the eyes of the Galatians. Instead, the testimony of the Jerusalem apostles provides the occasion for Paul to remind the Galatians subtly that they themselves, as the very products of God's activity through his mission, are in a privileged position to know the truth of the gospel. Hence, although the Jerusalem apostles no doubt carry considerable authority in the eyes of the Galatians, a fact that can only help in Paul's case here, the genius of Paul's presentation of his encounter with them is the way in which it elevates the Galatians above the Jerusalem pillars as "authorities" on the "gospel of the uncircumcision." Paul encourages the Galatians to see themselves as co-experts along with him on the uncircumcision gospel and in this way also predisposes them to listen to him rather than to the agitators.

The story of the Jewish Christians at Antioch is in many ways styled after Paul's view of the Galatians. The Jewish Christians at Antioch were faithful to the gospel until certain outsiders arrived promoting the law and lured them into disloyalty (cf. Gal 1:6-10). Furthermore, although the issue at Antioch is not the same as that at Galatia, the two situations are theologically related, since both the content of the gospel and the question of fidelity to the gospel are themes of the Antioch story that bear on the Galatian situation. In the first part of his "speech" Paul defends the former practice of the Jewish Christians (sharing the Gentile table) by articulating its theological basis (2:14-18). Jewish Christians are *not* to "Judaize" in a mixed church, and Paul leaves it to his readers to see the obvious significance of this for themselves. If Jewish Christians at Antioch are not to Judaize, it is foolish for Gentile Christians to imagine that lawkeeping (which entails Judaizing) on their part will meet with divine approval and blessing. At the same time the Galatians are to reject the negative example of the Jewish (and Gentile?) believers at Antioch and follow the positive example of the heroic Paul, who depicts himself throughout the narrative as the model par excellence of both a right self-understanding in the gospel and what it means to be a loyal servant of the gospel. The fact that Paul, as apostle to the Gentiles, is also apostle to the Galatians puts weight behind his exemplary ethos.

This last point gets at the heart of the autobiography. In the narrative and speech of Galatians 1–2 Paul is engaged in (re)establishing his apostolic identity. That identity includes his apostolic authority, to which the Galatians must submit—unless they are prepared to deny that God was in fact at work through Paul among them. By stressing his identity as apostle to the uncircumcised, Paul puts the Galatians' *own* identity at stake in their response to *his* apostolic identity and authority over them. Put positively, by heeding his authority the Galatians shall affirm their own primordial identity in Christ. The apostle also seeks to predispose the community to take his side in the controversy with the agitators by depicting himself as the one apostle, indeed the one Jewish Christian, who has demonstrated genuine loyalty to the Gentile cause. Even when everyone else abandoned the Gentiles, Paul stood up for them. In fact, the Galatians' very existence in Christ owes itself to the fact that despite every pressure, Paul never once yielded, "that the truth of the gospel might be preserved for you" (2:5).

Finally, while Paul's development and implementation of his apostolic ethos functions as a powerful emotional (*pathos*) appeal, his ethos also carries exemplary force in the narrative. Both Paul's fidelity to the gospel and his self-understanding in Christ serve as models for the Galatians to imitate. The emphatic 'I'-style in verses 19-20 suggests both aspects. Paul is still stressing his own faithfulness to the gospel (in contrast to Peter and the rest), but he is also giving expression to a self-understanding that is directly relevant to the issue at Galatia. The law does not mediate eschatological life in the Spirit. On the contrary, it is crucifixion with Christ as death to the law that inaugurates life in Christ. Thus, in Galatians 1–2 the establishment of Paul's *ethos*, which lends the letter its persuasive force, is closely linked with Paul's *word* to the community. Therefore, if "what counts most in deliberative oratory is the authority of the speaker" (Quintilian), one should mark in Galatians where the speaker declares:

I through the law died to the law, that I might live to God.

CHAPTER 5

The Apostolic Exhortation

And as, nevertheless, freedom over the world is dependent
on our union to God in Divine sonship (Rom. viii. 20),
so its basis, too, may properly be placed in the Holy Spirit.
We should be forbidden to take this view
only if the influence of the Holy Spirit
had always to be conceived as implying moral action.
For experiences of freedom over the world are not related
to the course of moral activity as its consequences,
even though they are conditioned
by the proper exercise of that activity.

—Albrecht Ritschl[1]

Since we live by the Spirit, let us also walk by the Spirit.

—Galatians 5:25

IN THE PRECEDING CHAPTER we considered Paul's apostolic autobiography in the light of the letter-body middle, 3:1–4:30, for which
it prepares. We shall now do the same for the apostolic exhortation. But
unlike the autobiography, the material we are about to consider does not

---

[1]*The Christian Doctrine of Justification and Reconciliation: The Positive Development of the Doctrine,* 2nd ed., ET ed. H. R. Mackintosh and A. B. Macaulay (Edinburgh: T. & T. Clark, 1902) 534.

prepare for the body middle; the body middle prepares for it. Therefore, in examining 4:31–6:10 we shall have to consider not only how Paul's preceding discussions shed light on this section (for us as "outside readers") but how they pave the way for it.

The apostolic exhortation depends on the theological argumentation that precedes it, but we shall see that it also furthers Paul's argument in two ways. Materially it clarifies the relationship between living by the Spirit and ethical activity. But it also has a more subtle rhetorical function, namely, to encourage the Galatians emotionally into heeding Paul's letter. Beginning with the confidence statement in 5:10, Paul treats the debate as settled and resumes normal pastoral relations with the Galatians by adopting the paraenetic mode of discourse. The effect is to re-create in the letter an atmosphere of pastoral care that simply assumes, and thereby encourages, the community's readiness to heed his word.

The Apostolic Warnings of 4:31–5:12

The very fact that the question of where the paraenesis[2] begins in Galatians is open to debate[3] draws attention to the transitional character of 4:31–5:12. Although the section contains little traditional paraenesis, the ethical theme of "love" that will dominate 5:13–6:10 does appear here for the first time in the letter (5:6). Furthermore, after the little diatribe in 5:7-12, where Paul issues brief statements regarding all the parties involved in the debate, this theme is immediately resumed, together with the motif of freedom announced already in 4:31.

In a statement that we have called a kind of "exhortative indicative," Paul declares that the Galatians are children of the *free* woman (4:31). The point, which the apostle immediately reformulates as an imperative in 5:1, is that the community should stand firm in freedom and not return to the old slavery in which they once found themselves (see especially 4:8-11). Now there are many ways in which a Gentile be-

---

[2]"Paraenesis" means here moral exhortation that makes use of traditional ethical materials. Paul's paraenesis in Galatians evidences creative use of stock sayings, which the apostle weaves into extended ethical arguments that are informed throughout by his own theological assumptions.

[3]See Otto Merk, "Der Beginn der Paränese im Galaterbrief," *ZNW* 60 (1969): 83-104.

liever might exchange freedom in Christ for bondage to the powers of the present age, but in Galatians this exchange threatens to take place when the community seeks the Spirit from the Torah, which in Paul's judgment amounts to treating Christ (and especially Christ's death) as insufficient for new life in the Spirit. That is why the reception of circumcision signifies apostasy from the gospel (5:2,4; cf. 1:6-9). No doubt the Galatians did not see things in quite these terms, but this is how Paul interprets their interest in the Torah and why he accuses them of having lost their minds (3:1).

After warning the Galatians in 5:2 that circumcision threatens to cancel their relationship with Christ, Paul makes a curious statement: "And I testify moreover (or "again") that anyone who gets circumcised is obliged to keep the whole law" (5:3). Most commentators think this sentence aims to discourage the Galatians from lawkeeping by stressing the quantitative magnitude of the obligation that circumcision entails: to do the *entire* law.[4] But after the forceful advances in verses 1 and 2, what a tentative step in the argument this would be, as if the Galatians would surely feel themselves unequal to a task that the obedient Jew takes for granted! It should be borne in mind that the chief hesitation encountered by Jews among potential Gentile proselytes was never the sheer number of the law's demands, which was hardly the burden that the non-Jew tends to imagine today, but circumcision itself.[5] The Gentile who submitted to circumcision had come to terms with the hard part of the Torah as far as he was concerned. Perhaps, then, we should understand the remark in verse 3 as an *ironic* challenge addressed to any of the Galatians who have already gotten circumcised that they should behave in accordance with their professed fidelity to the To-

---

[4]For a recent defense of this view, see Hans Hübner, *Law in Paul's Thought*, trans. James C. G. Greig and ed. John Riches (Edinburgh: T. & T. Clark, 1984) 18-19 and 36-39.

[5]See Neil J. McEleney, "Conversion, Circumcision and the Law," *NTS* 20 (1974): 332-33. According to Philo, circumcision was felt by pagans to be the most repugnant of all the Jewish laws (*Spec.* 1.1-11). W. L. Knox points out that the Septuagint tones down the references to circumcision in Deut 10:16 and 30:6. See Knox, *Paul and the Church of the Gentiles* (Cambridge: Cambridge University Press, 1961) 62 n. 3. The reluctance of would-be proselytes to get circumcised certainly had less to do with the pain than the shame involved.

rah by keeping the whole law, which Paul has taught them is fulfilled by *love* (cf. 5:6 and 5:14). Nevertheless, we are in a poor position to discern the precise sense of Paul's thought in verse 3, since he does not develop it any further but moves immediately to the theme of justification and the Spirit (5:4-6).

Verse 4 varies the warning of verse 2 but in so doing inaugurates a line of thought that leads Paul to his first positive statement of what the Galatians ought to be doing. The argument of verses 4-6 (note the use of γάϱ) defends the view that freedom in the Spirit exercised in love is the basis of future righteousness or justification. In putting his position on justification, the Spirit, and ethics in this way Paul reverses the "Galatian" way of ordering righteousness and the Spirit. Where they think of Torah-righteousness as a "ground" of ongoing life in the Spirit, Paul understands life in the Spirit to be the precondition of authentic ethical engagement, the ultimate justification of which remains future. At first sight this conception appears to stand in tension with Paul's assumption that righteousness is a precondition of receiving the Spirit. For he maintains that the curse of the law upon unrighteousness blocks the flow of the promise (3:10-14) and argues that God gives the blessing of the Spirit to the justified (3:6-9). But the tension dissolves once it is seen that Paul does not use the terminology of righteousness/justification strictly in his letters and that he speaks of two distinct justifications. The first is an initiatory eschatological event of reconciliation in which God accepts the ungodly as "sons" in Christ. The second is a final eschatological event of salvation, in which God vindicates cruciform existence.[6]

In verse 4 Paul calls the Galatians "you who are righteous in the law" and tells them that they are cut off from Christ and have fallen from grace. To take the verb δικαιοῦσθε ("you are righteous") as a conative present ("you want to be righteous") and then to interpret it as stating the express aim of the Galatians is to force the sense of Paul's sentence.[7] The phrase is descriptive, like Paul's "being blameless ac-

[6]See Cosgrove, "Justification in Paul: A Linguistic and Theological Reflection," *JBL* 106 (1987): 653-70.

[7]Most commentators and translators treat the δικαιοῦσθε as a conative present (so

cording to righteousness in the law'' in Phil 3:6,[8] and the sentence expresses the irony that the "Torah-righteous" Galatians are going to get quite the opposite of what they expect from the law. Although it may be that very few of the Galatians have already submitted to circumcision, Paul's present tense ("you are righteous in the law") suggests that many of them are practicing the law at least to some extent already (see also 4:10). Moreover, it may be that Paul simply treats the Galatians as if they had in fact gone ahead with the law, an assumption that the apostle might have adopted in view of the long interval between the departure from Galatia of those who brought him news about the Galatian "crisis" and the arrival of Paul's letter in Galatia (at least two weeks and probably well over a month or more[9]). That is, Paul really must reckon with "two" Galatian situations, the situation as it was when the report left Galatia and the situation as it will be when the Galatians get Paul's letter. That being the case, it is not surprising that at some points he speaks as if the Galatians had not fully acted on the agitators' advice (1:6; 4:21) and at other points treats them as lawkeepers (4:10; 5:4; cf. 5:7). The apostle's temporal and geographical distance from the Galatians occasions within him an uncertainty about the community that finds heartfelt expression in 4:20 ("I wish I could be there with you and change my tone, for I am perplexed about you"), but there is also some rhetorical advantage to treating the community now under one assumption, now under the other. It lets Paul pronounce the severest of judgments on the Galatians without closing the door on their future in Christ. It lets

---

the *RSV:* "you who would be justified by the law"). The almost universal assumption that the Galatians are interested in the law "for justification" as an end in itself and not as a means to something else lies behind this tendency to find here the relatively rare conative use of the present.

[8]The passive form διχαιοῦσθαι typically means "be righteous" in the Septuagint, and we may have a "subjective" present. Cf. Theophylact, ὡς ὑπολαμβάνετε (*PG* 984B).

[9]If Paul was at Ephesus and the Galatians were in "South Galatia," the round-trip correspondence would have required at least two weeks by government (military) post. If, as is far more likely, a greater distance lay between them and the correspondence was delivered by persons traveling on foot, then we should reckon with at least seven weeks and probably longer. My calculations are based on the information about letter carrying in the Roman world in *A Dictionary of the Bible,* Extra Volume, ed. James Hastings (New York: Charles Scribner's Sons, 1909) 375-402.

him underscore the seriousness of what they are doing (by speaking as if all is lost) and at the same time express confidence in them (5:10).

The use of the verb "to be justified" in verse 4 indicates that the "hope of righteousness" in verse 5 includes the hope of future justification. If we read verses 4-6 in the light of the Galatian letter's specific occasion, the following interpretation suggests itself. The agitators advocate living justly according to the law in order to promote ongoing life in the Spirit. Paul reiterates that life in the Spirit comes from faith and emphasizes that justification is ultimately a future hope that depends upon whether one has lived a life characterized by "faith working through love" (v. 6). According to this interpretation, "by faith" in verse 5 modifies not the verb but the dative noun "by/in the Spirit" (πνεύματι). The expression, "by the Spirit from faith," is shorthand for the now familiar axiom that the Spirit comes from faith (3:2, 5, 14), the phrase "from faith" functioning adjectivally in this construction. Burton is one of the few commentators who even considers this possibility. He observes that the interpretation "by a Spirit which is received by faith" is "neither gramatically impossible . . . nor un-Pauline in thought," although in his judgment "the nature of the relation which this interpretation assumes between πνεύματι and ἐκ πίστεως is such as would probably call for πνεύματι τῷ ἐκ πίστεως."[10] But it must be pointed out that the article is indicated only when the adjective defines, restricts, or limits its substantive. In Galatians 5:5 "the Spirit" is not being defined or restricted, hence the predicate position is most appropriate:

> attributive position: "the Spirit which is from faith"
> predicate position: "the Spirit, which is from faith, . . . "

As a predicate adjective, the prepositional phrase makes an additional statement about the Spirit, namely, that one receives it by faith.[11]

---

[10]*A Critical and Exegetical Commentary on the Epistle to the Galatians* (Edinburgh: T. & T. Clark, 1921) 278.

[11]Cf. ἡ ἐπαγγελία ἐκ πίστεως in 3:22; ἡ δέησις πρὸς τὸν θεὸν in Rom 10:1. See Herbert Weir Smyth, *Greek Grammar,* rev. G. M. Messing (Cambridge: Harvard University Press, 1956) 295; Nigel Turner, *Syntax,* vol. 3 of James H. Moulton, *A Grammar of New Testament Greek* (Edinburgh: T. & T. Clark, 1963) 221-23. Because πνεύματι is anarthrous, the ἐκ πίστεως could still be taken as attributive. But we should understand πνεύματι as definite here, since it is the Spirit (cf. 5:25).

The statement "We wait in (or by) the Spirit" describes believers as ethically engaged (cf. "walking by the Spirit," 5:25) in expectation that their labors will find fulfillment and vindication in the future kingdom. The verb "wait" (ἀπεκδέχεσθαι) points to the eschatological judgment (cf. 1 Cor 1:7; Phil 3:20; Heb 9:28; Rom 8:19, 23, 25). As in Romans 8:25, this "waiting" means obedient living for the future and not merely "expectation" by itself. Verse 6 specifies this "ethical waiting in the Spirit" as "faith working through love" and implies that "faith working through love"[12] is what "counts" (ἰσχύει) not simply in a general sense but in the specific sense of "for justification." Since the debate in Galatians is not over "justification" as such, Paul can use justification language in a variety of ways (2:16,17; 3:8; 3:11; 3:24; 5:4-5) without clarifying how all of his justification statements hang together. In 5:4-6 he is on the offensive. If the Galatians are interested in getting more of the Spirit by "being righteous in the law," Paul wants them to know that the order by which the Spirit and personal righteousness are related to one another is quite the reverse: "By the Spirit, which we have from faith, we wait for the hope of righteousness." Ethical life in the Spirit forms the basis for future righteousness (justification); present righteousness (right living)—and certainly not the righteousness the Galatians think they have in the law—does not bring the Spirit.[13]

Paul follows up the argument of 5:4-6 with a flurry of somewhat disjointed declarations and warnings that are held together by the fact that they touch on all the parties in the debate: the Galatians, the agitators, and Paul himself. The apostle expresses confidence in the Galatians, castigates the agitators, and depicts himself as faithful to the crucified Christ. We will have occasion to consider this last motif in chapter 6. What interests us here is Paul's statement of confidence in the Galatians, which he reinforces by insinuating that the agitators (not the Ga-

---

[12]In 6:15 Paul calls it "new creation," an expression which suggests new life in the Spirit, particularly in view of the way in which τῷ κανόνι τούτῳ στοιχήσουσιν (6:16) recalls πνεύματι καὶ στοιχῶμεν in 5:25. The use of the term κανών may be for the sake of alliteration: καινὴ κτίσις . . . τῷ κανόνι.

[13]Cf. the comment of Chrysostom on Gal 5:5: "Faith suffices to obtain the Spirit for us and through it (the Spirit) righteousness" (ἀρκεῖ γὰρ ἡ πίστις ἡμῶν πνεῦμα παρασχεῖν καὶ δι' αὐτοῦ δικαιοσύνην). See *PG* 61.666.

latians) are really to blame for everything. In 5:10 Paul declares his
certainty that "you will take no other view than mine" and from this
point on never expresses another doubt about whether the Galatians will
heed his word, although he does level additional harsh criticism at the
agitators. It is as if he has won the debate with the Galatians and must
now get on with the business of pastoral upbuilding. We shall consider
the rhetorical significance of this in connection with the paraenetic exhortation as a whole, to which we now turn.

Pastoral Exhortation (5:13-6:10)

Three questions related to the paraenesis have proved particularly
vexing to interpreters of Galatians in the past. (1) Why does Paul find
it necessary to issue ethical exhortation to lawkeepers? (2) How can Paul
proclaim freedom from the law in Galatians 1–4 and then go on to "lay
down the law" in Galatians 5–6? (3) What is the relation of the ethical
demands in Paul's exhortation to the ethical demands of the Torah? Each
of these questions rests on the assumption that the debate over the law
in Galatians concerns its value or appropriateness as a way of regulating
the ethical life of those in Christ. But if the issue in Galatians is rather
the efficacy of the law in promoting eschatological life in the Spirit, these
questions are cast in a different light. As we shall see, the first question
is not as puzzling as it seems, the second question depends on a misunderstanding of "freedom from the law" in Galatians, and the third,
although legitimate, is not a concern of the letter.

The Occasion and Rhetorical Function of the Exhortation

We may begin with the question of the occasion or motivation for
the paraenesis. James H. Ropes put the problem by asking what place
an attack on the dangers of libertinism (5:13ff.) has in a letter aimed at
Judaizers?[14] According to F. C. Baur, Paul adds the exhortative portion
to the letter in order to forestall any libertinistic misinterpretation or
misrepresentation of "freedom from the law" as set forth in the "dog-

---

[14]*The Singular Problem of the Epistle to the Galatians,* HTS 14 (Cambridge MA:
Harvard University Press, 1929).

matic'' part of the epistle.[15] But sentences such as 5:15, ''If you bite and devour one another, take care that you are not destroyed by one another,'' would be out of place if the paraenesis were simply a preventative or defensive measure. Wilhelm Lütgert, and after him Ropes, maintained that in Galatians Paul argues on two fronts, on one hand against Judaizers and on the other hand against libertines. The ethical exhortation is said to be aimed at the second group.[16] The artificiality of this solution was soon exposed by Walter Schmithals, among others, whose own solution is in effect to conflate the two factions posited by Lütgert and Ropes into one group of ''Jewish-Christian gnostics.'' According to Schmithals, the agitators are not Judaizers but libertinistic spiritualists who advocate circumcision as a rite of gnostic initiation.[17] Finally, we should mention H. D. Betz, who interprets the paraenesis as a ''defense of the Spirit.'' According to him, the Galatians, far from being libertines, are very much concerned about problems of the ''flesh'' and have turned to the Torah to remedy them.[18] He concludes:

> One cannot escape the impression that it [the problem as the Galatians saw it] was related to emancipation (cf. 3:26-28) and to lack of a new code of law which would specify for the Christian what is right and what is wrong.[19]

---

[15]*Paul, the Apostle of Jesus Christ,* ET of 2nd German ed. issued post. by E. Zeller, 2 vols. (London/Edinburgh: William and Norgate, 1873 and 1875) 1:263.

[16]See Ropes, *The Singular Problem of the Epistle to the Galatians;* Lütgert, *Gesetz und Geist: Eine Untersuchung zur Vorgeschichte des Galaterbriefes* (Gütersloh: Bertelsmann, 1919).

[17]''Die Häretiker in Galatien,'' *ZNW* 47 (1956): 25-67; revised in *Paulus und die Gnostiker,* TF 35 (Hamburg/Bergstedt: Herbert Reich, 1965) 9-46; further revised by the author and translated by John E. Steely in *Paul and the Gnostics* (Nashville/New York: Abingdon Press, 1972) 13-64. See also ''Judaisten in Galatien?'' *ZNW* 74 (1983): 27-58.

[18]*Galatians: A Commentary on Paul's Letter to the Churches in Galatia,* Hermeneia (Philadelphia: Fortress Press, 1979) 8-9, 28-33. See also J. Louis Martyn, ''Apocalyptic Antinomies in Paul's Letter to the Galatians,'' *NTS* 31 (1985): 410-24.

[19]*Galatians,* 273.

Paul is said to respond by demonstrating the ethical sufficiency of authentic life in the Spirit.[20]

Both Schmithals and Betz succeed in reconstructing a plausible occasion *at Galatia* for Paul's paraenesis. If the Galatians have come under the sway of "pneumatic libertinism" (Schmithals), it makes perfect sense that Paul should say, for instance: "If we live by the Spirit, let us *also* walk by the Spirit" (5:25). But a sentence like this is equally intelligible under the assumption that the Galatians are turning away from the Spirit to the law in order to manage problems with the flesh (Betz), a theory that fits especially well with the following declaration: "But I say, walk by the Spirit and you will not fulfill the passions of the flesh" (5:16). Nevertheless, Schmithals's reconstruction has one distinct advantage over that of Betz. It accounts for Paul's *paraenetic warnings* in a way that Betz's theory cannot. Each subsection (paragraph) of the paraenesis contains one of these warnings:

> If you bite and devour one another, take care that you do not destroy one another. (5:15)
>
> I warn you, just as I have already told you, that those who do such things (the works of the flesh) shall not inherit the kingdom of God. (5:21)
>
> Look to yourself, lest you be tempted as well. (6:1b)
>
> Do not be deceived; God is not mocked. (6:7)

Why does Paul find it necessary to issue these warnings, if the Galatians, far from taking transgressions lightly, are "quite concerned that such instances would destroy their hope of salvation in Christ" (Betz)?[21] The statement in 5:21, with its weighty introduction ("I am warning you just as I told you before . . . "),[22] is especially damaging to Betz's theory.

---

[20]Ibid., 28 and 277-78 (on 5:16); also idem, "In Defense of the Spirit: Paul's Letter to the Galatians as a Document of Early Christian Apologetics," in *Aspects of Religious Propaganda in Judaism and Early Christianity,* ed. E. Schüssler Fiorenza (Notre Dame IN: University of Notre Dame Press, 1976) 99-114.

[21]*Galatians,* 273.

[22]David E. Aune suggests that 5:21 reproduces a prophetic oracle that Paul pronounced when he was first with the Galatians. He now repeats it in a letter that is to be read aloud in public worship. See Aune, *Prophecy in Early Christianity and the Ancient Mediterranean World* (Grand Rapids: Eerdmans, 1983) 258.

The advantage of Schmithals's reconstruction is that by positing moral laxity on the part of the Galatians as a *consequence* of the agitators' teaching, it allows one to interpret the warning tone of the paraenesis as an integral part of Paul's response to the Galatian problem. In what follows we shall attempt to preserve this insight by seeking to discern the relationship between the problem at Galatia and Paul's ethical exhortation, without adopting the unlikely assumption that the Galatians have become both lawkeepers and libertines.

On close examination, it is not at all certain that 5:13ff. concerns itself with the sorts of practices one associates with libertinism. In fact, if the paraenesis has a recurring refrain, it is the exhortation against *rivalry* and its concomitants: "enmity, contention, jealousy, anger, disputes, dissensions, party strife, envy." The enumeration just cited belongs to a list of vices ("works of the flesh") in 5:19-21. This list begins with "fornication, impurity, licentiousness, idolatry, and magic" and concludes with "drunkenness, revelry, and the like." One gets the impression that Paul has loaded a traditional vice list (cf. 1 Cor 6:9-10) with sins of community strife, in order to make the point that *rivalry* is to be taken as seriously as the more obvious "sins of the flesh."[23] This interpretation finds confirmation in the fact that Paul announces the theme of rivalry already in 5:13-15 by exhorting the community to mutual love and warning them against "biting and devouring one another." Not only that, the section on the "two ways" (5:19-26) closes with the rhetorical cohortative, "Let us not be conceited, provoking one another and envying one another" (5:26).

The sentence just quoted leads to a more specific exhortation in 6:1, where Paul addresses the Galatians, or a group of them, with what is evidently their own self-description: "the pneumatic ones."[24] We should note that the apostle introduces this appellation midsentence in a construction already introduced by a vocative ("brothers") and that the content of his statement is the use of gentleness in dealing with acts of

---

[23]Cf. Burton Easton, "New Testament Ethical Lists," *JBL* 51 (1932): 5.

[24]See also Betz, *Galatians,* 297; Schlier, *Der Brief an die Galater,* 5th ed., MeyerK 7/14 (Göttingen: Vandenhoeck & Ruprecht, 1981) 271; Schmithals, "Die Häretiker in Galatien," 58ff. (original essay); Lütgert, *Gesetz und Geist,* 13. Of course, it cannot be proven that this is a community self-designation.

transgression in the community. Paul is insinuating that it is precisely in understanding themselves as "spiritual ones" that the Galatians tend to be self-righteously heavy-handed in community discipline. The remainder of the paragraph reinforces this inference, particularly the warning, "If anyone thinks he is something, when he is nothing, he deceives himself" (6:3), which is followed by an admonition not to boast through comparisons of oneself with one's neighbor (6:4).

It is certainly not difficult to imagine that divisions were caused at Galatia over the question of taking up the Torah, especially if some members of the community had already begun practicing the law and were claiming that God "supplies the Spirit" to them and "works wonders" among them because of their lawkeeping. Division and rivalry belong characteristically among the consequences of the entry of a new and highly-charged impulse into the life of a social group, and the outsiders who have come to Galatia introduce exactly that. The very fact that Paul uses the terms "agitate" (ταράσσω) and "unsettle" (ἀναστατόω) to characterize the activity of the outside teachers (1:7 and 5:10,12) suggests that from what he has heard the Galatians have not made a peaceable transition to a Torah-ordered existence but are in a state of commotion. In that case, the Torah-promoting campaign of the teachers at Galatia occasions both the "dogmatic" portion of the letter and the paraenesis. Nevertheless, we should not assume that the paraenesis is simply a piece of concerned pastoral advice "addressed to persons who really needed it."[25] It is to Paul's advantage to find occasion for pastoral exhortation in Galatians, for the mode of exhortation has its own rhetorical value.

We may begin our consideration of the rhetorical function of the paraenesis by recalling the confidence statement in 5:10. This statement inaugurates a mood in the letter that will prevail to the end. With this announcement Paul begins to create an epistolary atmosphere of normalcy in his pastoral-apostolic relations with the community. He treats the debate as settled and turns to address the problem of community rivalry and dissension that it has occasioned (5:13ff.). This explains why the exhortation in 5:13–6:10 seems somewhat disconnected from the

---

[25]Ropes, *The Singular Problem of the Epistle to the Galatians,* 23.

main body of argument in the letter.[26] The move to extended ethical exhortation is in part a rhetorical tactic whereby Paul pretends to put the arguments of Galatians 3–4 behind himself and the community as a way of demonstrating confidence that the Galatians are indeed on his side and will remain loyal to the gospel. Thus the continuation of the letter in a paraenetic mode represents a strategy of positive emotional (*pathos*)[27] appeal to the community.

At the same time, the tone of the exhortation is often harsh and accusatory. Such attacks on the Galatians' honor carry the implied message that Paul does not doubt for a moment their readiness to submit to his authority. For outside the context of an intact relation of dependence, such statements would constitute a challenge to which the community and especially its leaders would probably feel socially obliged to meet by demonstrating that they are in the right.[28] But as the apostle to the Gentiles and the founder of the community, two facts that he has already underscored in the letter, Paul has every right in the eyes of his audience to speak to them in this way, and by speaking to them in the pastoral voice of exhortation he binds them to his word. To this extent the exhortation in 5:13–6:10 reestablishes Paul's authority in the community not by arguing for it but by *exercising it*. It lets him restore an atmosphere of normalcy in his pastoral relations with the Galatians in which they are likely to find themselves assenting to what he says and in assenting submitting themselves once again to his apostolic author-

---

[26]The problem of the ostensible disconnection of the paraenesis from the letter body is the subject of a dissertation by Douglas K. Fletcher, "The Singular Argument of Paul's Letter to the Galatians" (Ph.D. diss., Princeton Theological Seminary, 1982).

[27]On specific instances of *pathos* appeals in Galatians 5–6, see Steven John Kraftchick, "Ethos and Pathos Appeals in Galatians Five and Six: A Rhetorical Analysis" (Ph.D. diss., Emory University, 1985). Kraftchick considers the paraenesis from the standpoint of how ethos and pathos appeals were used in classical rhetoric as integral elements of persuasion. Although he does not make the specific point that I am pressing, his understanding of 5:1-12 tends in the same direction: "First Paul attempts to reestablish a sense of communion with the readers by means of an extended interaction between ethos and pathos appeals (5:1-12)" (231).

[28]A challenge to honor can occur only between persons who perceive themselves as equals in status. See Bruce J. Malina, *The New Testament World: Insights from Cultural Anthropology* (Atlanta: John Knox Press, 1981) 25-50 ("Honor and Shame: Pivotal Values of the First-Century Mediterranean World").

ity. Thus the paraenetic mode of address is as important as the material content of the paraenesis, which suggests that Paul may well engage in exhortation at the end of Galatians for the sake of the rhetorical advantages it affords him.

Freedom and Obligation in Galatians

In discussing Galatians 5–6 C. K. Barrett comments on what he calls the "paradox of Paul's ethics," that by stressing freedom in Galatians 3–4 in such apparently uncompromising terms, the apostle makes it difficult for himself "to pass over into the realm of ethics."[29] But this widely held view of "freedom" and "ethics" in Galatians misses the point of Paul's statements about "redemption" and "freedom." The freedom of which Paul speaks in 4:31 and 5:1 is not freedom from commandments[30] as such but freedom from slavery "under sin." To be sure, Paul equates being under the power of sin with existence "under the law," but this has nothing to do with whether believers are obligated to conform to certain ethical norms, whether these norms happen to be found in the law or not. In Galatians Paul develops the metaphor of slavery under the law-pedagogue as a way of expressing the idea that existence under the law means waiting for (not possessing) the "inheritance" (the Spirit), hence life without access to the Spirit. This situation is desperate because those in waiting have no hope in themselves that they will come of age and receive "the goods of the estate." They are bound by the power of sin and legally sealed under the verdict of God's righteous law. This verdict, which is the curse of the law, blocks the blessing and keeps it from flowing to those under the law. Freedom from the law in Galatians means redemption from this subjection, not from law or commandments as such. The status of the Torah as *ethic* is touched by this redemption not because Christ frees believers from material ethical norms but because this redemption is for both Jew and

---

[29]*Freedom and Obligation in Paul: A Study of the Epistle to the Galatians* (Philadelphia: Westminster Press, 1985) 56.

[30]According to Rudolf Bultmann, e.g., Christian obedience as Paul conceives it is characterized by "*freedom from all human conventions and norms of value.*" See Bultmann, *Theology of the New Testament*, 2 vols. trans. K. Grobel (New York: Charles Scribner's Sons, 1951 and 1955) 1:343.

Gentile. Since the ethos of the law is ethnically exclusive, the law is superseded by the gospel and has no authority in the church. In this sense also believers are free from the law. "Death to the law" effects both kinds of freedom from the law. It transfers a person out of the sphere of the law, where the curse has fallen irrevocably and where the people of God are defined ethnically. Freedom from the curse is a *liberation;* freedom from the commandments that define Judaizing is an *obligation* of both Jew and Gentile in Christ. To confuse this second freedom with the first leads to the mistaken impression that the gospel means liberation from commandments (or from "legalism"). But where Paul speaks of freedom from specific ethical norms he never means freedom as liberation but always freedom as ethical obligation.[31]

The Relation of Material Obligations in Christ to the Torah

The question that arises out of the preceding discussion is how the specific ethical norms that are to govern the life of the church are to be understood in relation to the law. This question arises *for us* when we observe Paul issuing ethical admonition in the form of Hellenistic-Jewish paraenesis, quoting Leviticus 19:18 ("love your neighbor") as an obligation binding upon the believer (5:14), and introducing the concept of "Christ's law" (6:2).[32] Most interpreters treat the paraenesis in Galatians as if it purported to address questions regarding the ethical value of the law, the nature of Christian ethics, the ethical shape of free-

---

[31] 1 Cor 9:19-23 is the *locus classicus* for Paul's theology of freedom for service. See among other helpful discussions of this topic, Birger Gerhardsson, *The Ethos of the Bible,* trans. Stephen Westerholm (Philadelphia: Fortress Press, 1981) 63-92.

[32] Various meanings for this expression have been suggested. See Donald Stoicke, "The 'Law of Christ': A Study of Paul's Use of the Expression in Galatians 6:2" (Th.D. diss., School of Theology at Claremont, 1971); C. H. Dodd, "ΕΝΝΟΜΟΣ ΧΡΙΣ-ΤΟΥ," in *Studia Paulina: In Honorem J. de Zwaan* (Haarlem: Bohn, 1953) 96-110; W. D. Davies, *Paul and Rabbinic Judaism,* 4th ed. (Philadelphia: Fortress Press, 1980) 144; Peter Stuhlmacher, *Reconciliation, Law, & Righteousness: Essays in Biblical Theology,* ET (Philadelphia: Fortress Press, 1986) 116-19 with 123-28 (on p. 87 of the same volume, in a later essay, he proposes a different interpretation). In my own view, Paul himself introduces this language into the discussion and means by it the law of love as exemplified by Christ. Rom 15:1-4 provides the closest parallel to our text (cf. 2 Cor 8:9; Phil 2:5ff.). See also Richard B. Hays, "Christology and Ethics in Galatians: The Law of Christ," *CBQ* 49 (1987): 268-90.

dom from the law, and so forth, when Paul's views on such matters are not the subject but the presupposition of what he says in the paraenesis. The very fact that Paul makes no effort to defend his appeals to "law" in Galatians 5–6 shows that he does not view the problem at Galatia to be a dispute over ethics, hence the questions that arise in our minds are not within his epistolary purview. It is surely in part for this reason that it is so difficult to reconstruct Paul's "ethical theory" from Galatians, which explains why those who have attempted to do so have tended either to produce artificial reconstructions in an attempt to demonstrate the unity and logic of Paul's ethical reflection or to conclude that the apostle is at best unsystematic in his thinking and perhaps simply incoherent.[33]

Any attempt to do justice to Paul's ethical theory in Galatians would have to begin by recognizing that whatever theory guides his exhortation, from his use of the "love commandment" (Lev 19:18) to his appeal to the "law of Christ" (Gal 6:2), belongs for the most part to that great domain of assumptions that the apostle presumes to share with his readers. It is important to observe that Paul appeals to the love commandment and the law of Christ without any explanation or justification. This makes sense only if the apostle had already, presumably during his founding visit, taught the Galatians how one's ethical obligation in Christ relates materially to the teachings of the Torah. This is not to say that the assumptions Paul presumes to share with his readers on this point must comprise a neat and perfectly consistent theory. We simply are not sufficiently informed by Paul on this question. In Galatians, for example, Paul does not address the *question* of ethics; he issues ethical exhortation. Furthermore, the theoretical question that does lie near at hand is not how concrete ethical obligations in Christ relate to the commandments of the law, but how the Spirit is related to the fulfillment of concrete ethical obligations in Christ. Yet Paul does not address this

---

[33]See E. P. Sanders, *Paul, the Law, and the Jewish People* (Philadelphia: Fortress Press, 1983) 93-122 and Heikki Räisänen, *Paul and the Law,* WUNT 29 (Tübingen: J. C. B. Mohr [Paul Siebeck], 1983). Both Sanders and Räisänen present telling criticisms of all attempts to unify Paul's statements about law and ethics into a coherent whole, even when coherence is posited only for each letter separately in a developmental scheme. But neither Sanders nor Räisänen considers the possibility that the coherence they find lacking (especially in Galatians) may exist in the assumptions Paul shares with his readers based on his previous teaching.

question either. Instead he simply orders the Spirit and obedience in such a way that the material connection of the exhortation with the preceding argumentation of the letter is manifest to the reader. It is this connection that we have now to explore.

Obedience and Life in the Spirit

There are six statements about the Spirit within the paraenesis:

Walk by the Spirit and you will not satisfy the passion of the flesh. (5:16)

For the flesh wars against the Spirit and the Spirit against the flesh— for these two are opposed to each other—so that you would not do the things (the fleshly works?) that you want to do. (5:17)

And if you are led by the Spirit, you are not under the law. (5:18)

But the fruit of the Spirit is love, joy . . . ; against such there is no law. (5:22-23)

Since we live by the Spirit, let us also walk by the Spirit. (5:25)

The one who sows to the Spirit shall reap from the Spirit eternal life. (6:8)

Each of these statements (except 6:8) belongs to a relatively unified section stretching from 5:16 to 5:25-26. Paul begins this section of exhortation by declaring, "But I say *walk by the Spirit* . . . ," and he concludes with the cohortative, "If we live by the Spirit, let us also *walk by the Spirit*," which thus forms an inclusio. Therefore, we may understand 5:16 as a kind of topic sentence for the unit and 5:25 as a brief summary of Paul's exhortation. This observation underscores the significance of 5:25 for the paraenesis as a whole.[34] Not only does 5:25 give a summary statement to what is manifestly the central core of Paul's exhortation, it serves as the general imperative upon which Paul's specific paraenetic attack on infighting rests (see v. 26). Therefore, we may view 5:25 as both a summary of the preceding and a topic sentence for

---

[34]Cf. Schlier: "Noch einmal nimmt der Apostel in V. 25 den Grundgedanken des ganzen Abschnittes [5:13-6:10] auf . . . " (*Der Brief an die Galater*, 268).

what follows.[35] According to 5:16-24, the Spirit is itself the power that enables "walking by the Spirit" (vv. 16-18), and believers are summoned to live in accordance with the aims of the Spirit (5:19-24). Thus, 5:16-24 indicates the relationship between "living by the Spirit" and "walking by the Spirit," while verse 26, together with 6:1-10, spells out explicitly what "walking by the Spirit" means.

Since Paul's paraenesis can be summed up in the words of 5:25, we shall make this sentence the focus of our examination of the Spirit as a central theme of the apostolic exhortation: "If (since) we live by the Spirit, let us also walk by the Spirit." We begin with the observation that living by the Spirit and ethical walking by the Spirit, although they belong together, are nevertheless distinct from one another. "Walking by the Spirit" is an activity in the Spirit in which human subjects are both active and passive. They are active in that they "do" the "walking" or "sowing" (see 6:9) but passive in that what they do is "fruit of the Spirit" made possible by the fact that the Spirit wins out over the flesh in their lives (5:16-17). "Living by the Spirit" is an activity in the Spirit in which human beings are "led," and it is the sign that they are not "under the law" (5:18).

The language of "being led" (ἄγεσθαι) recalls 1 Corinthians 12:2, where Paul says, "You know that when you were Gentiles you were drawn astray to voiceless idols, however you were led (ἤγεσθε)." The implication of this statement is that life in the Spirit and pagan religious ecstasy have enough in common on the experiential plane so as to be confused with one another.[36] One thinks of the strong language in Mark 1:12 ("The Spirit drove him out into the desert . . . "), modified in

---

[35]Some commentators construe 5:25 with what precedes (e.g., Mussner, *Der Galaterbrief*, 391), while others take 5:25 with what follows (e.g., Betz, *Galatians*, 293). Still other interpreters rightly recognize the close links that 5:25 has with both: Albrecht Oepke, *Der Brief des Paulus an die Galater*, 4th ed., ThHK 9 (Berlin: Evangelische Verlagsanstalt, 1979) 185; Kraftchick, "Ethos and Pathos Appeals in Galatians Five and Six: A Rhetorical Analysis," 255.

[36]As Johannes Weiss correctly stresses about 1 Cor 12:2, Paul's point is not to distinguish the outward manifestations of the Spirit from pagan ecstasy but precisely to draw an analogy: "ihr wisst ja aus eigener Erfahrung, wie willenlos der Mensch ist, wenn er in Gewalt eines πνεῦμα ist." See *Der erste Korintherbrief*, MeyerK 5/9 (Göttingen: Vandenhoeck & Ruprecht, 1910) 296.

Matthew 4:1 ("Jesus was led into the desert by the Spirit") and Luke 4:1 ("being led in the Spirit"). The fact that stories circulated in the early church about people mistaking Jesus' "Spirit-possession" for "demon-possession" (ἔλεγον γὰρ ὅτι ἐξέστη, Mark 3:21; cf. 3:22; Matt 12:24; 9:34; Luke 11:15) is another indicator of how "being in the Spirit" was conceived in the early church. Paul himself points out that if outsiders were to enter the Corinthian congregation while all were speaking in tongues at once, they would surely conclude that the Corinthians had gone mad (1 Cor 14:23).

To live in the Spirit or be led by the Spirit is to experience the power of the Spirit, and apparently the first thing that comes to mind as "life in the Spirit" for a member of one of Paul's churches is miraculous manifestations of the Spirit as divine power. Thus, although the Spirit gives gifts for the sake of building up the church, living by the Spirit is not ethical activity as such, otherwise it could not be cut off from ethics in the life of the church (see 1 Cor 12-14).[37] That is, when Paul admonishes the Galatians, "If we live by the Spirit, let us *also* walk by the Spirit," he acknowledges that living by the Spirit is not itself walking by the Spirit (Gal 5:25).[38] Nowhere does Paul indicate that if a manifestation of the Spirit does not serve to upbuild the church, it is *therefore* not a genuine manifestation of the Spirit.

---

[37]As James D. G. Dunn observes, "Paul does not dispute that the Corinthians experienced genuine charismata. . . . But *even genuine charismata of the most striking nature when exercised without love made for strife within the community and stunted the growth of the body.*" See Dunn, *Jesus and the Spirit: A Study of the Religious and Charismatic Experience of Jesus and the First Christians as Reflected in the New Testament* (Philadelphia: Westminster Press, 1975) 271. 1 Cor 13:1-3 is a remarkable statement of Paul's own view. Powerful manifestations of the Spirit may indeed be performed "without love," in which case these very manifestations of God's liberating power count for nothing.

[38]Both the "also" (καί) and the choice of words, "living" (ζῆν) in the first clause and "walking" (στοιχεῖν) in the second, indicate this distinction. It is therefore incorrect of Bultmann to use this verse as an example of the paradoxical unity of indicative and imperative in Paul. Gal 5:25 is not a paradox ("Become what you are") but a summons to obey the Lord who has given believers new life and freedom from the powers of the present evil age. See Bultmann, "Das Problem der Ethik bei Paulus," *ZNW* 23 (1924): 123-40.

Living by the Spirit is what Paul describes in 3:5, when he speaks of God supplying the Spirit and working "miracles" (δυνάμεις) in the community. In Galatians 3–4 Paul has argued that doing the law does not bring the Spirit, which raises the question whether there is some other activity or obedience that does. To sharpen this question, if doing the law does not promote charismatic life in the Spirit, where does the problem lie—in the inappropriateness of the law as an ethic for the church or in the very idea that the blessing of the Spirit can be increased or promoted by obedience? In order to grasp the significance of this question one must bear in mind that for Paul the Spirit represents the totality of eschatological life and divine presence in the earthly sphere. The Spirit is itself the "presence of the future" and as such is *the* divine blessing in Christ in which all other blessings are found.[39] It represents God's sustaining help in the midst of life's trials and temptations, which is to say that the Spirit is the life of God against the powers of death and sin, suffering and "the flesh."

We have reason to believe that some of Paul's converts tended to celebrate the power of the Spirit over suffering and death, without taking seriously the ethical aims of the same Spirit, its war against the flesh. Evidently the Corinthians inclined in this direction. It appears that some of them disjoined the flesh and the Spirit in such a way as to render conventional ethical norms obsolete. These spiritualists viewed the Spirit as *freedom* from ethical norms governing the bodily order (the order of creation), and celebrated this freedom in what appear to be antinomian ways: "All things are lawful" (1 Cor 10:23).[40] But the problem Paul confronts in Galatians is somewhat different. In Galatians the question is whether doing the works of the law, a form of ethical activity, promotes ongoing life in the Spirit, God's ongoing gift of the Spirit as sustaining presence and "miracle." The theory that informs this project

---

[39]As the "downpayment" (2 Cor 1:22; 5:5) or "first-fruits" (Rom 8:23), the Spirit is not only the guarantee but also the substance of future salvation as it appears under the conditions of present earthly existence.

[40]See further, E. Earle Ellis, "Paul and His Opponents," in his *Prophecy and Hermeneutic in Early Christianity* (Grand Rapids: Eerdmans, 1978). But compare also the cautions of John Hurd regarding reconstructions of antinomianism at Corinth: *The Origin of 1 Corinthians,* new ed. (Macon GA: Mercer University Press, 1983) 273-88.

derives from the Old Testament and Jewish tradition, according to which God crowns the Torah-faithfulness of his people with blessing. Paul contests the applicability of this theology to the sphere of Christ, and he disputes that the law bears any such relation to the eschatological blessing of the Spirit. The apostle complements this negative argument with a positive one. Believers enjoy the blessing of the Spirit because they belong to Christ, believe in Christ, are crucified with Christ, and so forth. In effect, Paul's letter is a call to the community to return to the way of life in Christ that it pursued before the arrival of the agitators and the law.

Since Paul intends for the Galatians to return to the assumptions on which they formerly understood their life in the Spirit, assumptions that the letter itself reinforces and clarifies in many respects, he never comes to address the question whether there is some other obedience, if not the works of the law, upon which ongoing life in the Spirit depends. Of course, it is clear that the power of the Spirit against the flesh is not to be won by ethical obedience, which would be contradictory. Every act of obedience is empowered, hence preceded, by the Spirit (see 5:16-17). That is the assumption behind the exhortation, "Since we live by the Spirit, let us also walk by the Spirit." But it is not immediately clear how Paul understands the relation of obedience ("walking by the Spirit") to the ongoing presence of the Spirit as the fount of charismatic gifts and eschatological joy, the Spirit as an active power against suffering and the frailty of earthly existence. Is the problem with the Galatian theory of how to promote life in the Spirit that they have adopted the wrong ethic ("works of the law") or, more fundamentally, that they are operating under a false assumption about how obedience and blessing are ordered in the earthly sphere for those in Christ? Since we do not really know what the Galatians themselves were thinking, we cannot determine how Paul's letter might have provided them with an answer to this question. It is nevertheless appropriate to inquire whether any of the things Paul names as the sufficient conditions by which the Galatians enjoy the life of God's Spirit *constitute conditions to be fulfilled in obedience*. This is the question that shall occupy us in the final chapter, where we shall explore the meaning of crucifixion with Christ as the sole and irreplaceable ground of life in the Spirit.

CHAPTER 6

The Cross
and the Spirit

For while we live
we are always being handed over to death because of Jesus,
that the life of Jesus might be manifested
in our mortal flesh.

—2 Corinthians 4:11

This is Paul's physical experience,
constant peril, infirmity and physical suffering,
probably by persecution and even violence, in order that
the healing, restoring, and sustaining power and life of Jesus
might be manifested in His very body
for the encouragement of suffering saints. . . .

—A. B. Simpson[1]

IT USED TO BE COMMON for interpreters to argue that Paul's rejection of the law for salvation implies the rejection of the idea that anything of religious value can be earned or achieved. Since the publication of E. P. Sanders's landmark study, *Paul and Palestinian Judaism,*[2] this

---

[1]*The Gospel of Healing* (New York: The Christian Alliance Pub. Co., 1888; rev. 1915) 27-28.

[2]*A Comparison of Patterns of Religion* (Philadelphia: Fortress Press, 1977).

way of conceiving Paul's rejection of the law has become increasingly less popular. This holds true especially for recent treatments of Galatians. Evidently, Sanders has convinced most interpreters that the problem Paul attacks in Galatians does not concern "works-righteousness" as "boasting in one's achievements" or "seeking to establish one's righteousness (and thus one's salvation) through works." Some who have given up this old paradigm for interpreting the law in Paul tend now to understand Paul's rejection of the law almost exclusively in terms of his commitment to the ethnic universality of the gospel. Thus, Galatians is now being interpreted as defending the position that the Gentile does not have to become a Jew (get circumcised and keep the law as the Jewish lifestyle) in order to belong to God's people in Christ.[3] In the preceding chapters of the present study it has been argued that this position is in fact *not* at stake in Galatians but represents an *assumption* that Paul presumes to share with his readers. Nowhere in Galatians does Paul *defend* the idea that the Galatians (or Gentile believers as such) belong to Christ, although he asserts this view and assumes it at various points in developing arguments that have another aim. That aim is to show that life in the Spirit does not depend upon works of the law, a thesis that provokes the following question: Does Paul mean to replace the works of the law with some other form of obedience as the genuinely effective means of promoting life in the Spirit?

A positive answer to this question would not necessarily imply that good works in Christ *earn* the charismatic presence of the Spirit, only that God keeps on "supplying the Spirit" and "working wonders" in proportion to the obedience of his people. This way of thinking about the relation of righteousness to the power of the Spirit accords well with the sort of popular piety expressed in James 5:16, which conceives of personal righteousness as the conduit through which divine healing (life) flows to those among God's people who are suffering or afflicted by ill-

---

[3]See Sanders, *Paul, the Law, and the Jewish People* (Philadelphia: Fortress Press, 1983) 17-18; James D. G. Dunn, "The New Perspective on Paul," *BJRL* 65 (1983): 95-122; idem, "Works of the Law and the Curse of the Law (Galatians 3.10-14)," *NTS* 31 (1985): 523-42; Sam K. Williams, "Justification and the Spirit in Galatians," *JSNT* 29 (1987): 91-100; cf. Richard B. Hays, "Christology and Ethics in Galatians: The Law of Christ," *CBQ* 49 (1987): 289.

ness: "The petition of a righteous man is strong and effective." Such a premise may lead to any number of theological constructions, depending on the other theological axioms with which it is combined. For example, it could be made the basis of a theology that regards debility as a sign of sin and prosperity as a sign of righteousness (cf. John 9:2 and Luke 13:1-5). It would be a distortion to say that James supports such a religious outlook, since James also takes quite seriously another equally axiomatic tradition of ancient Judaism, namely, the tradition of the suffering righteous, who must wait for ultimate deliverance and vindication from God.[4] It is important to stress that both traditions, the one joining prosperity and righteousness and the one concerned with the problem of the suffering righteous, depend on the premise that blessing belongs to righteousness. Paul reveals that he shares this premise, when he argues that the curse of the law blocks the blessing and that eschatological blessing flows from justification.[5] Therefore, it would not be inconsistent of Paul were he to affirm that ongoing blessing in Christ attaches to "new obedience" in Christ. And such a view would not necessarily have to be conceived in casuistic terms. Moreover, to develop this hypothetical line of thought a bit further, one might expect Paul to hold such a view in dialectical tension with his understanding of sharing Christ's sufferings.

Now on one level it is evident that in Galatians Paul does not advocate another form of obedience in place of works of the law as a means of promoting life in the Spirit. As we have seen, Paul grounds the community's life in the Spirit in the fact of their belonging to Christ. Moreover, when he comes to speak of ethical responsibility in Christ, he orders obedience ("walking by the Spirit") not before but after blessing ("living by the Spirit"). But at the close of the preceding chapter we ob-

---

[4]This tradition is exceedingly diverse. Examples are: Pss 22, 31, 69; Job; Isa 50:4-9 and 52:13-53:12; Wis 2:10-5:43; 4 Maccabees; 1QH 8:26-27 and 1QS 8 (interpreting the Isaianic figure of the suffering servant collectively). See further Lothar Ruppert, *Der leidende Gerechte: Eine motivgeschichtliche Untersuchung zum Alten Testament und zwischentestamentlichen Judentum*, FB 5 (Würzburg: Echter-Verlag; Stuttgart: Katholisches Bibelwerk, 1972).

[5]See "The Law Is Not Against the Promises of God" in ch. 2. Cf. also "The Law, the Promise, and the Spirit" in ch. 3, the discussion of 5:4 in ch. 5 and the discussion of 2:21 in ch. 4.

served that among the ways in which Paul speaks about belonging to Christ as the ground of life in the Spirit is one that assumes an ongoing and specifically ethical form, namely, participation in the cross of Christ. This observation appears especially interesting in view of the hypothetical line of reflection just developed. For it suggests that perhaps Paul does not simply qualify a more or less traditional understanding of the relationship of righteousness and blessing by placing it in tension with his notion of cruciform existence but views cruciform existence itself as the new form of obedience from which the ongoing blessing of the Spirit flows.

With this last statement we approach the thesis of this chapter: For Paul *participation in the crucifixion of Christ is the sole condition for ongoing life in the Spirit.* In working our way toward this thesis we shall begin by considering what is meant concretely by "life in the Spirit" and then explore the specific conditions for ongoing life in the Spirit as they are enumerated in Galatians. This second line of inquiry will lead us directly into a discussion of the cross and the Spirit, an investigation that we shall broaden beyond Galatians to include the Pauline corpus as a whole with special attention to 2 Corinthians. This broadening is necessitated by the nature of the question before us as it arises out of our investigation of the Galatian letter. Paul's argument in Galatians is essentially a negative one. He seeks to persuade the Galatians *not* to take up the law and tells them that life in the Spirit can *not* be accessed through the law. The question at hand, however, requires a positive answer. Paul supplies this positive answer in Galatians but only in the course of making his negative point. For this reason there is practically no *development* in Galatians of the theme that interests us here. Evidently in Paul's judgment the occasion does not require it. His aim is to persuade the community to return it to its former pattern of life in Christ, in which all the conditions for ongoing life in Christ were met apart from works of the law. But this approach, which may have succeeded with the Galatians, only makes us all the more curious about these "conditions," hence the inclusion of Paul's other writings in our field of investigation. Finally, it must be stressed that the question before us arises out of Paul's argument and does not necessarily represent a question that the Galatians were asking or even one that they would have found meaningful.[6]

---

[6]For a review of this point, see the introduction to ch. 3 above.

Life in the Spirit and Its Conditions

To this point in our study of Galatians we have used the expression "life in the Spirit" as a convenient designation for a range of language employed in the letter to express the believer's share in "life" and the "Spirit" in Christ. Included under "life in the Spirit" are ongoing reception of the Spirit from the God "who supplies the Spirit and works wonders" in the community (3:5), "Christ living in me" (2:20), "living to God" (2:19), "new creation" (6:15), "living by the Spirit" (5:25), "being led by the Spirit" (5:18), "being free as children of the free woman" (4:26, 31), coming into the inheritance ("realized heirship" as possessing the Spirit, 3:29 and 4:6-7), and "living by Faith" (3:11; cf. 2:20). Intimately related to life in the Spirit is ethical engagement in the power of the Spirit. The Spirit wages war on "the flesh" in the life of the community and in this way supports ethical life as "fruit of the Spirit" (5:17-18, 22-23).

As we have seen, however, it is possible for life in the Spirit to proceed with little positive outcome for ethics, since ethical engagement in the Spirit depends on the decision of the community to "walk" by the Spirit (5:25) or "sow" to the Spirit (6:8). We have no reason to think that in Paul's view the Galatians' understanding of life in the Spirit is so distorted that they imagine themselves to be lords of the new age who are free from ethical responsibility in the body. Were that Paul's opinion, his almost exclusive emphasis on the "realized" aspects of eschatological life in Christ would make little sense.[7] Nevertheless, the apostolic warnings and admonitions in 5:13–6:10 suggest that, in Paul's judgment, ongoing life in the Spirit is not issuing as it should in mutual love and service within the community. What, then, is the nature of this "life in the Spirit," which Paul can affirm, despite his concern that the Galatians have not taken its ethical implications and aims seriously enough?

We are interested specifically in the concrete experience of "living by the Spirit," a reality that Paul need not describe, inasmuch as the

---

[7]"Realized eschatology" in Galatians is expressed in the following themes: the presence of the Spirit in power as the fulfillment of God's promise to Abraham (realized heirship), present citizenship in the "Jerusalem above," the death of the world and new creation, deliverance from this present evil age (1:4), "Christ living in me" as eschatological "living to God."

Galatians know it firsthand. Therefore, we will have to reconstruct the nature of this experience from the one place in the letter where Paul speaks about it in relatively descriptive terms. He does that in 3:5. Fortunately, the language Paul uses here occurs also in other letters, particularly in 1 Corinthians, where the apostle sets forth with some precision a "theology" of life in the Spirit (1 Cor 12-14).[8] In Galatians 3:5 Paul describes God as "the one who supplies you with the Spirit and does mighty works among you." As we have seen, the use of the present tense (ἐπιχορηγῶν and ἐνεργῶν) is not "general" ("the supplier . . . the worker") but "progressive" ("the one who is supplying . . . and working").[9] God is presently at work among the Galatians, "giving his holy Spirit to them," to borrow the language of 1 Thessalonians 4:8. This ongoing gift of the Spirit is the way in which God sustains the community. The verb ἐπιχορηγέω, which we have been translating "supplies," probably carries the more specific sense of "provides in support."[10] The gift of the Spirit as continual divine support surely includes in principle every "manifestation" (φανέρωσις) of the Spirit "for the common good" (1 Cor 12:7). But the construction in Galatians 3:5 is a hendiadys[11] and thus spells out more clearly the specific form of help that Paul has in view: "and effects mighty works (δυνάμεις) among you."

Paul refers to "mighty works" as manifestations of the Spirit's power elsewhere in his letters (1 Cor 12:10, 28-29; 2 Cor 12:12), but we are not in a position to know precisely what they are. The following observations by James Dunn give a succinct statement of the problem:

---

[8]The following studies are of particular help here: Hermann Gunkel, *The Influence of the Holy Spirit: The Popular View of the Apostolic Age and the Teaching of the Apostle Paul*, trans. Roy A. Harrisville and Philip A. Quanbeck (Philadelphia: Fortress Press, 1979 [German ed. 1888]) and James D. G. Dunn, *Jesus and the Spirit: A Study of the Religious and Charismatic Experience of Jesus and the First Christians as Reflected in the New Testament* (Philadelphia: Westminster Press, 1975).

[9]Contra Ernest De Witt Burton, *A Critical and Exegetical Commentary on the Epistle to the Galatians*, ICC (Edinburgh: T. & T. Clark, 1921) 152.

[10]See Paul W. Meyer, "The Holy Spirit in the Pauline Letters: A Contextual Exploration," *Interp* 33 (1979): 10. Note the cognate construction in Phil 1:19, "the support (ἐπιχορηγίας) of the Spirit of Jesus Christ." Cf. also Rom 1:11.

[11]Since Paul numbers δυνάμεις among the workings of the Spirit (1 Cor 12:10, 28-29; 2 Cor 12:12), we are justified in concluding that the second participial clause interprets the first.

What these *dunameis* included we are unfortunately now unable to determine. In the Synoptics *dunameis* is used for the whole range of Jesus'
healings and also for the "nature miracles" (though probably only by
the evangelists). Paul, however, seems to distinguish *dunameis* from
"gifts of healing" in 1 Cor. 12:9f., and it may be that in *dunameis* he
is thinking primarily of exorcisms. Nor may we exclude the possibility
that *dunameis* here includes "nature miracles."[12]

Dunn concludes that "by *dunameis* Paul is evidently thinking of
events in which people (and things?) were visibly and beneficially af-
fected in an extraordinary way by a nonrational power through the me-
dium of Paul and other believers."[13] This definition appears especially
appropriate when one takes into account Paul's use of δύναμις in the
singular for the generic "power" of the Spirit (e.g., Rom 15:13) and
the fact that in Romans 15:19 he associates this generic power with the
working of signs (σεμεῖα) and wonders (τέρατα). Therefore, we
conclude that in Galatians 3:5 Paul is describing God as the one who
supports and helps the Galatians by effecting extraordinary works on
their behalf by the power of the Spirit. These are works of *life* for the
community, performed by the life-giving Spirit of the one who raised
Jesus from the dead (see Rom 8:11). The Corinthians are "eager for
manifestations of the Spirit," and Paul encourages them to be "eager
for the greater gifts" of the Spirit and to make edification of the community their aim (1 Cor 14:12 and 12:31). The Galatians (in our reconstruction of them) are eager for life-giving manifestations of the Spirit
and seek to secure or promote these "by works of the law." Paul denies
that doing the law can have any positive effect upon ongoing life in the
Spirit, which raises the question whether it is possible by some other
more appropriate means to increase prosperity in the Spirit. We turn,
therefore, to examine the specific conditions for life in the Spirit that are
mentioned in Galatians.

We have already ascertained what these "conditions" for receiving
the Spirit are. They include "the hearing of faith" (3:2,5), "faith" (3:9,
14), "justification by God" (3:8, 11), "sonship" (3:29; 4:6-7), bap-

---

[12]*Jesus and the Spirit*, 210.
[13]Ibid., 210.

tism (as "putting on Christ," being "one" in Christ, being "of Christ;" 3:26-29), and "crucifixion with Christ" (2:19-20; 6:14-16). All of these have in common a locus in the *initiatory* stage of Christian existence. The Galatians heard the gospel of the crucified Christ and believed (3:1-2). When they believed, they were justified, just like Abraham (3:6-8). They were baptized into Christ and thus came to be "of Christ" (3:28-29), which includes "crucifixion with Christ" (2:19-20; 5:24).[14] As baptized persons who belong to Christ and wear Christ as a "garment," they are "sons of God" (3:26-27). In short, initiation into Christ, being a Christian, appears to be the sole condition for "receiving the Spirit." Nevertheless, since the reception of the Spirit (3:2) is *ongoing* (3:5), the question arises whether all of the conditions we have just enumerated belong *exclusively* to the moment of initiation. That is, does Paul in any way suggest that instead of "works of the law" there is something else the Galatians should be doing in order to promote the powerful activity of the Spirit among them?

As a first response to the question just posed, we observe that among the various conditions enumerated above only two might be construed as forms of action that lie within the power of believers. These are "faith" and "crucifixion with Christ." Although "faith" in Galatians is primarily Faith as an eschatological reality (Jesus-Christ-Faith)[15] and crucifixion with Christ is above all an "event" in which believers are passive,[16] believers are also themselves active in faith and in sharing Christ's passion.[17] Moreover, the two, faith and the cross, are also closely connected with one another in Galatians. Not only is Faith the "Faith of the Son of God who loved me and gave himself for me" (2:20),

---

[14]We will leave aside the question of whether baptism constitutes a "sacrament" for Paul.

[15]On "Faith" as an eschatological reality, see ch. 2.

[16]The passivity of the suffering subject in crucifixion is expressed both in statements that speak of Christ and those that express the idea of believers' participation in Christ's death. See the following passages: Rom 3:25; 4:25; 6:3-4; 8:32 (8:36); 2 Cor 4:11-12; 12:7-10; 13:4; Gal 2:20; 6:14.

[17]Christ is also active (obedient) in his death: Rom 5:6; 5:18; 2 Cor 5:15; Gal 1:4; 2:20; Phil 2:8. The same holds for existential participation in Christ's suffering: Phil 1:29-30; 2:5; Rom 8:17?; 2 Cor 5:14-15.

but faith in Christ means faith in the crucified Christ (3:1-2; 3:13-14).[18] Therefore, in order to answer the question to what extent the fulfillment of the conditions for receiving the Spirit remains an ongoing task of the community, we must obtain a clear understanding of the relationship between the cross and the Spirit.

The Cross and the Spirit

One of the most remarkable things about the epistle to the Galatians is that it mentions the resurrection of Christ only once. This reference occurs in the prescript, where Paul identifies himself as "an apostle . . . through Jesus Christ and God the Father who raised him from the dead" (1:1). By contrast, statements about the death of Jesus appear again and again (1:4; 2:19-20; 2:21; 3:1; 3:13; 5:11; 5:24; 6:12; 6:14; 6:17). How is it that in a letter otherwise dominated by an air of realized eschatology—a realized eschatology that Paul does not criticize but affirms—Paul stresses the cross, rather than the resurrection, as the event that inaugurates eschatological life and new creation?

We can sharpen this question. At first sight, the occasion of the epistle would seem to call for a discussion of the connection between the resurrection of Christ and the gift of the Spirit. In Romans Paul treats the resurrection as a deed of God's Spirit (Rom 1:4; 8:11; cf. 1 Tim 3:16 and 1 Peter 3:18), an idea that accords well with the Jewish view that God's Spirit gives life.[19] Furthermore, according to a very old but evidently quite persistent Jewish-Christian tradition, it is the *resurrected* Jesus who receives and bestows the Spirit (John 20:22; Acts 2:33).[20] Now

---

[18]We shall not consider further here the extent to which "Christ-Faith" (πίστις Χριστοῦ) includes the idea of faithfulness unto death as instantiated in Jesus' own faith. As we shall see, the idea of cruciform existence bubbles beneath the surface of the text, breaking through at points, but not in terms that suggest this as a primary meaning of "Christ-Faith."

[19]See ch. 3.

[20]Since the statement in Acts 2:33 stands in tension with Luke's own stress on Jesus' reception of the Spirit at his baptism (Luke 3:21-22) and his ministry in the full power of the Spirit (Luke 4:14), it must represent a pre-Lukan tradition. The association of the Spirit with the resurrected Jesus in New Testament creeds and hymns (Rom 1:4; 8:11; 1 Tim 3:16; 1 Ptr 3:18) suggests that the tradition belongs to a primitive two-stage Christological reflection which has not yet applied the predicates of the risen Lord to the earthly Jesus.

in Galatians it is indeed Jesus, the one seed, who receives the promise (3:16, 19), yet nowhere does Paul indicate that the Spirit (blessing, and so forth) flows in consequence of the resurrection, much less that the resurrected Jesus dispenses the Spirit. It is God who gives the Spirit (3:5), and the redemptive act of God that brings the Spirit is the *cross* (3:13-14; cf. 2:19-20; and cf. 1:4 with 4:4-7). These observations indicate that Paul's interpretation of the problem at Galatia is not simply "dogmatic," as if "the problem with the law is [simply] that it is not Christ."[21] The apostle's concentration on the link between the cross and the Spirit suggests that he has a more complex and nuanced understanding of the Spirit's relation to Christ.

The centrality of the cross in Paul's conception of the Spirit's relation to Christ is especially evident in 3:1-14, that chain of argumentation that has turned out to be so crucial for our understanding of the letter. Paul calls the Galatians "foolish" for failing to grasp the meaning of Christ's death (3:1), and by the end of the argument it is clear that what the Galatians fail to understand is the link between the Spirit and the crucified Christ. According to 3:13-14, the blessing or promise of the Spirit "flows" from the cross. Hence, Paul can speak of "dying in order to live" and stresses that "being crucified with Christ" is a condition that coincides with experiencing the eschatological reality of "Christ living in me" (2:19-20). It is therefore incorrect to say that "the justification of the ungodly is for Paul the fruit of Jesus' death, and nothing else."[22] The fact is, in Galatians 3:13-14, where we might well expect the death of Jesus to mean the justification of the ungodly, inasmuch as Paul employs the juridical motif of Christ's substitutionary act of "becoming a curse for us," the apostle names not "justification" but the blessing-promise of the Spirit as the fruit of the cross.

These observations about the Spirit and the cross in Galatians suggest our thesis: participation in the cross of Christ is the sole condition for life in the Spirit. If we are to test this thesis we must first of all be clear about what "participation in the cross of Christ" means. Robert

---

[21]Sanders, *Paul and Palestinian Judaism*, 551.

[22]Ernst Käsemann, *Perspectives on Paul*, trans. Margaret Kohl (Philadelphia: Fortress Press, 1971) 46.

C. Tannehill, in his book *Dying and Rising with Christ*,[23] points out that in Paul's letters the motif of "dying with Christ" falls into two groups of texts: "the texts which refer to dying with Christ as a decisive, past event, and those which refer to dying with Christ as a present experience, especially in suffering."[24] Therefore, we must determine not only whether participation in the cross is the "sole condition" for life in the Spirit but whether our thesis holds for both or only one of these two forms of participation in the cross. In what follows we shall treat these two aspects of participation in the cross in turn. For reasons that will become clear below, we shall refer to the first form of "dying with Christ" as "cosmic crucifixion with Christ" and to the second form as "existential crucifixion with Christ."

The most important statements about Jesus' death, to judge from their placement, occur in the prescript, the central argument of 3:1-14, and in the final autograph. These three statements are alike in that each treats the death of Jesus as an "epochal" event. They differ in that the first and the third speak of that event in cosmic terms, while the second appears to have a salvation-historical focus (cf. 4:4-5).

> Jesus Christ who gave himself for our sins to deliver us from the present evil age. (1:4)
>
> Christ delivered us from the curse of the law, having become a curse for us . . . that the blessing of Abraham for the Gentiles might be in Christ Jesus. (3:13-14)
>
> But as for me, let it not be that I should boast except in the cross of Christ, through whom the world has been crucified to me and I to the world. For neither circumcision nor uncircumcision is anything, but only new creation. (6:14-15)

We have already concluded from such statements that Paul wishes to stress the cross as the fundamental "ground" of life in the Spirit. But Paul does not always speak of the cross in identifying the grounds of eschatological life. Galatians 4:4-7 is a good example, especially in view of the fact that the apostle might well have mentioned the crucifixion in

---

[23]BZNW 32 (Berlin: Alfred Töpelmann, 1967).

[24]Ibid., 6.

verse 4 or 5, where it is certainly implied theologically. The use of baptismal traditions in 3:26-29 is another. According to what Paul says in Romans 6:1-11 (cf. Col 2:12), baptism means "baptism into Christ's death," and the apostle can even think of "putting on Christ" (the baptismal metaphor employed in Gal 3:27) as donning the *crucified* Christ (2 Cor 5:1-5).[25] But he makes no mention of the cross when he speaks of baptism in Galatians 3:26-29. The argument is more generally Christological: "and if you are *of Christ,* then you are seed of Abraham, heirs according to promise" (3:29).

In the light of these considerations we may now state more precisely a question posed earlier in this discussion. Why does Paul stress the cross and not the resurrection in Galatians, if his argument is basically *Christological*— in which case one would expect at least some balance between statements about Christ's death and those concerning his resurrection—and if the aim of the letter is to locate the source of the Spirit exclusively and sufficiently in Christ—in which case one would expect the resurrection, as the *life* side of the Christ event, to figure more prominently? We have already considered the fact that in Galatians Paul accents the realized aspect of his eschatology. It is true that the future is not altogether eclipsed (note 5:5; 5:21; 6:5; 6:8), but there is nothing to suggest that the future-oriented statements serve explicitly as words of eschatological reservation, much less that the theme of the cross speaks against tendencies among the Galatians to think in categories of overly realized eschatology. The point of Paul's stress on the cross lies elsewhere. In fact, far from qualifying the realized aspect of redemption in Christ, certain statements about the cross tend to express the realized eschatology of Galatians in its boldest form.

Galatians 6:14-15 is a case in point. In 6:14 Paul expresses in elevated tones one of his favorite themes: boasting in the cross alone. The counterpoise to this idea is boasting in the flesh, which Paul describes as the secret aim of the agitators: "They want you to be circumcised so that they might boast in your flesh" (v. 13b). The apostle introduces the

---

[25]So Paul Meyer ("The Holy Spirit in the Pauline Letters," 13), who builds on the work of J. F. Collange, *Enigmes de la deuxième épître de Paul aux Corinthiens* (Cambridge: Cambridge University Press, 1972) 199-225. See also Chrysostom, who expands the metaphor as "being clothed with his blood" (*PG* 59.257-62).

idea of boasting here for the first time in the letter, and he does so in a polemical jab that prepares for his own antithetical statement in verse 14. But the elevated style of verses 14-15, the language of benediction in verse 16, together with the almost detached mood of verse 17 suggest that these closing statements have to do less with their immediate polemical context than with the larger themes of the epistle. In short, they set the stage for Paul's statements about the relation between the crucifixion of Christ and "new creation." As in 2 Corinthians 5:14-17, it is the death of Jesus that inaugurates new creation, what we have become accustomed to calling "realized eschatology."

In an essay that is very suggestive for the discussion at hand, J. Louis Martyn argues that in Galatians 6:14-15 Paul speaks in apocalyptic terms of nothing less than the death of the cosmos.[26] According to him, the decisive clue that the language of verse 14 ("the world has been crucified to me") is to be taken in an apocalyptic sense is found in verse 15, where Paul declares that "neither circumcision nor uncircumcision is anything." Observing how pervasive in the ancient Mediterranean world the idea is that the cosmos is structured in "pairs of opposites" (τἀναντία), Martyn suggests that statements like 3:27-28 ("There is neither Jew nor Greek . . . ") and 6:15 ("neither circumcision nor uncircumcision is anything . . . ") must signify that the cosmos, at least as the Jew will have conceived it, has suffered its death. For if the fundamental structural polarities of the world (Jew/Gentile, male/female, slave/free) no longer exist, then the creation has collapsed in which "all the works of the Most High are in pairs, one the opposite of the other" (Sir 33:15). In Martyn's view, the point of Paul's assertion that the old world has died lies in its consequences for two pairs of opposites in particular, "circumcision and uncircumcision" and "the law and the fleshly Impulse."[27] In short, what the Galatians need to understand is that the law is no longer the "God-given antidote to the fleshly Impulse" (rather, the Spirit is), hence becoming one of the circumcised is not the solution to combatting the power of the flesh.[28] But it is not at all clear that Paul

---

[26]"Apocalyptic Antinomies in Paul's Letter to the Galatians," *NTS* 31 (1985): 410-24.

[27]Ibid., 415-16.

[28]Ibid., 416.

addresses the question of whether the law is an "antidote" to the evil inclination, much less that he views the law and the evil impulse as "a pair of opposite characteristics of the *old* cosmos" now "radically re-aligned" so that the law has *become* an "ally of the Flesh."[29] Without repeating discussions conducted in the preceding chapters, we may simply reiterate that the problem of "the flesh" is raised for the first time in the paraenesis, and even then not in a way that suggests it plays a significant role in the teaching of the agitators.

The significance of Paul's statement in 6:15 ("Neither circumcision nor uncircumcision is anything") lies in its function as support (γάρ) for the statement about the death of the cosmos (v. 14), which Paul qualifies by the restriction "to me" (ἐμοί). Paul is able to draw upon a traditional formula, the baptismal tradition cited in 3:28, which he expresses here and in 5:6 in his own words (cf. also 1 Cor 7:19). The value of this tradition for the argument at hand lies in the sharp distinction it makes between the cosmos, to which the law belongs, and the new creation, to which believers belong in Christ. It is instructive to note that Paul appeals to this tradition three times in Galatians (3:27-28; 5:6; 6:15) and each time makes a different point with it. In 3:26-29 he uses it to argue that Christ's *singular* "sonship/seedship" (3:16, 19), which makes him the sole heir of the promise, means that believers share in that (realized) heirship solely by virtue of being *one* in him. In 5:4-6 Paul exploits the same confession to make a point about ethics and future justification. And in 6:14-15 he appeals to this confession to defend the assertion that the cosmos has "died," at least as far as believers are concerned.

The idea that believers are no longer subject to the basic structural realities of the cosmos and therefore not in need of a law that supplies the rules for successful living in the cosmos has close affinities with what Paul says about the law and the "elements of the cosmos" in 4:8-11. The expression "the elements of the cosmos" represents Paul's way of speaking about the cosmic order. The calendrical observances ordained by the law enable the Jew to live according to the nature of the cosmos. But the Torah calendar ("days, months, seasons, years") no longer applies to persons who have been delivered from "the present evil age" (1:4) or, as 6:14 has it, to those for whom the cosmos has died. The re-

---

[29]Ibid., 416.

alized apocalyptic eschatology expressed in this conception raises a host of questions, not the least of which concerns how it is that those who have died to the present cosmic order remain subject nonetheless to the power of death. But Paul's use of the idea is governed not by considerations of the believer's relation to death-dealing powers but by his focus on the believer's access to life-giving ones. Does fidelity to the law, living in tune with the cosmos, have anything to do with the powers of the *new creation?* Does the link between Torah-faithfulness and blessing hold for blessings belonging to a world not made "through the Torah"? Can the promise that "the one who does them *shall live* by them" be applied to *eschatological* life? This is how Paul addresses the specific question, "Does the one who supplies the Spirit and works miracles among you do so because of works of the law?"

The apostle uses the language of death (crucifixion) in order to express the discontinuity between life in Christ and life "in this present evil age" (1:4). His purpose in emphasizing this discontinuity is to show that the rules that promote life in the present cosmic order do not promote life in Christ. He has in view the rules ordained by the Torah ("the works of the law") for life in this world ("the one who does them shall live by them"). Hence he can speak of both death to the cosmos and death to the law. In stressing that the gift of the Spirit flows in consequence of the eschatological death of Christ, "in" which the believer and the world die to one another, Paul makes clear that the cosmic order of the Torah does not specify the conditions for "receiving the Spirit." By contrast, the "resurrection of Christ," as a theological concept, does not lend itself naturally to the apostle's argument for discontinuity. For unless the stress is placed on resurrection *from the dead,* the fact that participation in Christ's *life* presupposes a radical break with the old determiners of one's existence is not expressed. It is the idea of death, present implicitly in the concept of resurrection, that carries this notion of an end, a dissolution, a disruption. Therefore, Paul attends to the symbol of death in making his case against the theory that works of the law promote eschatological life. This accounts for the fact that in a letter dominated by an air of realized eschatology, the resurrection of Christ gets mentioned only once—and even here as resurrection *from the dead* (1:1), while the death of Christ receives repeated emphasis.

We may summarize the significance of the preceding discussion for our central thesis as follows. At the most general level of expression we may say that being in Christ is the sole condition of life in the Spirit. But the crisis in Galatia leads Paul to stress a particular aspect of being in Christ as most fundamental for receiving the Spirit, namely, participation in Christ's death. This aspect of being in Christ expresses the discontinuity of life in the Spirit with cosmic existence as such and therefore the impossibility of promoting life in the Spirit through any earthly activity or obedience. For life in the Spirit begins with death to the cosmos. Nevertheless, the matter is not quite so simple, inasmuch as those who have died to the world continue to live in it and are called to do so in ethically responsible ways by the power of the Spirit. Not only that, cosmic crucifixion carries existential implications for life in the world that bear directly on ethics. Hence, the very condition that appears in the first instance to exclude every conceivable earthly activity or obedience as requisite for ongoing reception of the Spirit turns out to have worldly implications of its own. That is, the fact that crucifixion with Christ extends itself into the world as existential participation in the cross would seem to imply that obedient participation in the sufferings of Christ is a fundamental condition for ongoing life in the Spirit. It is this aspect of participation in the cross of Christ that we have now to explore.

In Galatians cosmic crucifixion with Christ is affirmed explicitly as a condition for ongoing life in the Spirit, but existential participation in Christ's death (suffering with Christ) is treated as a condition of life in the Spirit at best only implicitly.[30] In fact we are led to reflect on the relation of existential crucifixion to life in the Spirit only because we assume that cosmic crucifixion manifests itself in the existential consequence of suffering.[31] This prompts us to inquire whether Paul views

---

[30]Note that Tannehill does not treat any passages from Galatians under the aspect of suffering with Christ (*Dying and Rising with Christ*, 84-129), except to list Gal 6:17 in a note (91 n. 2).

[31]See, for example, Tannehill, *Dying and Rising with Christ*, 74-129; Norbert Baumert, *Täglich Sterben und Auferstehen: Der Literalsinn von 2 Kor 4:12-5:10*, SANT 34 (Munich: Kösel Verlag, 1973); Wolfgang Schrage, "Leid, Kreuz, und Eschaton. Die Peristasenkataloge als Merkmale paulinischer theologia crucis und Eschatologie," *EvTh* 34 (1974): 141-75; John Howard Schütz, *Paul and the Anatomy of Apostolic Authority*, SNTSMS 26 (Cambridge: Cambridge University Press, 1975) 238-48.

sharing Christ's sufferings as the existential "condition" for manifestations of the Spirit in the church's experience. In 1 Thessalonians 1:6 Paul reminds his readers how they became "imitators" of him and of the Lord by receiving the word "in much affliction with joy in the Holy Spirit." This statement suggests not only that imitating Christ involves especially conformity to him in suffering (cf. 2:13-16), but also that mimetic suffering is the characteristic locus of *eschatological joy in the Spirit*. Thus Paul can go on to say that the Thessalonians' "joy in the Spirit in the midst of affliction" has made them an example (παρά-δειγμα) to all the believers in Macedonia and Achaia (v. 7). Evidently Paul thinks that "affliction" is the characteristic lot of those who receive the word of Christ and that the Spirit's supporting presence makes itself felt among those who suffer for Christ's sake (see 2 Cor 7:4; 8:1 ff.; Phil 2:17; cf. Col 1:24). If this assumption is basic to his understanding of Christian existence, so basic that it becomes virtually an article of catachesis (1 Thess 3:4), then it is not so surprising that Paul, without any preparation or explanation, refers to the sufferings of the Galatians in immediate connection with statements about their life in the Spirit.

I have in mind Galatians 3:4, which speaks clearly enough about suffering[32] but is rarely translated that way because "no sufferings are mentioned in the near or larger context."[33] Paul asks,

> Have you suffered so much in vain, if it really is in vain? Does, then, the one who supports you with the Spirit and works mighty works among you do so because of works of the law or because you heard and believed (the gospel of the crucified Christ; cf. v. 1)?

If receiving the word of the gospel draws the believer into a sphere of conflict, where sharing the sufferings of Christ is the rule and the power and joy of the Spirit sustain those under assault, then it is only natural

---

[32]Elsewhere in Paul the verb πάσχειν always means "suffer": 1 Cor 12:26; 2 Cor 1:6; Phil 1:29; 1 Thess 2:14 (cf. 2 Thess 1:5). W. Michaelis points out that πάσχειν, when used absolutely, always means suffering, except where the context makes clear that a neutral or pleasant "experience" is intended (*TDNT* 5:905).

[33]I cite myself and thereby revise my previous opinion. See Cosgrove, "The Law and the Spirit: An Investigation into the Theology of Galatians" (Ph.D. diss., Princeton Theological Seminary, 1985) 101.

that Paul speaks of the Galatians' sufferings in connection with both their conversion and their experience of the Spirit's support. The reference to suffering, which follows an ironic remark about "beginning with the Spirit and ending up with the flesh" (v. 3), sounds almost sarcastic. Paul asks, in effect, what the point of all that suffering has been, if the power of the Spirit can be had simply by doing the law.

The suggestion that Paul makes a connection in 3:1-5 between suffering and the Spirit brings to mind a number of other texts in Galatians and casts them in a fresh light. For example, in 4:29 Paul declares, "Just as at that time the one born according to the flesh persecuted the one born according to the Spirit, so it is now." Paul does not say in this passage that suffering persecution occasions the sustaining presence of the Spirit; he suggests that being born according to the Spirit marks believers out for conflict in the world. But a close connection between suffering and the Spirit is nonetheless affirmed. Suggestive as well are certain calculated recollections in the personal appeal of 4:12-20. After asking the Galatians to imitate him, a motif in Paul's letters that often means imitation of the suffering apostle,[34] Paul reminds the community that it was his own suffering that occasioned his preaching of the gospel to them:

> You know that it was because of a weakness of the flesh that I first preached the gospel to you. But although my flesh was a trial to you, you did not scorn or despise me. On the contrary, you received me as an angel of God, as Christ Jesus. What, then, has become of your joy? (4:13-15a)

The Galatians' acceptance of the weak and suffering Paul was an occasion of blessing (μακαρίσμος) for them. In receiving him and his message they received Christ himself, who is throughout this letter above all the crucified Christ, just as Paul portrays himself throughout Galatians as the crucified apostle. One thinks especially of the autograph in 6:11-18, where Paul speaks of his crucifixion to the world in its extension in the world as experiences of suffering for the cross of Christ (cf.

---

[34]See 1 Thess 1:6; 2:14; 1 Cor 11:1 (where the reference to Paul's imitation of Christ suggests the cross); Phil 3:17 (note the reference to the cross in v. 18).

5:11): "Let no one give me any trouble, for I bear on my body the marks of Jesus."[35]

If Galatians associates participation in Christ's sufferings with sharing Christ's eschatological life, this accords well with the way in which Paul characteristically applies the death and life of Christ to believers. Dying and rising with Christ belong together in Christian experience. A moving expression of this thought is found in 2 Corinthians 4:11, where Paul discerns the death and life of Jesus in his own experience as an apostle:

For while we live we are always being given up to death for Jesus' sake,
so that the life of Jesus may be manifested in our mortal flesh.

Yet the theme of suffering and the Spirit never becomes an object of reflection in Galatians. It appears at most implicitly in passages like 6:14-16, where "peace and mercy" constitute presumably blessings of eschatological life[36] pronounced upon those who walk by the "canon of the cross," or 3:3-4, where loss of the Spirit and ending up with the flesh is associated with "suffering so many things in vain" (see above). But nowhere does Paul suggest that the Galatians spurn participation in Christ's weakness and suffering, as the Corinthians came to do. The last passage mentioned, recalling as it does other places where Paul acknowledges that his churches share in Christ's affliction (1 Thess 1:6; 2 Cor 1:7; Rom 8:35-36; Phil 1:29), indicates that what Paul questions is not the Galatians' readiness to suffer with Christ but their understanding of the relationship between that suffering and the Spirit.

Let us review what we have learned so far about the theme of the cross in Galatians. First, the most important and explicit references to

---

[35]These "marks" (στίγματα) are probably wounds received as suffering for Christ (cf. 2 Cor 11:23-25). Werner Kramer points out that when Paul uses the simple name "Jesus," it is "in statements about participation by Christians in the death and resurrection of Christ." See Kramer, *Christ, Lord, Son of God*, trans. B. Hardy, SBT 50 (London: SCM, 1966) 200; further F. F. Bruce, *The Epistle to the Galatians: A Commentary on the Greek Text*, NIGTC (Grand Rapids: Eerdmans, 1982) 275-76; Udo Borse, "Die Wundmale und der Todesbescheid," *BZ* (NF) 14 (1970): 88-111.

[36]The benediction is not simply a word of approbation applied to those who follow the canon of the crucified Christ. Paul wishes eschatological blessing (the saving mercy and *shalom* of God) upon those who walk by this rule.

the cross are "epochal" in orientation. Second, most of the statements that speak in some way of sharing in the cross have cosmic crucifixion in view. We have explored the way in which this theme of cosmic death with Christ as the "event" that brings the Spirit gives expression to the radical discontinuity between the world of the Spirit and the present world order. Third, we do find references to suffering, weakness, and persecution for the cross (3:4; 4:13-14; 4:29; 5:11; 6:12; 6:17), and these references are consistent with Paul's understanding that cosmic crucifixion with Christ has cruciform existence as one of its consequences for Christian experience in the world. But existential crucifixion never becomes an explicit theme in Galatians. Therefore, if we are to understand what form of action or obedience may be entailed in crucifixion with Christ as the ground of ongoing life in the Spirit, we need to explore the idea of sharing Christ's sufferings as it is treated elsewhere in the Pauline corpus.

In 2 Corinthians Paul speaks of the relation of existential participation in the cross (suffering, weakness) to power (life, resurrection, deliverance, glory, the Spirit) in two ways. The first and most readily comprehensible is the idea that just as Jesus' death was the occasion for God's life-giving intervention, so existential participation in Christ's death occasions the experience of Christ's resurrection life as transcendent power:

> We had this sentence of death among us [cf. v. 5: "the sufferings of Christ abound in us"], in order that we might trust not in ourselves but in the God who raises the dead. (2 Cor 1:9)

> We have this treasure [the glory of God] in earthen vessels, in order that the transcendent power might be of God and not of ourselves. . . . We are always carrying around in the body the death of Jesus, in order that the life of Jesus might be manifested in our bodies. For we are always being given up to death for Jesus' sake, in order that the life of Jesus might be manifested in our mortal flesh. So death is at work in us but life in you. (4:7-11)

> For he was crucified in weakness, but he lives by the power of God. For we are weak in him, but in dealing with you we shall live by the power of God. (13:4)

In each of these passages Paul interprets his own life and ministry as participation in the death and life of Jesus, and in each example the manifestation of Jesus' life is visible and tangible: deliverance from mortal danger (1:9),[37] the pneumatic life of the Corinthians (4:12),[38] the effective exercise of apostolic authority and discipline in the church in demonstrations of divine power (13:4).[39] That is, in this first way of understanding participation in Christ's death and life, the cross and divine power are related consecutively: the cross *occasions* the manifestation of divine power. But at what we may justly term a deeper level of conception Paul relates the symbols of death and life *paradoxically*. Here the cross and divine power are not treated as polar opposites, as if the cross were simply that negative reality which the resurrection overcomes. Instead the cross comes to be viewed as virtually coincident with the life of Jesus. At this level of conception Paul is able to make statements like the following.

> When I am weak, then I am strong. (2 Cor 12:10)

> We preach Christ crucified, a stumbling block to Jews and foolishness to Gentiles, but to those who are called . . . Christ the power of God and the wisdom of God. (1 Cor 1:23-24)

Or he can speak as he does in 2 Cor 4:17 of existential crucifixion as a kind of immanent power "preparing in us an eternal weight of glory" (αἰώνιον βάρος δόξης κατεργάζεται).

For Paul, Jesus' resurrection life is so inextricably bound to his death that when the apostle thinks of participation in either Christ's death or his resurrection he always keeps the two together, even where their interconnection is not *evident* in experience. For instance, it is one thing

---

[37]The God who raises the dead is here the God "who delivered us from mortal peril" (1:10a).

[38]Although Paul wants the Corinthians to understand properly their eschatological life in the Spirit, he never disputes that what they regard as the power of the Spirit among them truly is a manifestation of the Spirit ("So life is at work in you"). Compare 2 Cor 13:8-9, where Paul raises the question whether Christ is indeed among the Corinthians, but then says: "We cannot do anything against the truth, but only for the sake of the truth. For we rejoice when we are weak, and you are powerful. What we pray for is this: your maturity (τὴν ὑμῶν κατάρτισιν)."

[39]Paul warns the Corinthians: "For we are weak in him but we shall live with him by the power of God toward you" (13:4b; cf. 13:2; 10:6, 11; 1 Cor 4:21; 5:3-5).

for the apostle to think of an extraordinary rescue from mortal danger as a manifestation of Jesus' death and resurrection in his ministry experience and quite another for him to connect his sufferings on the missionary road with the Corinthians' experience of life as 2 Corinthians 4:12 avers. How does death at work in Paul occasion life for the Corinthians? It is not that Paul's suffering mediates life to the Corinthians by displaying the death and life of Christ on the stage of Paul's life, which will communicate life to them *if they accept it*. Although such an idea may be implied by the language of "manifestation" in verses 7-11, verse 12 transcends this logic, for it suggests that although the Corinthians disdain Paul's weakness, Paul's *present* suffering is nevertheless positively related to the eschatological life they *presently* enjoy (cf. 13:9). Yet Paul does not explain the logic of the "so" (ὥστε) in verse 12. Just as remarkable is the idea that suffering *works* glory (4:17), as if Paul finds his own idea that weakness and suffering serve as the occasion for divine help and deliverance ultimately inadequate to comprehend the full extent to which the death and life of Jesus are at work in the existence of believers. Evidently, as Paul understands it, the death and life of Jesus are present not only in those moments of weakness in which the visible, tangible power of God appears as life in the midst of death but in suffering and weakness as such, which amounts to saying that the life of God lies hidden at points under its very opposite.[40] Paul never pits the paradoxical conception of Jesus' death and life against the consecutive ordering of the two. He is prepared to discern the presence of Jesus' *life*, in both divine deliverance from extremity and subjection to weakness that does not lead to deliverance, and formulations like "the cross . . . is the power of God" and "power is perfected in weakness" give expression to his total conception, without partiality toward either form.

We cannot pursue here in full detail the intricacies and profundities of Paul's understanding of participation in Christ's death and life, about

---

[40]Cf. Ernst Käsemann on the similar Pauline logic in Rom 8: "Like all that God does, the love of Christ also manifests itself in time under its opposite" (*Commentary on Romans*, trans. G. W. Bromiley [Grand Rapids: Eerdmans, 1980] 250). Käsemann's language echoes a favorite formulation of Luther: *abscondita sub contrariis* (see, e.g., *WA* 4.82.17-18; 4.243.7-13; 4.451.25-27).

which there is considerable divergence of scholarly opinion.[41] Nevertheless there are certain additional aspects of his conception of sharing Christ's crucifixion and life that will illumine our understanding of his treatment of this motif in Galatians. Although "sharing Christ's sufferings" is essentially an expression of obedience to God (participation in Christ's "obedience unto death," Phil 2:8), Paul never formulates ethical participation in Christ's death as an imperative. He comes closest in the summons, "imitate me," which often includes sharing Christ's sufferings. But this imperative is not a command to suffer, but a call to "be receptive to the fullness of God's power which never is to be separated from weakness and suffering."[42] Existential crucifixion does not lie at the immediate discretion of the believer. It remains, even as obedience, part of the gospel "indicative." As Philippians 1:29 puts it, "What has been granted (ἐχαρίσθη) to you for the sake of Christ is not only to believe in him but also to suffer for him." To that extent it is not an action that can be performed but something passive in the radical sense of the word. The active (ethical) side of this suffering is the obedience that exposes one to suffering, but the experience of suffering itself is something that *overtakes* believers.[43]

---

[41]See especially the following: W. Grundmann, *Der Begriff der Kraft in der neutestamentlichen Gedankenwelt*, BWANT 4/8 (Stuttgart, 1932); Ernst Käsemann, "Die Legitimität des Apostels: Eine Untersuchung zu II Korinther 10-13," *ZNW* 41 (1942): 33-71; Werner Bieder, "Paulus und seine Gegner in Korinth," *ThZ* 17 (1961): 319-33; Wolfgang Schrage, "Leid, Kreuz, und Eschaton: Die Peristasenkataloge als Merkmale paulinischer theologia crucis und Eschatologie," *EvTh* 34 (1974) 141-75; Jacob Jervell, "Der schwache Charismatiker," in *Rechtfertigung: Festschrift für Ernst Käsemann*, ed. J. Friedrich et al. (Tübingen: J. C. B. Mohr [Paul Siebeck], 1976; Göttingen: Vandenhoeck & Ruprecht, 1976); Helge Kjaer Nielsen, "Paulus' Verwendung des Begriffes Δύναμις: Eine Replik zur Kreuzestheologie," in *Die paulinische Literatur und Theologie*, ed. Sigfried Pedersen, TS 7 (Århus: Forlaget Århus, 1980; Göttingen: Vandenhoeck & Ruprecht, 1980); Karl A. Plank, *Paul and the Irony of Affliction* (Atlanta: Scholars Press, 1987).

[42]Schütz, *Paul and the Anatomy of Apostolic Authority*, 231. This receptivity finds expression in obedient thought (self-understanding) and action. Furnish points out how different Paul's conception is from the Stoic idea of "performing" suffering: "We afflict ourselves, we distress ourselves" (Epictetus *Disc.* 1.25.28). See Victor Paul Furnish, *II Corinthians*, AB 32A (Garden City NY: Doubleday, 1984) 282.

[43]Tannehill's comments on 1 Thess 1:5-8 and 2:13-16 are especially discerning in this connection (*Dying and Rising with Christ*, 100-104).

It is the essentially passive aspect of existential participation in Christ's cross that prevents a Pauline slogan like "When I am weak, then I am strong" from becoming a formula for power or success. Although Paul celebrates his weakness ("that the power of Christ may rest upon me"), he never says that he makes himself weak, as if weakness and suffering in Christ could be acted out or orchestrated, so as to promote the operation of God's transcendent power on the stage of Paul's frail flesh. Existential participation in Christ's death *happens* to Paul; witness his passive formulations (2 Cor 1:6; 4:11; cf. 1 Thess 2:14).

Paul's letters to Corinth suggest that the Corinthians tended to resist again and again—and under various theological conceptions—the idea that being in Christ involves ongoing participation in the cross. To put it generally and at the risk of oversimplification, where 1 Corinthians suggests that the community accepts Paul as a suffering apostle but fails to see that the weakness of the cross applies to *them*, 2 Corinthians 10-13 (together with other letter sections or fragments in 2 Cor 1-9) suggests that they eventually come to reject *Paul's* cruciform weakness as well, his apostolic participation in the cross.[44] In both cases the Corinthians sever the link between the "death" and "life" of Jesus by rejecting the cross as a constitutive symbol of existence in Christ. Paul's argumentative projection of the problem at Galatia suggests that the Galatians also violate the unity of Christ's death and life, but in a different way. By attaching the life-giving Spirit of Christ to "works of the law" they in effect replace the cross with the law as the fundamental reality by which the Spirit is mediated. It is not that the Galatians spurn the cross as a symbol of Christ's identity or refuse to share in his sufferings. The problem is that they have lost sight of the meaning of the cross: "Oh foolish Galatians! Who has bewitched you—you before whose eyes Jesus Christ was publicly portrayed as crucified?" What the Galatians are to understand about the cross is that it alone mediates the Spirit, a fact that has both a positive and a negative significance. Negatively, the cross as the death of the cosmos to the believer (and vice versa) means that life in the Spirit depends on nothing in the present world order, since being in the Spirit lies on the far side of death to the world. Therefore, nothing

---

[44]See the astute observations of Scott Hafemann, *Suffering and the Spirit,* WUNT Reihe 2/19 (Tübingen: J. C. B. Mohr [Paul Siebeck], 1986) 65-67.

belonging to the present cosmos, however good or righteous, can mediate the life of the Spirit: "I through the law (Christ's death under the curse of the law) *died to the law* (as part of the present world to which I have died with Christ—6:14-15) that I might *live to God*" (2:19). Positively, the cross itself is the beginning of new creation and life in the Spirit, which means that life in the Spirit belongs to those who are crucified with Christ. Just as Jesus' death "occasioned" the coming of the Spirit upon both Jews and Gentiles (3:13-14), so participation in his death "occasions" eschatological life in the Spirit as "living to God" (2:19) or "Christ living in me" (2:20).

The preceding reflection leads us to a final, more nuanced answer to the question of how the Galatians might promote the powerful presence of the Spirit in their lives. We have seen that every ground of the Spirit's advent, on both the epochal and the existential planes, lies decisively in the believer's *past,* where it is therefore beyond the scope of any human willing and doing, except one: crucifixion with Christ. Paul expresses this conduit of the Spirit's arrival in the perfect tense (2:20 and 6:14), which suggests that dying with Christ has a present dimension that "occasions" life in the Spirit. Moreover, we know that one way in which crucifixion with Christ manifests itself existentially in the "present" is in the form of "sharing the sufferings of Christ." But although the theme of suffering percolates to the surface of Paul's discourse at a number of points in Galatians, existential crucifixion with Christ never becomes an explicit theme of the letter, much less an imperative in Paul's exhortation.

We have accounted for the absence of the theme of existential participation in Christ's death by making two observations. First, Paul does not think that the Galatians have rejected sharing Christ's sufferings as a fundamental aspect of existence in Christ. Rejecting existential participation in the cross is a Corinthian, not a Galatian problem. What Paul asks the Galatians is whether they have suffered (for Christ) in vain, as if to suggest that their suffering will end up being for nothing, since they are in danger of losing Christ (and the Spirit) and winding up with the flesh (3:3-4). Second, existential crucifixion is not something that can be acted out in life, hence it does not lie at the discretion of the Galatians to make it a reality in their own lives. What does lie at their discretion is the active dimension of the cross, which entails the risk of sharing the sufferings of Christ. That active dimension is the love, sacrifice, or self-giving that meets with assault from the powers of death. This love is weak in the world, for it is subject to death ("He was crucified out of weakness," 2 Cor 13:4), and as an ethical act Paul calls it "obedience unto death, even death on a cross" (Phil 2:8). In Galatians he expresses this ethical act of Christ as "love" and "self-giving" (2:20). These considerations reveal that for Paul existential participation in the cross has *its* occasion in obedience to Christ. Hence, if there is any action that can be construed as promoting the power of the Spirit, it is obedience to Christ's lordship (walking by the Spirit), since obedience to the crucified Lord draws one into the sphere of Christ's sufferings, where God is always at work bringing life out of death. Therefore, in the context of Christian existence living and walking by the Spirit do in fact mutually determine one another. Living by the Spirit is the motive and power of walking in accordance with the Spirit's aims. Walking in accord with the Spirit leads believers to the place where the life of the Spirit upholds those under assault.

But this link between obedience and blessing is a decidedly unstable one, since the cross, which constitutes it, is a symbol of both death and life. As far as the eschatological future is concerned, Paul is prepared to assert unhesitatingly that "those who sow to the Spirit shall reap eternal life from the Spirit" (Gal 6:8). For present existence in Christ, however, no such formula holds, since the "location" of eschatological life in the present is the cross, which represents not only the birth of that life but also the assault on its bearers by the powers of death that crucified the Lord of glory. It may be a universal human logic to think, despite every contradiction, that blessing must somehow follow upon the heels of righteousness in this world. Paul has a different understanding. In his view righteousness (in Christ) finds itself subject more often than not to powers of death, and the life of Jesus sustains those who share Christ's sufferings in both manifest and powerful workings of the Spirit as well as in hidden and paradoxical ways. "Life" *is* firmly attached to the Crucified, but for that very reason the form this life will assume in any given moment of the church's existence, as well as the fate of that life in the world, lies outside the control and calculation of believers.

Bibliography

1. Commentaries on Galatians

Becker, Jürgen. *Der Brief an die Galater*. NTD 8. Göttingen: Vandenhoeck & Ruprecht, 1981.

Betz, Hans Dieter. *Galatians: A Commentary on Paul's Letter to the Churches in Galatia*. Hermeneia. Philadelphia: Fortress Press, 1979.

Bonnard, Pierre. *L'Épître de Saint Paul aux Galates*. Second edition. Commentaire du Nouveau Testament 9. Neuchâtel: Delachaux et Niestle, 1972.

Bring, Ragnar. *Commentary on Galatians*. Translated by Eric Wahlstrom. Philadelphia: Muhlenberg Press, 1961.

Bruce, F. F. *The Epistle to the Galatians: A Commentary on the Greek Text*. NIGTC. Exeter: Paternoster Press, 1982.

Burton, Ernest De Witt. *A Critical and Exegetical Commentary on the Epistle to the Galatians*. ICC. Edinburgh: T. & T. Clark, 1921.

Ellicott, Charles J. *A Commentary, Critical and Grammatical, on St. Paul's Epistle to the Galatians*. Second edition. Boston: Draper and Holliday, 1867.

Lagrange, Marie-Joseph. *Saint Paul, Épître aux Galates*. Second edition. Études bibliques. Paris: J. Gabalda, 1925.

Lietzmann, Hans. *An die Galater*. HNT 10. Tübingen: J. C. B. Mohr (Paul Siebeck), 1910.

Lightfoot, Joseph Barber. *The Epistle of St. Paul to the Galatians*. Reprint of 1865 edition: Grand Rapids MI: Zondervan, 1957.

Mussner, Franz. *Der Galaterbrief*. Fourth edition. HTKNT 9. Freiburg/Basel/Vienna: Herder, 1981.

Oepke, Albrecht. *Der Brief des Paulus an die Galater*. Fourth edition. Posthumously edited and enlarged by Joachim Rohde. ThHK 9. Berlin: Evangelische Verlagsanstalt, 1979.

Ridderbos, Herman. *The Epistle of Paul to the Churches of Galatia*. Translated by H. Zylstra. NIC. Grand Rapids: Wm. B. Eerdmans Publishing Co., 1953.

Schlier, Heinrich. *Der Brief an die Galater*. Fifth edition. MeyerK 7/14. Göttingen: Vandenhoeck & Ruprecht, 1971.

Sieffert, Friedrich. *Der Brief an die Galater*. MeyerK 7/9. Göttingen: Vandenhoeck & Ruprecht, 1899.

Zahn, Theodor. *Der Brief des Paulus an die Galater*. Second edition. KNT 9. Leipzig: A. Deichert, 1907.

2. Other Literature

Bammel, Ernst. "Gottes ΔΙΑΘΗΚΗ (Gal. III 14-17 und das jüdische Rechtsdenken." *New Testament Studies* 6 (1959–1960): 313-19.

Bandstra, Andrew John. *The Law and the Elements of the World: An Exegetical Study in Aspects of Paul's Teaching*. Kampen: J. H. Kok, 1964.

Barrett, Charles Kingsley. "The Allegory of Abraham, Sarah, and Hagar in the Argument of Galatians." In *Rechtfertigung: Festschrift für Ernst Käsemann*. Edited by J. Friedrich et al. Tübingen: J. C. B. Mohr (Paul Siebeck), 1976. Göttingen: Vandenhoeck and Ruprecht, 1976.

——————. "Pauline Controversies in the Post-Pauline Period." *New Testament Studies* 20 (1974): 229-45.

Beker, J. Christiaan. *Paul the Apostle: The Triumph of God in Life and Thought*. Philadelphia: Fortress Press, 1980.

Betz, Hans Dieter. "In Defense of the Spirit: Paul's Letter to the Galatians as a Document of Early Christian Apologetics." In *Aspects of Religious Propaganda in Judaism and Early Christianity*. Edited by E. Schüssler Fiorenza. Notre Dame IN: University of Notre Dame Press, 1976.

——————. "The Literary Composition and Function of Paul's Letter to the Galatians." *New Testament Studies* 21 (1975): 353-79.

Blinzler, Josef. "Lexikalisches zu dem Terminus τὰ στοιχεῖα τοῦ κόσμου bei Paulus." In *Studiorum Paulinorum Congressus Biblicus*. Volume 2. Rome: Pontifical Biblical Institute, 1963.

Brinsmead, Bernard Hungerford. *Galatians— Dialogical Response to Opponents.* SBLDS 65. Chico CA: Scholars Press, 1982.

Bultmann, Rudolf. *Theologie des Neuen Testaments.* Fifth edition. Tübingen: J. C. B. Mohr (Paul Siebeck), 1965. ET: *Theology of the New Testament.* Two volumes. Translated by Kendrick Grobel. New York: Charles Scribner's Sons, 1951 and 1955.

_____. "Zur Auslegung von Galater 2,15-18." In *Exegetica: Aufsätze zur Erforschung des Neuen Testaments.* Edited by Erich Dinkler. Tübingen: J. C. B. Mohr (Paul Siebeck), 1967.

Cosgrove, Charles H. "Arguing Like a Mere Human Being: Gal. 3:15-18 in Rhetorical Perspective." *New Testament Studies* 34 (1988): 536-49.

_____. "Justification in Paul: A Linguistic and Theological Reflection." *Journal of Biblical Literature* 106 (1987): 653-70.

_____. "The Law Has Given Sarah No Children (Gal. 4:21-30)." *Novum Testamentum* 29 (1987): 219-35.

Crownfield, Frederic R. "The Singular Problem of the Dual Galatians." *Journal of Biblical Literature* 64 (1945): 491-500.

Dahl, Nils. *Studies in Paul: Theology for the Early Christian Mission.* Assisted by Paul Donahue. Minneapolis: Augsburg, 1977.

Danker, Frederick W. *Benefactor. Epigraphic Study of a Graeco-Roman and New Testament Semantic Field.* St. Louis: Concordia Publishing House, 1982.

Davies, W. D. *Paul and Rabbinic Judaism: Some Rabbinic Elements in Pauline Theology.* Fourth edition. Philadelphia: Fortress Press, 1980.

_____. *Torah in the Messianic Age and/or Age to Come* JBLMS 7. Philadelphia: The Society of Biblical Literature, 1952.

Delling Gerhard. "στοιχέω." In *Theological Dictionary of the New Testament,* volume 7. Edited by Gerhard Kittel and Gerhard Friedrich. Translated by G. W. Bromiley. Nine volumes. Grand Rapids: Wm. B. Eerdmans, 1964–1974.

Dodd, Charles Harold. "ΕΝΝΟΜΟΣ ΧΡΙΣΤΟΥ." In *Studia Paulina: In Honorem Johannis de Zwaan,* 96-110. Edited by J. N. Sevenster and W. C. van Unnik. Haarlem: Bohn, 1953.

Donaldson, T. L. "The 'Curse of the Law' and the Inclusion of the Gentiles: Galatians 3.13-14." *New Testament Studies* 32 (1986): 94-112.

Dülmen, Andrea van. *Die Theologie des Gesetzes bei Paulus.* SBM 5. Stuttgart: Verlag Katholisches Bibelwerk, 1968.

198   THE CROSS AND THE SPIRIT

Dunn, James D. G. "I Corinthians 15:45—Last Adam, Life-Giving Spirit." In *Christ and the Spirit in the New Testament: In Honour of C. F. D. Moule.* Edited by B. Lindars and S. Smalley. Cambridge: Cambridge University Press, 1973.

_____. *Jesus and the Spirit: A Study of the Religious and Charismatic Experience of Jesus and the First Christians as Reflected in the New Testament.* Philadelphia: The Westminster Press, 1975.

_____. "The New Perspective on Paul." *Bulletin of the John Rylands University Library of Manchester* 65 (1983): 95-122.

_____. "Once More—Gal 1,18 ἱστορῆσαι Κηφᾶν. In Reply to Otfried Hofius." *Zeitschrift für die neutestamentliche Wissenschaft* 76 (1985): 138-39.

_____. "The Relationship between Paul and Jerusalem according to Galatians 1 and 2." *New Testament Studies* 28 (1982): 461-78.

_____. "Works of the Law and the Curse of the Law (Galatians 3.10-14)." *New Testament Studies* 31 (1985): 523-42.

Easton, Burton S. "New Testament Ethical Lists." *Journal of Biblical Literature* 51 (1932): 1-12.

Gaventa, Beverly Roberts. "Galatians 1 and 2: Autobiography as Paradigm." *Novum Testamentum* 28 (1986): 309-26.

Georgi, Dieter. *Die Geschichte der Kollekte des Paulus für Jerusalem.* TF 38. Hamburg/Bergstedt: Herbert Reich, 1965.

_____. "Theologische Auseinandersetzung mit den Einwänden gegen die Thesen der Bruderschaften." In *Christusbekenntnis im Atomzeitalter,* 109-13. ThEh 70. Munich: Chr. Kaiser Verlag, 1959.

Gunkel, Hermann. *The Influence of the Holy Spirit.* Translated by Roy A. Harrisville and Philip A. Quanbeck. Philadelphia: Fortress Press, 1979 (German edition, 1888).

Hafemann, Scott J. *Suffering and the Spirit: An Exegetical Study of II Cor. 2:14–3:3 within the Context of the Corinthian Correspondence.* WUNT Reihe 2/19. Tübingen: J. C. B. Mohr (Paul Siebeck), 1986.

Harvey, A. E. "The Opposition to Paul." In *Studia Evangelica.* Volume 4. Edited by F. L. Cross. TU 102. Berlin: Akademie-Verlag, 1968.

Hays, Richard B. "Christology and Ethics in Galatians: The Law of Christ." *The Catholic Biblical Quarterly* 49 (1987): 268-90.

_____. *The Faith of Jesus Christ: An Investigation of the Narrative Substructure of Galatians 3:1-4:11*. SBLDS 56. Chico CA: Scholars Press, 1983.

Hengel, Martin. *Die Zeloten: Untersuchungen zur jüdischen Freiheitsbewegung in der Zeit von Herodes I. bis 70 n. Chr.* AGSU 1. Leiden/Köln: E. J. Brill, 1961.

Hofius, Otfried. "Gal 1,18: ἱστορῆσαι Κηφᾶν." *Zeitschrift für die neutestamentliche Wissenschaft* 75 (1984): 73-85.

Holmberg, Bengt. *Paul and Power: The Structure of Authority in the Primitive Church as Reflected in the Pauline Epistles*. Coniectanea biblica. New Testament Series 11. Lund: CWK Gleerup, 1978.

Howard, George. *Paul: Crisis in Galatia: A Study in Early Christian Theology*. SNTSMS 35. Cambridge/New York: Cambridge University Press, 1979.

Hübner, Hans. *Law in Paul's Thought*. Translated by James C. G. Greig. Edited by John Riches. Edinburgh: T. & T. Clark, 1984.

Jervell, Jacob. "Das Volk des Geistes." In *God's Christ and His People: Studies in Honour of Nils Alstrup Dahl*. Edited by Jacob Jervell and Wayne Meeks. Oslo/Bergen/Tromsö: Universitetsforlaget, 1977.

_____. "Der schwache Charismatiker." In *Rechtfertigung: Festschrift für Ernst Käsemann*. Edited by G. Friedrich et al. Tübingen: J. C. B. Mohr (Paul Siebeck), 1976; Göttingen: Vandenhoeck & Ruprecht, 1976.

Jewett, Robert. "The Agitators and the Galatian Congregation." *New Testament Studies* 17 (1971): 198-212.

Kennedy, George A. *Classical Rhetoric and Its Christian and Secular Tradition from Ancient to Modern Times*. Chapel Hill: The University of North Carolina Press, 1980.

_____. *New Testament Interpretation through Rhetorical Criticism*. Chapel Hill and London: The University of North Carolina Press, 1984.

Kilpatrick, G. D. "ΙΣΤΟΡΗΣΑΙ ΚΗΦΑΝ." In *New Testament Essays: Studies in Memory of T. W. Manson*. Edited by A. J. B. Higgins. Manchester: Manchester University Press, 1959.

Klein, Günter. "Individualgeschichte und Weltgeschichte bei Paulus: Eine Interpretation ihres Verhältnisses im Galaterbrief." In *Rekonstruktion und Interpretation: Gesammelte Aufsätze zum Neuen Testament*. BET 50. Munich: Chr. Kaiser Verlag, 1969.

Kraftchick, Steven John. "Ethos and Pathos Appeals in Galatians Five and Six: A Rhetorical Analysis." Ph.D. dissertation, Emory University, 1985.

Kremer, Jacob. " 'Denn der Buchstabe tötet, der Geist aber macht lebendig'. Methodologische und hermeneutische Erwägungen zu 2 Kor 3,6b." In *Begegnung mit dem Wort: Festschrift für Heinrich Zimmermann*. Edited by S. Konijewski and E. Nellessen. BBB 53. Bonn: Peter Hanstein, 1980.

Lambrecht, Jan. "The Line of Thought in Gal. 2:14b-21." *New Testament Studies* 24 (1977–1978): 484-95.

_____. *New Testament Interpretation through Rhetorical Criticism*. Chapel Hill and London: The University of North Carolina Press, 1984.

Lips, H. von. "Der Apostolat des Paulus—ein Charisma? Semantische Aspekte zu χάρις–χάρισμα und anderen Wortpaaren im Sprachgebrauch des Paulus." *Biblica* 66 (1985): 305-43.

Lohmeyer, Ernst. "Gesetz und Werk." In *Grundlagen paulinischer Theologie*. BHT. Tübingen: J. C. B. Mohr (Paul Siebeck), 1929.

_____. "Gesetzeswerke." In *Probleme paulinischer Theologie*. Tübingen: H. Kaupp, n.d.

Louw, J. P. *Semantics of New Testament Greek*. SBLSS. Philadelphia: Fortress Press, 1982; Chico CA: Scholars Press, 1982.

Lührmann, Dieter. "Tage, Monate, Jahreszeiten, Jahre (Gal 4, 10)." In *Werden und Wirken des Alten Testaments: Festschrift für Claus Westermann*. Göttingen: Vandenhoeck & Ruprecht, 1980.

Lull, David John. " 'The Law Was Our Paidagogos': A Study in Galatians 3:19-25." *Journal of Biblical Literature* 105 (1986): 481-98.

_____. *The Spirit in Galatia: Paul's Interpretation of PNEUMA as Divine Power*. SBLDS 49. Chico CA: Scholars Press, 1980.

Lütgert, Wilhelm. *Gesetz und Geist: Eine Untersuchung zur Vorgeschichte des Galaterbriefes*. Gütersloh: Bertelsmann, 1919.

Lyons, George. *Pauline Autobiography: Toward a New Understanding*. SBLDS 73. Atlanta: Scholars Press, 1985.

Martyn, J. Louis. "Apocalyptic Antinomies in Paul's Letter to the Galatians." *New Testament Studies* 31 (1985): 410-24.

_____. "A Law-Observant Mission to Gentiles: The Background of Galatians." *Michigan Quarterly Review* 22 (1983): 221-36.

Marxsen, Willi. *Introduction to the New Testament: An Approach to Its Problems*. Translated by G. Buswell. Philadelphia: Fortress Press, 1964.

Meyer, Paul W. "The Holy Spirit in the Pauline Letters: A Contextual Exploration." *Interpretation* 33 (1979): 3-18.

Michaelis, Wilhelm. "πάσχω." In *Theological Dictionary of the New Testament,* volume 5. Edited by Gerhard Kittel and Gerhard Friedrich. Translated by G. W. Bromiley. Nine volumes. Grand Rapids: Wm. B. Eerdmans, 1964–1974.

Nolland, John. "Grace as Power." *Novum Testamentum* 38 (1986): 26-31.

Plank, Karl A. *Paul and the Irony of Affliction.* SBLSS. Atlanta: Scholars Press, 1987.

Räisänen, Heikki. *Paul and the Law.* WUNT 29. Tübingen: J. C. B. Mohr (Paul Siebeck), 1983.

Reicke, Bo. "The Law and the World according to Paul." *Journal of Biblical Literature* 70 (1951): 259-76.

Reumann, John. " 'Stewards of God'— Pre-Christian Religious Application of *OIKONOMOS* in Greek." *Journal of Biblical Literature* 77 (1958): 339-49.

Ropes, James Hardy. *The Singular Problem of the Epistle to the Galatians.* HTS 14. Cambridge MA: Harvard University Press, 1929.

Sanders, E. P. *Paul and Palestinian Judaism: A Comparison of Patterns of Religion.* Philadelphia: Fortress Press, 1977.

_____. *Paul, the Law, and the Jewish People.* Philadelphia: Fortress Press, 1983.

Schäfer, Peter. *Die Vorstellung vom Heiligen Geist in der rabbinischen Literatur.* SANT 28. Munich: Kösel-Verlag, 1972.

Schmithals, Walter. "Die Häretiker in Galatien." *Zeitschrift für die neutestamentliche Wissenschaft* 47 (1956): 25-67. Revised under the same title in *Paulus und die Gnostiker.* TF 35. Hamburg and Bergstedt: Herbert Reich, 1965. Further revised by the author and translated by John E. Steely under the title, "The Heretics in Galatia," in *Paul and the Gnostics.* Nashville and New York: Abingdon Press, 1972.

_____. "Judaisten in Galatien?" *Zeitschrift für die neutestamentliche Wissenschaft* 74 (1983): 27-58.

Schuppe, E. "Paidagogos." In *Paulys Real-Encyclopädie der classischen Altertumswissenschaft,* volume 18/1. Twenty-four volumes. Reedited by Georg Wissowa. Stuttgart. J. B. Metzler, 1894–1963.

Schütz, John Howard. *Paul and the Anatomy of Apostolic Authority.* SNTSMS 26. Cambridge: Cambridge University Press, 1975.

Schweizer, Eduard. "Die 'Elemente der Welt' Gal. 4, 3. 9; Kol. 2, 8. 20." In *Verborum Veritas: Festschrift für Gustav Stählin*. Edited by O. Bocher and K. Haacker. Wuppertal: Rolf Brockhaus, 1970.

_____. "Observance of the Law and Charismatic Activity in Matthew." *New Testament Studies* 16 (1970): 213-30.

Smith, D. Moody. "Ο ΔΕ ΔΙΚΑΙΟΣ ΕΚ ΠΙΣΤΕΩΣ ΖΗΣΕΤΑΙ." In *Studies in the History of the Text of the New Testament in Honor of Kenneth Willis Clark*. Edited by B. Daniels and M. Jack Suggs. Salt Lake City: University of Utah Press, 1967.

Stählin, Gustav. "Galaterbrief." In *Religion in Geschichte und Gegenwart*, volume 2. Third edition. Six volumes. Tübingen: J. C. B. Mohr (Paul Siebeck), 1958.

Tannehill, Robert C. *Dying and Rising with Christ*. BZNW 32. Berlin: Alfred Töpelmann, 1967.

Tyson, Joseph B. " 'Works of the Law' in Galatians." *Journal of Biblical Literature* 92 (1973): 423-31.

Vielhauer, Philip. "Gesetzesdienst und Stoicheiadienst im Galaterbrief." In *Oikodome: Aufsätze zum Neuen Testament*, volume 2. Edited by G. Klein. TBNT 65. Munich: Chr. Kaiser Verlag, 1979.

Wilckens, Ulrich. "Was heisst bei Paulus: 'Aus Werken des Gesetzes wird kein Mensch gerecht'?" In *Evangelisch-Katholischer Kommentar zum Neuen Testament: Vorarbeiten*. Pamphlet 1. Edited by Eduard Schweizer et al. Neukirchen: Neukirchener Verlag, 1969; Zürich: Benziger Verlag, 1969.

Williams, Sam K. "Again *Pistis Christou*." *The Catholic Biblical Quarterly* 49 (1987): 431-47.

_____. "The 'Righteousness of God' In Romans." *Journal of Biblical Literature* 99 (1980): 241-90.

_____. "Justification and the Spirit in Galatians." *Journal for the Study of the New Testament* 29 (1987): 91-100.

Wilson, R. Mcl. "Gnostics—in Galatia?" In *Studia Evangelica*, volume 4/1. Edited by F. L. Cross. TU 102. Berlin: Akademie-Verlag, 1968.

Young, Norman H. "*Paidagogos:* The Social Setting of a Pauline Metaphor." *Novum Testamentum* 29 (1987): 150-76.

Index of Authors

Index of Passages Cited

Old Testament

Additional Sources

Additional Early Christian Sources